D0981097

ACCLAIM FOR *NOT OUT OF AFRICA*

"An anguished and eloquent cry against declining standards of historical scholarship and against the teaching of 'feel good' history."
—*Kirkus Reviews*

"With great eloquence, learning and compassion, *Not Out of Africa* shows how preferring myth to facts is a disaster for everyone."
—*Wall Street Journal*

"The real problem with Afrocentrism . . . is not that its 'truth' about Greece and Egypt are false. More dangerous is the underlying attitude that all history is fiction, which can be manipulated at will for political ends." —*Time*

"A careful and methodical response to one of Afrocentrism's central tenets: that the ancient Greeks hijacked much of their philosophy, theology, and science from the ancient Egyptians and passed it off as their own invention." —*Boston Globe*

"A painstaking refutation of the main Afrocentric mythologies which have come to prominence from their small beginnings in the 1950s to their high-water mark following Martin Bernal's *Black Athena* books in the 1980s." —*The Times* (London)

"Lefkowitz presents the evidence and arguments underlying classical scholars' objections to Afrocentric claims clearly and concisely."
—*American Historical Review*

"Lefkowitz is superb at lighting the dim corridors in which falsehood is transmuted into fact." —*Commentary*

"Should you read *Not Out of Africa*? Yes. It is a work of true merit and even unsettling knowledge is a useful tool." —*Virtual Dashiki*

"Mary Lefkowitz will make enemies. . . . Cassandras are, after all, inconvenient, especially when they show that a myth designed to help a particular community is in reality demeaning that community and helping to marginalize it." —*Times Literary Supplement*

"Written in reaction to a veritable firestorm of criticism and vituperation, sometimes quite ugly." —Glenn Loury, *Arion*

"Mary Lefkowitz's courageous book reminds us that history must be based on evidence, openly arrived at and openly argued, not a myth, ideology, or opinion. She further reminds us that if scholars abandon the canons of scholarship, then the university itself is in peril."
—Diane Ravitch, New York University

"*Not Out of Africa* combines a learned demolition of various 'politically correct' historical fantasies with a thoughtful inquiry into questions of historical method and of academic freedom. Anyone perplexed by multicultural education should read it." —Arthur Schlesinger, Jr., CUNY Graduate Center

NOT OUT OF AFRICA

NOT
OUT OF
AFRICA

HOW AFROCENTRISM
BECAME AN EXCUSE TO TEACH
MYTH AS HISTORY

MARY LEFKOWITZ

A New Republic Book
BasicBooks
A Member of the Perseus Books Group

Grateful acknowledgment is made for permission to reprint
portions of chapter 6 from Mary Lefkowitz, "Exploring the
Boundaries of Academic Freedom," *National Forum: The Phi Kappa
Phi Journal* 75, no. 2 (1995): 16–19.

Copyright © 1996, 1997 by BasicBooks,
A Member of the Perseus Books Group.

All rights reserved. Printed in the United States of America. No
part of this book may be reproduced in any manner whatsoever
without written permission except in the case of brief quotations
embodied in critical articles and reviews. For information, address
Basic Books, 387 Park Avenue South, New York, NY 10016–8810.

Library of Congress Cataloging-in-Publication Data
    Not out of Africa : how Afrocentrism became an excuse to
teach myth as history / Mary Lefkowitz.
        p. cm.
    "A New Republic Book."
    Includes bibliographical references and index.
    ISBN 0-465-09837-1 (cloth)
    ISBN 0-465-09838-X (paper)
    1. Africa—History—Study and teaching. 2. Afrocentrism. I.
Title.
DT14.L44   1996
960'.07—dc20   95-49109
                                                           CIP

03 04 05 06   15 14 13 12 11 10 9 8

For

Guy MacLean Rogers

. . . nunc uino pellite curas;

cras ingens iterabimus aequor.

CONTENTS

	Illustrations	ix
	Preface	xi
one	Introduction	1
two	Myths of African Origins	12
three	Ancient Myths of Cultural Dependency	53
four	The Myth of the Egyptian Mystery System	91
five	The Myth of the Stolen Legacy	122
six	Conclusion	155
	Epilogue	177
	Notes	195
	Supplementary Notes	239
	Bibliography	255
	Glossary	281
	Index	289

ILLUSTRATIONS

1. Map of the Eastern Mediterranean   15
2. The Family Tree of the Mythological Greek Heroes
   Danaus and Heracles   19
3. Cleopatra's Family Tree   37
4. The Ordeal of the Four Elements   123

PREFACE

In the fall of 1991 I was asked to write a review-article about Martin Bernal's *Black Athena* and its relation to the Afrocentrist movement.[1] The assignment literally changed my life. Once I began to work on the article I realized that here was a subject which needed all the attention, and more, that I could give to it. Although I had been completely unaware of it, there was in existence a whole literature that denied that the ancient Greeks were the inventors of democracy, philosophy, and science. There were books in circulation that claimed that Socrates and Cleopatra were of African descent, and that Greek philosophy had actually been stolen from Egypt. Not only were these books being read and widely distributed; some of these ideas were being taught in schools and even in universities. I soon discovered that one of the universities where students were being taught these strange stories about ancient Greece was my own alma mater, Wellesley College.

My article in the *New Republic* soon propelled me into the center of a bitter controversy.[2] For many years a course had been offered in Wellesley's Africana Studies department, called "Africans in Antiquity." I had always thought that the course was about historical Africa. But now as a result of my research, I realized instead that the ancient "Africans" in its subject matter were such figures as Socrates and Cleopatra, and that among the "facts" of "African" ancient history were the same bogus claims about Greek philosophy that I had previously uncovered. Because I had discussed why these ideas were wrong, I found myself fighting on the front lines of one of the most hotly contested theaters in the Culture Wars, both at home and on a national level.[3]

At first I was amazed that what I wrote had provoked hostility far beyond the range of ordinary scholarly disagreement. I was accused of being inspired by racist motives and later of being the leader of a Jewish "onslaught."[4] An influential Afrocentrist writer, Professor Molefi Kete Asante of Temple University, dismissed my whole discussion as an expression of white prejudice: "Lefkowitz and those who share her views are not interested in understanding Afrocentricity. Their intention is fundamentally the same projection of Eurocentric hegemony that we have seen for the past five hundred years."[5] Asante tried to cast doubt on everything that I said in my *New Republic* article. For instance, I reported that I had been surprised when one of my students told me that she had always thought Socrates was black and was concerned that I had never mentioned his African origins. Asante suggested that I had invented the incident, and that my surprise was motivated by "white racism."[6] Apparently Asante believed I could not endure the thought that Socrates might be black, whereas in reality I doubted that he was black because there was no evidence to support such a contention. Asante, in fact, is aware that there is no such evidence and says that for him the matter is "of no interest." Why didn't he imagine that I was responding in the same way as he was? Because there was no evidence, it was not an interesting question.

If Afrocentrist scholars could ward off criticism and even discussion of their claims and theories by calling their academic opponents racists, there seemed to be little hope of sponsoring the kind of debate that has until recently been a central feature of academic life. Rather than being encouraged to ask questions, to read widely, and to challenge any and all assumptions, students were being indoctrinated along party lines. What could be done to improve the situation before Afrocentrists walled their students off into a private thought-world of their own? It is not enough simply to raise questions about some of the more outlandish Afrocentric allegations. There is a need for explanation. There is a need to show why these theories are based on false assumptions and faulty reasoning, and cannot be supported by time-tested methods of intellectual inquiry. There is a need to explain why this misinformation about the ancient world is being circulated, and to indicate that the motives behind it are political, and that this politicizing is dangerous because it requires the end to justify the means.

In this book I want to show why Afrocentric notions of antiquity, even though unhistorical, have seemed plausible to many intelligent people. In part, the explanation lies in the present intellectual climate. There is a current tendency, at least among academics, to regard history as a form of fiction that can and should be written differently by each nation or ethnic group. The assumption seems to be that somehow all versions will simultaneously be true, even if they conflict in particular details. According to this line of argument, Afrocentric ancient history can be treated not as pseudohistory but as an alternative way of looking at the past. It can be considered as valid as the traditional version, and perhaps even more valid because of its moral agenda. It confers a new and higher status on an ethnic group whose history has largely remained obscure.

Thus ethnic, and even partisan, histories have won approval from university faculties, even though the same faculties would never approve of outmoded or invalid theories in scientific subjects. But the notion that there are many "truths" does not explain why Afrocentrists have chosen to concentrate on the history of ancient Greece, as opposed to the history of any other ancient civilization. Why are questions now being raised about the origins of Greek philosophy and the ethnicity of various ancient celebrities? How could anyone suppose that the ancient Greeks were not the authors of their own philosophy and scientific theory?

The explanation is that only 160 years ago it was widely believed that Egypt was the mother of Western civilization. Although shown to be untrue as soon as more information about Egypt became available, the earlier beliefs survive in the mythology of Freemasonry. The Masons believe that their rituals derive from Egypt, but in reality their rituals do not originate from a real Egyptian source and are not nearly so ancient as they suppose. Rather, they derive from the description in an eighteenth-century novel of an "Egyptian Mystery System," which served as a means of providing university-level education and as the source of ancient philosophy. This system, although wholly fictional, was in fact based on Greek sources. And, although no one knew it at the time, these ancient sources were themselves inaccurate, because their authors interpreted Egyptian culture in terms of Greek custom and experience.

Although the "Egypt" in these accounts never existed, the ancient writers nonetheless believed it, and the Freemasons still talk as if they had some direct connection with it. Because of their conviction that what they are saying is true, their reports can appear credible, especially to people who do not have an extensive knowledge of the ancient world. That is why an attempt to distinguish these plausible fictions from actual fact needs to be undertaken by a classical scholar who knows some ancient languages and who is familiar with the complex nature of ancient historical writing.

Even though I am not the only classicist who could have written a book about the Afrocentric myth of ancient history, I have one special qualification: a long-standing interest in pseudohistory. I have identified in ancient writings both deliberate and unconscious falsification of evidence. I have also studied the many and ingenious ways in which ancient writers created historical "facts" to serve particular purposes, some of them political.[7] It has been a fascinating exercise to bring my knowledge of fictional history to bear on the questions raised in this book, because the issues involved are of interest to all of us, not just to classical scholars.

As my readers will see from some of the incidents that I shall describe in the course of the book, working on such a contro-

versial subject has not made my life easier. I have not enjoyed
having to explain, even to people who have known me for many
years, that I am not attempting simply to preserve the traditions of an outmoded discipline; I am defending academic standards. I am not writing about Afrocentrist misconceptions of
the past in order to show that Greek civilization is superior to
that of Egypt, or any other African nation. I would like to assure
anyone who is prepared to make such allegations that, on the
contrary, I am deeply grateful for the opportunity to have
learned more about Egypt than I might have done had I not
taken on this special project. I have only the highest respect for
the advanced civilization and accomplishments of ancient
Egypt.

This book thus has both a negative and a positive purpose. The
negative purpose is to show that the Afrocentric myth of ancient
history is a myth, and not history. The positive purpose is to
encourage people to learn as much about ancient Egypt and
ancient Greece as possible. The ancient Egypt described by
Afrocentrists is a fiction. I would like our children and college students to learn about the real ancient Egypt and the real ancient
Africa, and not about the historical fiction invented by Europeans.

Any work of this kind must inevitably take its readers into
unfamiliar territory. For that reason I have tried to provide
as many guideposts as possible along the way. I specify when
writers wrote and where they came from. All quotations in
foreign languages are translated (by me, unless otherwise
noted). I have sought not to encumber the reader with
learned references and footnotes; the narrative can be read
straight through without a glance at the back of the book.
But the references are there for anyone who wants to know

them. A work on such a controversial subject requires thorough documentation.

This book was written with the support of grants from Wellesley College, the Bradley Foundation, and the John M. Olin Foundation.

Among the many people who have urged me to write this book, and to discuss these controversial issues, I am particularly grateful to the following for their support, advice, and encouragement: Harold Brackman, Deborah B. Cohen, Henry Louis Gates, Jr., Glen Hartley, Barbara S. Held, Heather R. Higgins, Kermit Hummel, Diane Ravitch, Frank M. Snowden, Jr., and Leon Wieseltier. The late F. W. Sternfeld alerted me to the importance of the work of the Abbé Jean Terrasson. Kelly J. King spent many hours in Boston libraries tracking down obscure books. Beatrice Cody, Christopher Korintus, Sir Hugh Lloyd-Jones, and Stephanie O'Hara made many valuable suggestions about the manuscript. I could not have written the book without their help.

Wellesley, Massachusetts
July 1995

The paperback edition contains corrections, additions, and improvements. Among these are a full bibliography, with suggestions for further reading; a glossary of names to help people sort out who is who in the ancient writings mentioned in this book; and supplementary notes keyed to pages in the text, which provide more information and answer questions raised by reviewers and correspondents (these may be found after the endnotes). I have corrected some minor errors and typos. I have added an epilogue in which I discuss the central issues raised by the book, examine the rather curious arguments that have been presented by critics and reviewers, and suggest topics for further discussion. My thanks to the friends, colleagues, and correspondents who have offered much helpful advice: John Baines, Harold Brackman, Brian Burrough, Beverly Coleman, Matthew Dickie, George M. Hollenback, Erich Martel, Jørgen Mejer, John Morgan, and Robert Renehan.

Wellesley, Massachusetts
January 1997

ONE

INTRODUCTION

In American universities today not everyone knows what extreme Afrocentrists are doing in their classrooms. Or, even if they do know, they choose not to ask questions.[1] For many years I had been as unwilling to get involved as anyone else. But then, when I learned what was going on in this special line of teaching, my questions about ancient history were not encouraged. There was no sense that as a faculty we were all involved in a cooperative enterprise, that of educating all of our students. Intellectual debate was in fact actively discouraged, even though the questions raised were reasonable and fair. Ordinarily, if someone has a theory that involves a radical departure from what the experts have professed, he or she is expected to defend his or her position by providing evidence in its support. But no one seemed to think it was appropriate to ask for evidence from the instructors who claimed that the Greeks stole their philosophy from Egypt.

Normally, if one has a question about a text that another instructor is using, one simply asks why he or she is using that book. But since this conventional line of inquiry was closed to me, I had to wait until I could raise my questions in a more public context. That opportunity came in February 1993, when Dr. Yosef A. A. ben-Jochannan was invited to give Wellesley's Martin Luther King, Jr., memorial lecture. Posters described Dr. ben-Jochannan as a "distinguished Egyptologist," and indeed that is how he was introduced by the then president of Wellesley College. But I knew from my research in Afrocentric literature that he was not what scholars would ordinarily describe as an Egyptologist, that is, a scholar of Egyptian language and civilization. Rather, he was an extreme Afrocentrist, author of many books describing how Greek civilization was stolen from Africa, how Aristotle robbed the library of Alexandria, and how the true Jews are Africans like himself.

After Dr. ben-Jochannan made these same assertions once again in his lecture, I asked him during the question period why he said that Aristotle had come to Egypt with Alexander and had stolen his philosophy from the library at Alexandria, when that library had only been built after his death. Dr. ben-Jochannan was unable to answer the question, and said that he resented the tone of the inquiry. Several students came up to me after the lecture and accused me of racism, suggesting that I had been brainwashed by white historians. But others stayed to hear me out, and I assured Dr. ben-Jochannan that I simply wanted to know what his evidence was: so far as I knew, and I had studied the subject, Aristotle never went to Egypt, and while the date of the library of Alexandria is not known precisely, it was certainly built some years after the city was founded, which was after both Aristotle's and Alexander's deaths.

A lecture at which serious questions could not be asked, and in fact were greeted with hostility—the occasion seemed more like a political rally than an academic event.[2] As if that were not disturbing enough in itself, there was also the strange silence on the part of many of my faculty colleagues. Several of them were well aware that what Dr. ben-Jochannan was saying was factually wrong. One of them said later that she found the lecture so "hopeless" that she decided to say nothing. Were they afraid of being called racists? If so, their behavior was understandable, but not entirely responsible. Didn't we as educators owe it to our students, all our students, to see that they got the best education they could possibly get? And that clearly was what they were not getting in a lecture where they were being told myths disguised as history, and where discussion and analysis had apparently been forbidden.

Good as the myths they were hearing may have made these students feel, so long as they never left the Afrocentric environment in which they were being nurtured and sheltered, they were being systematically deprived of the most important features of a university education. They were not learning how to question themselves and others, they were not learning to distinguish facts from fiction, nor in fact were they learning how to think for themselves. Their instructors had forgotten, while the rest of us sat by and did nothing about it, that students do not come to universities to be indoctrinated, at least not in a free society. As Arthur Schlesinger says in *The Disuniting of America*:

> The purpose of history is to promote not group self-esteem, but understanding of the world and the past, dispassionate analysis, judgment and perspective, respect for divergent cultures and traditions, and unflinching protection for those unifying ideas of tolerance, democracy, and human rights that make free historical inquiry possible.[3]

So it seemed to me that being called a racist was not my principal problem, false and unpleasant as the charges were. Such attacks could easily be repelled, as long as my colleagues were prepared to reconstruct what happened in the past on the basis of historical evidence. The trouble was that some of my colleagues seemed to doubt that there was such a thing as historical evidence, or that even if evidence existed, it did not matter much one way or the other, at least in comparison with what they judged to be the pressing cultural issues and social goals of our own time. When I went to the then dean of the college to explain that there was no factual evidence behind some Afrocentric claims about ancient history, she replied that each of us had a different but equally valid view of history. When I stated at a faculty meeting that Aristotle could not have stolen his philosophy from the library of Alexandria in Egypt, because that library had not been built until after his death, another colleague responded, "I don't care who stole what from whom." How could I persuade these colleagues, and many others like them, that evidence does matter, that not every interpretation of the past is equally probable, and that I was not trying to teach about the history of the ancient world in order to pre-serve or transmit racist values?

The present book is an attempt to answer these difficult questions, at least so far as the understanding of ancient history is concerned. There is an urgent need for a book that discusses the nature of the charges against the Greeks and provides a complete discussion of the reasons why they are without foundation. Hardly a week goes by when an article does not appear by an Afrocentrist writer observing that the discoveries attributed to the Greeks rightly belong to the an-cient Egyptians. But while many of us have responded to var-ious individual assertions about the Greeks, no one so far has taken the trouble to respond fully to all of them, and to ex-plain why it is that these ideas are now being circulated. I can understand this reluctance on the part of classicists and Egyptologists. To respond to the kinds of allegations that are now being made requires us in effect to start from the begin-ning, to explain the nature of the ancient evidence, and to dis-cuss what has long been known and established as if it were now subject to serious question. In short, we are being put on the defensive when in ordinary circumstances there would have been nothing to be defensive about. Worst of all, making this sort of defense keeps us from going on to discover new material and bring our attention to bear on real interpreta-tive problems. Instead of getting on with our work, we must rehearse what has long been known. But nonetheless, the case for the defense must still be made.

Afrocentrist writers have suggested many ways to revise the teaching of European history and science.[4] But in this book I have chosen to concentrate on the way modern writers have misrepresented the achievement of the ancient Greeks. Throughout European history many different groups have claimed affinity with the ancient Greeks, because they have admired particular aspects of their civilization, whether intellectual, military, or athletic. But Afrocentrists are not content with establishing a special relationship to the ancient Greeks. Instead, they seek to remove the ancient Greeks from the important role they have previously played in history, and to assign to the African civilization of Egypt the credit for the Greeks' achievements.

Any attempt to question the authenticity of ancient Greek civilization is of direct concern even to people who ordinarily have little interest in the remote past. Since the founding of this country, ancient Greece has been intimately connected with the ideals of American democracy.[5] Rightly or wrongly, since much of the credit belongs to the Romans, we like to think that we have carried on some of the Greeks' proudest traditions: democratic government, and freedom of speech, learning, and discussion.[6] But it is from the Greeks, and not from any other ancient society, that we derive our interest in history and our belief that events in the past have relevance for the present.[7]

So, in spite of what my colleague said, it does matter to all of us whether or not Aristotle stole his philosophy from Egypt, even though that event (or rather, nonevent) supposedly took place as long ago as the late fourth century B.C. It matters, because if Aristotle had done such a thing, we should give the ancient Egyptians, rather than the ancient Greeks, credit for the development of conceptual vocabulary and formal arguments. It matters, because extreme Afrocentrists accuse historians of antiquity like myself of being party to a major cover-up in behalf of the ancient Greeks.

Instead, I will try to show that no such cover-up operation has ever existed. Afrocentrism is not simply an alternative interpretation of history, offered on the basis of complex data or ambiguities in the evidence: there is simply no reason to deprive the Greeks of the credit for their own achievements. The basic facts are clear enough, at least to dispassionate observers. In effect, Afrocentrists are demanding that ordinary historical methodology be discarded in favor of a system of their own choosing. This system allows them to ignore chronology and facts if they are inconvenient for their purposes. In other words, their historical methodology allows them to alter the course of history to meet their own specific needs.

In asserting that important aspects of Greek civilization were derived from Egypt, modern Afrocentric writers are, however, following a long-established pattern. Some two thousand years ago Jews in Alexandria insisted that the Greeks had been inspired by their own earlier civilization: Plato, they said, had studied the works of Moses. The claim, at the time that they made it, did not sound as incredible as it does today. Their notion of chronology was vague, and their knowledge of Greek philosophy limited. But modern Afrocentric writers have no such excuse.

Although it is understandable that Afrocentrists, as certain Europeans have done before them, should want to take credit for the ancient Greek origins of Western civilization, the basic outlines of chronology in the Mediterranean are well known, and all the texts under discussion are readily available in translation in all university libraries. There is no reason why claims of a conspiracy should be credited, if no real evidence can be produced to support it. Despite allegations to the contrary, virtually all the claims made by Afrocentrists can be shown to be without substance. Anyone who is willing to look into the matter can see that it is utterly absurd to state (as some Afrocentrists have done) that Aristotle's treatise *On the Soul* was derived from the Egyptian "Book of the Dead."[8] In fact, all that the two texts have in common is that they mention souls. But that is true of a great many other ancient documents.

In this book I will show why these and many other claims about Greece's debt to Egypt are false. I will suggest that arguing that Afrocentric writers offer a valid interpretation of ancient history is like being comfortable with the notion that the earth is flat. But although such new and daring hypotheses about the past can easily win adherents, especially when they favor present cultural and political aspirations, everyone should be aware that there are real dangers in allowing history to be rewritten, even for culturally useful purposes. Even though it may inspire students with pride and self-confidence, writing and teaching such ethnic histories, each with its own brand of "ethnic truth," sanctions the invention of falsehoods.

What will happen some years from now, when students who have studied different versions of the past discover that their picture of events is totally incomparable with what their classmates have learned about their own ethnic histories? Will students of one ethnicity deny the existence of other "ethnic truths," with dire consequences akin to the ethnic conflicts in the former Yugoslavia? Perhaps they will be reassured that the differences do not matter because all history is a form of rhetoric, and narratives of the past can be constructed virtually at will. When that time comes, and I hope it never will, our students will be no better off than the Jews who claimed that Plato was a disciple of Moses: they will have no respect for evidence, no concern with chronology, no understanding of the differences between languages and cultures. In other words, they will have overlooked everything that has been learned about history since Herodotus in the fifth century B.C. began his famous inquiry into the human past. It is in the hope of helping to prevent such retrogression that I have written this book.

Since Afrocentrist assertions do not amount to a systematic revision of the history of ancient Greece, but rather focus on a small range of particular issues, it is possible to approach these issues as a series of interrelated questions. The second chapter deals with questions of "race." Is there any evidence that Egyptians invaded Greece during the second millennium B.C., evidence that might provide some support for the allegations that there was an African component in Greek civilization? I shall also address two particular questions about African ancestry: Was Socrates black? Was Cleopatra black? I shall show that there is no evidence for thinking so. I shall discuss the ancient perception of ethnicity and race. Here once again we can learn from the ancients. To them, culture was a far more important factor in human behavior than skin color or other "racial" characteristics.

The third chapter of the book turns to the broader and more complicated issue of whether Greek philosophy was stolen or in any way dependent upon Egyptian thought. I believe that the notion of an extensive Greek debt to Egypt originated in the mythology of eighteenth-century Freemasonry, and that for that reason, the Afrocentric claims about an Egyptian legacy are based on an honest misunderstanding. I shall show that although some ancient writers were told by Egyptian priests that the famous Greek philosophers studied in Egypt, these stories are more accurately understood as myths of cultural dependency.

In the fourth chapter I explain why certain Afrocentrist writers have come to believe that there was in ancient times an "Egyptian Mystery System." I will argue that in reality this "System" was an invention of an eighteenth-century French writer, the Abbé Jean Terrasson. The mysteries he described were in character Greco-Roman. In other words, when Afrocentrists accuse the Greeks of stealing from the Egyptians, the Egyptian ideas that they are describing are not actually Egyptian, but rather "Egyptian" as imagined by Europeans who had no direct or authentic knowledge about Egypt. To say that the Greeks stole their philosophy from Egypt is tantamount to saying that they stole their philosophy from themselves.

The fifth chapter deals with the origins of the myth that the Greeks stole their philosophy from Egypt. I suggest that the idea of a "Stolen Legacy" was first popularized by Marcus Garvey in the 1920s, and I describe how it was developed into a full-fledged theory in 1954 by a college teacher in Arkansas, George G. M. James. I also examine the evidence James provides in support of his thesis and show in general and in particular that it does not hold up to serious scrutiny.

In the conclusion I consider what (if anything) can be done to contradict the calumnies that are being spread about the ancient Greeks and about all of us who study the ancient world. I discuss the issue of responsible teaching and of academic freedom. I suggest some possible courses of action that schools and universities might adopt.

I believe it is essential for all of us to realize that some action needs to be taken. It is not simply a matter of doing justice to the ancient Greeks and their modern descendants. Universities must encourage free inquiry and debate, and not permit the classroom to be used as a means of political indoctrination. Even more important than that is our obligation to teach history, history that can be supported by warranted evidence.

TWO

MYTHS OF
AFRICAN ORIGINS

Who were the ancient Greeks? Where did they come from? Until recently, no one contested the basic answers to these questions. Because the Greeks spoke an Indo-European language, they were thought to have migrated to Europe from somewhere north of the Indian subcontinent. When, and over what periods of time, they did so is a more difficult question to answer; but we know that Greeks were established on the Greek mainland in the second millennium B.C. The Myceneans who had settled there during that time wrote in Greek, as the clay tablets they left behind them indicate. In the fifth century B.C. and after, most Greeks regarded themselves as indigenous, or to use their word for it, "autochthonous," from the land (*chthon*) itself (*auto-*). The only exceptions were some of the great families. In their myths, their founders came from Asia, like Cadmus the founder of Thebes, or Pelops the founder of the dynasty of Argos.

What did the ancient Greeks look like? From portraits on seal-rings, paintings on vases, and sculptures in clay and stone, it is possible to get a good sense of how they saw themselves.[1] Written texts describe a variety of hair color, ranging from brown to black, and skin color ranging from light to dark. Vase paintings, because of the limited colors available to the potters, give a more schematic impression. Women are usually portrayed with white faces. If the background of the vase is black, the men have black faces; if the background is the color of the clay from which the vase is made, men have reddish-brown faces. They distinguish themselves clearly from Egyptians and Ethiopian peoples in their art and literature. The Africans have flat noses, curly hair, and thick lips; their skin color is portrayed with black glaze or, on occasion, plain unglazed terra-cotta.[2] They regularly speak of the Egyptians' dark skin, and sometimes of their curly hair. Herodotus supposed that the Colchians (a people who lived on the eastern coast of the Black Sea) were Egyptian because they were dark-skinned (*melanchroes*) and curly-haired (*oulotriches*).[3] He identifies a pair of doves as Egyptian in origin because they are "dark" (*melainai*).[4]

But although the Greeks knew the Egyptians to be what we would now call "people of color," they did not think less or more or them (or any other Africans) on that account.[5] To them, the salient fact were that these other peoples were foreigners. The Greeks were careful to distinguish themselves from all foreigners, and referred to them rather indiscriminately as *barbaroi*, people who spoke unintelligibly. Because of their own sense of identity, the Greeks would have dismissed as nonsense any suggestion that they were of African descent. The inhabitants of Greek colonies that were established during the eighth century B.C. on the north coast of Africa, like Cyrene in Libya, invariably regarded themselves as Greeks (see figure 1).

Although the identity of the ancient Greeks seems to be well known, and supported by many different types of evidence, in recent years Afrocentric writers have argued that there were from earliest times Egyptian immigrants among the Greeks. Afrocentrist writers have claimed that the mythical founders of several ancient Greek city-states came from Africa. Afrocentrist writers also assume that the ancient inhabitants of the northern coast of Africa were black, even though it is known, for example, that many came from elsewhere in the Mediterranean. Carthage was settled by Phoenicians, a Semitic people; Cyrene was a colony of the Greek island Thera. Claims have also been made that some famous Greek historical figures had African ancestors: the philosopher Socrates of Athens (469–399 B.C.); Cleopatra VII (69–30 B.C.), queen of Egypt. In this chapter I shall review the arguments for all of these assertions, and explain why none stands up to careful scrutiny. My reason for doing so is not because I find the topic of "race" particularly interesting or important.[6] In assessing the nature of past achievement, it is much more important to know what people thought and did than what they looked like. If Socrates' skin had been darker than that of his Athenian neighbors, if his ancestors' origins were African or Phoenician or Indian, he would still be a great ancient Greek philosopher.

FIGURE 1

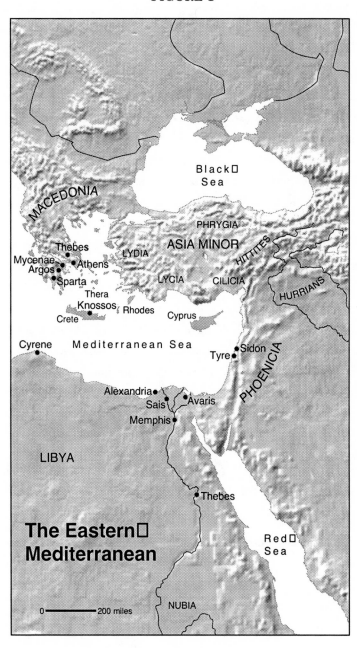

Black
Sea

MACEDONIA

PHRYGIA

ASIA MINOR

Thebes
Mycenae
Argos
Athens
LYDIA

Sparta

LYCIA

CILICIA

HITTITES

HURRIANS

Thera

Knossos
Rhodes
Cyprus

Crete

Cyrene
Mediterranean Sea

Tyre
Sidon

PHOENICIA

Alexandria
Sais
Avaris

Memphis

LIBYA

Thebes

**The Eastern
Mediterranean**

Red
Sea

0 ————— 200 miles

NUBIA

The question of race matters only insofar as it is necessary to show that no classicists or ancient historians have tried to conceal the truth about the origins of the Greek people or the ancestry of certain famous ancient figures. It has been suggested that classicists have been reluctant to ask questions about Greek origins, and that we have been so "imbued with conventional preconceptions and patterns of thought" that we are unlikely to question the basic premises of our discipline.[7] But even though we may be more reluctant to speculate about our own field than those outside it might be, none of us has any cultural "territory" in the ancient world that we are trying to insulate from other ancient cultures. If there had been in ancient Egypt a university system at which the Greeks might have studied, we would be eager to discuss it. In the last few years there has been renewed interest in influences on Greece from the Near East. Classicists are in fact eager to learn about the impact on Greece of other cultures in the eastern Mediterranean. Our problem is rather how to prevent the study of the past from being misused and misinterpreted as a result of modern politics.

DID EGYPTIANS INVADE GREECE IN THE SIXTEENTH CENTURY B.C.?

In his influential book *Civilization or Barbarism*, which was originally published in French in 1981, the Senegalese humanist and scientist Cheikh Anta Diop undertook to construct a usable past for African people.[8] He regarded Egypt as the source of much of what is called Western Civilization. He suggested that according to Greek mythology, the Egyptians brought their civilization to Greece during the time of the XVIIIth Dynasty in Egypt (1574–1293 B.C.):

> Indeed, the XVIIIth Dynasty was contemporaneous with Mycenaean Greece; even Athens was founded by a colony of Black Egyptians led by Cecrops, who introduced agriculture and metallurgy to continental Greece around the sixteenth century B.C., according to Greek tradition itself.
>
> Erechtheus, who unified Attica, also came from Egypt, according to Diodorus of Sicily, while the Egyptian Danaus founded at Argos the first royal dynasty in Greece. It was at the same time that the Phoenician Cadmus, an Egyptian subject, founded the city of Thebes in Boeotia and the royalty of that country.[9]

Later in the book Diop reiterates his claim that Cecrops, Aegyptus, Danaus, and Erechtheus were all "Egyptian Blacks," and that Cadmus was a "Negroid" who came from Canaan.[10] If this account of the origins of these Greek heroes is correct, a case could be made for thinking that Greek myths preserved through genealogy a sense of the Greeks' African heritage.

In fact, it easily can be shown that Diop's research is not so thorough as it might appear. Rather than follow the ordinary stories about the origins of the Greek heroes, he relies on one extraordinary account, and has uncritically repeated an ancient assertion of dubious accuracy. Diop's source for his claims that the Greek heroes came from Egypt is Diodorus of Sicily, who wrote in the first century B.C. And what were Diodorus's sources? Diop does not say, but Diodorus himself tells us. He is simply reporting what Egyptian priests told him when he visited that country during the 180th Olympiad (60–56 B.C.).[11] Diodorus does not imply that he believed them. The priests also told him that Egypt in early times colonized the whole of the Mediterranean world: Babylon, Colchis, and even the nation of the Jews. But this account of the origins of civilization is, to put it mildly, highly idiosyncratic, and almost certainly wrong. The Hebrews certainly did not agree with it, and neither did the Greeks. According to all known Greek sources, Cecrops was autochthonous, that is, he sprang from the soil of Attica. His lower body took the form of a snake.[12] Erechtheus, too, was a native of Athens, being descended from the earlier kings of Attica.[13]

Diop's suggestion that Danaus was Egyptian is slightly less farfetched. He was Egyptian, in the sense that he was born in Egypt. But according to the myth, his family was Greek in origin. His great-grandfather, Epaphus, was born in Egypt, after his mother, Io, the daughter of the river Inachus in Argos, had come to the Nile Delta (see figure 2). Io (Danaus's great-great-grandmother) had been compelled to leave Greece because the Greek god Zeus had fallen in love with her, and in jealousy his wife, Hera, turned her into a cow.[14] In that form, Io wandered from Greece to Asia Minor, and from there to Egypt. There she gave birth to Epaphus, Danaus's great-grandfather. Danaus and his fifty daughters returned to Argos from Egypt, because the daughters refused to marry their first cousins. These were the sons of Danaus's brother Aegyptus, whose name in Greek is the same as the country "Egypt" (see figure 2).

Even though Danaus's family had been in Egypt for several generations, when they wanted to escape they went to Argos

FIGURE 2

THE FAMILY TREE OF THE MYTHOLOGICAL

GREEK HEROES DANAUS AND HERACLES*

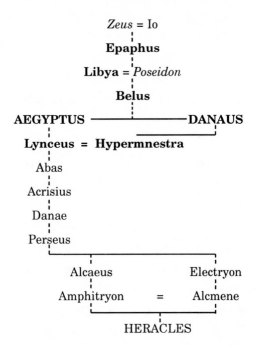

*The names of Greek gods are italicized. The mythological persons whose names appear in boldface were born in Egypt.

in Greece, because they were Greeks. For that reason, they found sanctuary there. Once they realized that Danaus's ancestors came from Argos, the Argives welcomed them. They were not deterred either by problems of language or appearance. In his drama *The Suppliants* (ca. 468 B.C.), Aeschylus portrays the moment of their arrival in Greece, describing them as a "dark, sun-struck family" (*melanthes helioktypon genos*, 154–156). And in *Prometheus Bound* Aeschylus describes the daughters' great-great-grandfather, Epaphus, as "dark" (*kelainos*, 851). Here is a clear indication that Athenians in the fifth century B.C. thought of the Egyptians as darker than themselves, and also that they thought of skin color as being determined by climate. Their clothing is different, too. The king of Argos comments on their "unhellenic garb, barbarian tunics and close-woven cloth" (234–236). He notices that they are both foreign and more adventurous than Greek women: Are they Libyan, or Egyptian, or nomads who live near Ethiopia, or are they Amazons who live in Colchis near the Black Sea (279–287)? But they assure him that they are descended from Io, daughter of the river Inachus in Argos, and of Epaphus, Io's son by Zeus who was born in Libya. The king acknowledges their ancestry and allows them to settle in Argos. The next drama in the trilogy, *The Egyptians*, tells the story of how the king is killed defending the daughters of Danaus against their cousins, and how Danaus then took his place as king.[15] This outcome suggests that to the fifth-century Athenians genealogy mattered more than any outward sign of ethnicity, and that they thought of the coming to Greece of Danaus and his daughters as a return of Greeks to Greece from exile, not as an Egyptian invasion.

Diop ignores the fact that the Greeks regarded Danaus as a Greek. In the case of the hero Cadmus, he overlooks the Greek tradition that Cadmus came to Thebes in Greece from Phoenicia and accepts instead a hybrid origin. According to Greek belief, Cadmus came from Tyre in Phoenicia (or Canaan) and founded the Greek city of Thebes. His daughter Semele was the mother, by the god Zeus, of the god Dionysus. According to Diop, Cadmus, although a Phoenician, was an Egyptian subject, who then founded the city of Thebes in Boeotia and the royalty of that country. He also says that Cadmus was "Negroid." Again, his ancient source is Diodorus of Sicily, but Diop does not report what Diodorus tells us. Diodorus says nothing about Cadmus's physical appearance. Like other Greeks, he would have assumed that Cadmus looked like other Phoenicians, and the Phoenicians were a Semitic people. Moreover, Diodorus does not say that Cadmus went from Egypt to Greece. Rather, the Egyptian priests told him that Cadmus was a citizen of *Egyptian* Thebes, and that his daughter Semele gave birth to the Egyptian god Osiris, whom they identified with Dionysus.[16] In other words, the priests told Diodorus that Cadmus emigrated from Greece to Egypt, and Diop has understood that to mean that Cadmus went in exactly the opposite direction, in order to provide documentation for his idea of an Egyptian invasion.

I shall say more in the next chapter about why the Egyptians in the first century B.C. wanted to assert the priority of their own civilization, and why Diodorus was ready to record what they told him. At the time of Diodorus's visit Egypt had been under the domination of Macedonian Greeks for more than a century. On their part, the Greeks had from earliest times an abiding respect for the antiquity of Egyptian civilization. Because of this respect, they were willing to report, if not to believe, that their religion originated in Egypt, and that some of their famous philosophers had studied there, even though neither they nor the Egyptians could provide evidence to support their ideas.

By now it should be clear that Diop has supplied his readers only with selected and to some extent distorted information. When he reports what the Egyptian priests told Diodorus, he says nothing about the Greeks' own earlier accounts of their origins. Nor does he advise his readers to remember that in any case all of these stories are myths, not history. As such, they cannot provide the precise information about the timing of events or the movements of peoples that we would now like to possess. At best they can give a general impression of the cultural ties among Mediterranean peoples; for more precise information we must rely on material remains.

In fact, archaeology does not provide any support for an invasion of Greece by Egyptians in the second millennium. Such information as we have suggests instead that settlers came to Egypt from Greece. A thousand fragments of frescoes in the Minoan Greek style have been found in the last several years at Avaris in the Nile Delta, dating from the seventeenth century, during the period when the Semitic (probably Canaanite) people known as the Hyksos ruled Egypt (1674–1566 B.C.).[17] In 1991, a fragment of a painted Minoan floor, dating from the sixteenth century, was discovered in Tell Kabri in Israel. These findings seem to suggest that an "invasion," whatever form it may have taken, went from Greece to Egypt, rather than in the other direction.[18] Perhaps the story of Io's journey to the Nile Delta is a distant reflection of this cultural influence from the north, as Egyptologist Donald Redford has suggested.[19] But the myth need not reflect history at all, since the Greeks used myths to account for all kinds of different phenomena. Here it may simply have been a means of explaining why Io resembled the Egyptian goddess Isis, who was often represented with cow's horns on her head. The fifth-century historian Herodotus, who had visited Egypt, remarks on the resemblance.[20] Whatever the origin of the story of Io's journey, the myths of the origins of Argos and Athens, as the Greeks knew them, before they were revised by the Egyptian priests in the first century, provide no indications of African roots or an Egyptian invasion.

Did the Greeks wish not to call attention to their foreign origins, "for reasons of cultural pride?" So argues Martin Bernal in volume 1 of *Black Athena*. Like Diop, he imagines that the myths of Danaus and Cecrops reflect actual historical events: "I am certain that all the legends contain interesting kernels of historical truth."[21] Like Diop, he argues that Egyptian culture and language were brought to Greece by the Semitic people known as the Hyksos during the seventeenth and sixteenth centuries B.C. He even imagines that the name *Hyksos* is related to the Greek word for suppliant (*hiketis*, the word from which Aeschylus's play about the daughters of Danaus takes its title). But as we have seen, recent archaeological discoveries suggest that the Hyksos came from Greece to Egypt rather than vice-versa, and the proposed etymology of *hiketis* from *Hyksos* simply does not work.[22] In fact, it is no more likely than Diop's fanciful attempt to link the Egyptian word *ba* (soul) with the Greek word *bia* (might, force).[23] If anyone could prove to the satisfaction of other scholars that a large number of Greek words were derived from Egyptian, he or she would be credited with a new and important discovery. But vague similarities do not prove any connection between words. The sound qualities of vowels and consonants alike change when words are gradually assimilated from one language to another, and even loanwords are transformed: for example, the Latinized Greek word *episcopus* became *bishop* in the mouths of Saxon converts in the ninth century A.D. Linguists have long since noted the relatively few words of Egyptian origin that have made their way into Greek. They object to Bernal's etymologies of Hyksos and many other words because he ignores other and more likely etymologies in favor of those that will best suit the purposes of his argument.

In volume 2 of *Black Athena*, Bernal attempts to fortify his argument by claiming that the river-god Inachus, Io's father, came from Egypt. But it turns out that this assertion is even less substantive than Diop's notions about the Egyptian origins of the Greek heroes. Bernal states that "the church father Eusebius referred to a tradition that Inachos, like Danaus, was a settler from Egypt." But, like the etymology of *hiketis*, this statement does not stand up to scrutiny. Bernal does not provide any reference to the place where Eusebius is supposed to have said that Inachus came from Egypt. It is not surprising that he fails to document the reference, because in fact Eusebius never says that Inachus had Egyptian origins. The idea that Inachus and his son Phoroneus were settlers from Egypt originated not in antiquity, but in the eighteenth century A.D. Its source is the historical novel *Anacharsis* (1788) by the Abbé Barthélemy.[24] Barthélemy was writing at a time when it was widely believed that many aspects of Greek culture were derived from Egypt. In an earlier novel, *Séthos* (1731), the Abbé Terrasson had described how Greek education and religious ritual (as he imagined it) had originated in Egypt. I shall discuss in chapter 4 how the mythology of

Freemasonry was based on the practices described in this novel and from there made its way into popular culture. Bernal is, of course, aware that *Anacharsis* and *Séthos* are fictional accounts, although loosely based on Greek and Roman sources, and he knows that neither of their learned authors had access to independent information about Egypt, because none was available to any historian until hieroglyphics were deciphered in 1836. But these are the only sources he cites for his claim about Inachus coming from Egypt.

In short, there is virtually no evidence to support modern notions of invasions of Greece from Africa, and there is no way to set the precise times when these imaginary invasions or migrations ought to have occurred. If the myths of Io and Danaus have any connection with history, they provide better support for the notion of a migration from Greece to Egypt. Another Afrocentric claim about Egyptian origins rests on even shakier ground than myth. This is the idea that the Greek hero Heracles was descended from Egypt on both sides of his family.[25] Authors who make this claim identify the source of this information as Herodotus, but in fact it is not Herodotus but Herodotus *in translation*. Every English translation that I know of says that Heracles was descended distantly "from Egypt." But the translation is incorrect. Herodotus is talking about Aegyptus the man rather than *Aigyptos* the country. Although the same word, *Aigyptos*, is used to designate both the man and the country, if Herodotus had meant Egypt he would have used a different Greek word for the preposition *from*, and specified that he meant natives of that country.[26] Herodotus is simply seeking to remind his readers that Heracles' mother Alcmene and father Amphitryon were both descendants of Perseus, who was a descendant of Danaus's brother Aegyptus (see figure 2). Herodotus is trying to explain why Heracles is worshipped in Egypt; by adducing this Greek connection with Egypt, he suggests that the cult of Heracles, and Heracles' very name, came to Greece through Heracles' "Egyptian" ancestors. Bernal argues that the name derives from "a sacred paranomasia [sic] [pun] or combination of three West Semitic roots all based on the consonants √ḥrr."[27] But in fact the etymology of Heracles' name is, as linguists would say, transparent. It is a compound of two Indo-European roots, *Hera* (the goddess) and *kleos* (fame), and means "whose fame is from/of/for Hera."[28]

In conclusion, no substantial arguments can be made for an African invasion of Greece in prehistoric times. The absence of evidence for such an invasion seriously undermines the Afrocentric argument that there was a significant African element in the population in Greece in the second millennium. Without such a presence in Greece, it is more difficult to argue that historical Greeks could have had African ancestors. As it is, such claims must rest on independent evidence. But this evidence also will prove to be both weak and circumstantial.

WAS SOCRATES BLACK?

I first learned about the notion that Socrates was black several years ago, from a student in my second-year Greek course on Plato's *Apology*, his account of Socrates' trial and conviction.[29] Throughout the entire semester the student had regarded me with sullen hostility. A year or so later she apologized. She explained that she thought I had been concealing the truth about Socrates' origins. In a course in Afro-American studies she had been told that he was black, and my silence about his African ancestry seemed to her to be a confirmation of the Eurocentric arrogance her instructor had warned her about. After she had taken my course, the student pursued the question on her own, and was satisfied that I had been telling her the truth: so far as we know, Socrates was ethnically no different from other Athenians.

What had this student learned in her course in Afro-American studies? The notion that Socrates was black is based on two different kinds of inference. The first "line of proof" is based on inference from *possibility*. Why couldn't an Athenian have African ancestors? That of course would have been possible; almost anything is *possible*. But it is another question whether or not it was probable. Few prominent Athenians claim to have had foreign ancestors of any sort. Athenians were particularly fastidious about their own origins. In Socrates' day, they did not allow Greeks from other city-states to become naturalized Athenian citizens, and they were even more careful about the non-Greeks or *barbaroi*. Since Socrates was an Athenian citizen, his parents must have been Athenians, as he himself says they were.[30]

Another reason why I thought it unlikely that Socrates (or any of his immediate ancestors) was a foreigner is that no contemporary calls attention to anything extraordinary in his background. If he had been a foreigner, one of his enemies, or one of the comic poets, would have been sure to point it out. The comic poets never missed an opportunity to make fun of the origins of Athenian celebrities. Socrates was no exception;

he is lampooned by Aristophanes in his comedy *Clouds*. Aristophanes did not hesitate to say that the playwright Euripides' mother was a vegetable-seller, that is a poor woman, possibly even a slave or freed-woman, even though Euripides, like the other famous poets, came from a propertied Athenian family.[31] Other comic poets alleged that Aristophanes himself was a foreigner. They accused him in their comedies of being a native of the island of Rhodes, and of the island of Aegina, where his father owned property.[32] If comic poets enjoyed teasing Aristophanes for his alleged connection with other Greek city-states, think of what they would have said about Socrates if he had been known to have even the remotest connection to a foreign civilization, such as Egypt or Ethiopia! If Socrates or his parents had had dark skin, some of his contemporaries would have been likely to mention it, because this, and not just his eccentric ideas about the gods, and the voice that spoke to him alone, would have distinguished him from the rest of the Athenians. Unless, of course, he could not be distinguished from other Athenians because they all had dark skin; but then if they did, why did they not more closely resemble the Ethiopians in their art?

Those are the arguments I put forward in my article about Bernal and the Afrocentrists in the *New Republic*. But since, admittedly, they are only arguments from probability, some readers found my discussion unpersuasive. One reader suggested that Socrates' ancestors might have come to Athens before the law was passed in 451–450 B.C. that limited Athenian citizenship to persons who had two native Athenian parents.[33] If so, they would have had to come before 470, when Socrates was born. But since we have no information that any

of Socrates' ancestors came from anywhere other than
Athens, why should we assume that they came from somewhere else? And if they came from a foreign place, why assume that they came from Egypt or Nubia rather than from
Phoenicia, Palestine, or Scythia? In fact, the need to establish
that Socrates' ancestors came from Africa is strictly a twentieth-century phenomenon, specific to this country and to our
own notions of race.

Another line of argument in favor of Socrates' African ancestry has been offered by Martin Bernal: Socrates was said
by eyewitnesses, his pupils Plato and Xenophon, to have resembled a silenus—an imaginary creature like a bearded
man with a horse's tail and ears. In portrait sculptures dating
after his lifetime, Socrates is shown with a snub nose, broad
nostrils, and a wide mouth, features that may also be found in
portrayals of Ethiopian types on vase paintings. Athenians
appear to have identified these facial characteristics with
Ethiopians, because on a vase from the fourth century B.C. the
faces of an Ethiopian and a white satyr (a creature with a
man's body, except for pointed ears, and a goat's legs and a
horse's tail) are made from the same mold.[34]

This argument is ingenious, but like the argument about
Socrates' possible ancestors, it is an argument from inference
that does not stand up to scrutiny. First of all, nothing certain
can be deduced about Socrates' actual physical appearance
from how it is portrayed in sculpture. None of the portraits is
drawn from life; rather they were inspired by jokes in his
pupils' writings about his being flat-nosed and bald. In
Xenophon's *Symposium* Socrates describes himself as "snub-
nosed" (*simotes*, 5.6). In Plato's *Symposium* Socrates' pupil

Alcibiades compares him to a silenus and to a satyr (215b). None of these traits proves anything about his ethnic origins. In order to show that a joke about his looking like a silenus or satyr meant that Socrates had African origins, it would be necessary to establish that snub noses, broad nostrils, and wide mouths in Athenian vase painting were exclusive characteristics of African types. But, in fact, they are by no means exclusive. Greeks thought that the Scythians were snub-nosed, and they lived in what is now south Russia—about as far from Africa as anyone at the time could have been imagined to live.[35] In vase paintings, by far the largest number of faces with these features belong to silenoi and satyrs. These creatures are usually depicted with the same skin color as other Greek males on the vases; they were in fact believed to be natives of the Greek countryside. Saying that Socrates looks like a silenus means that Socrates looks like a silenus, not like an African. If we were to use his resemblance to a silenus as an indication of his origins, it would clearly be equally logical to infer that he was descended from bearded men with horse's ears and tails.

WERE THE NATIVES OF ANCIENT NORTH AFRICA BLACK?

Joel A. Rogers, in *World's Great Men of Color* (1946) includes on his list of ancient "Black personalities" Aesop, Hannibal, and the Roman playwright Terence. Rogers appears to think that anyone who was born on the continent of Africa was black, and uses the term black to describe anyone who has African blood, or who can by virtue of location be presumed to possess it. But Aesop and Hannibal do not belong on the list. Aesop probably never existed. The ancient accounts of his "life" say that he was dark (*melas*, or in Latin, *niger*) and flat-nosed, but they also state explicitly he came not from Africa but from Phrygia in Asia Minor.[36] Only one late source suggests that Aesop was of African origin; this is Maximus Planudes, a scholar of the late thirteenth century A.D. Relying on the description in the earlier lives, Planudes imagines that Aesop also had prominent lips and that Aesop meant *dark* in Ethiopian.[37] Hannibal was an aristocratic Carthaginian, whose ancestors came from Phoenicia (or Canaan), as the *baal* in his name suggests, and the Phoenicians were a Semitic people.

A better case can be made for the Roman poet Terence. The ancient biographer Suetonius says that Terence had a dark complexion (*fusco colore*).[38] So it is certainly possible that Terence was black, because the same term (*fuscus*) is used in a first-century poem to describe the skin color of a woman who is unambiguously of "African descent."[39] But we cannot be absolutely certain, since Terence, like Hannibal, came from Carthage,[40] and the Carthaginians were of Phoenician origin. The term *fuscus*, or "dark," can also be used to describe the skin color of Mediterranean people.[41] The Greeks and Romans were less precise in their use of color terms than we would wish, because skin color to them was no more important than the color of a person's eyes or hair.[42]

Unfortunately, nothing about Terence's ethnicity can be determined from his name, Publius Terentius Afer or "Terence the African." What the Romans called "Africa" was only the north coast of that continent. The native population of the North were the ancestors of the modern Berbers; they are shown in Egyptian art with light hair and facial coloring. Their land was colonized by Phoenicians, Greeks, and finally by Romans. For that reason it is unlikely that most natives of what was called "Africa" in antiquity, that is North Africa, were "black" in the modern sense of the word. Afrocentrist writers tend to overlook this distinction. In *African Origins of the Major "Western Religions"* (1970), Yosef A. A. ben-Jochannan certainly does:

> Indigenous Africans, in this work, specifically refers to the ancestors of and present Africans who are today called "Negroes, Bantus, Hottentots, Pygmies, Bushmen," etc.; even "Niggers" by some.[43]

So defined, his list of "indigenous Africans" includes St. Augustine (354–430 A.D.) and his mother, Monnica; Saints Cyprian, Perpetua, and Felicity; and Tertullian of Carthage. He also includes a certain Namphamo, whom he calls "the first of the Christian martyrs."

Ben-Jochannan does not point out that the only reason to think that these Africans were black comes from the presumption that the ancient term "Africa" applied to all the rest of the continent. Such information as we have about them suggests instead that they were actually Carthaginian or Roman, rather than African in the modern sense of the word. During the early centuries A.D., when these Christian martyrs lived, the population of Carthage included native Berbers and Romans. The Romans were the descendants of the settlers who, in the first century B.C., had been sent to rebuild the city. Carthage had been destroyed by the Romans in 146 B.C., but many people of Phoenician ancestry remained in the area. As a result, the ethnic mix of people in ancient Tunisia was varied, and in the absence of other evidence, no assumptions can be made about anyone's background.

Such information as we have suggests that the martyrs on ben-Jochannan's list were not what people today would call Africans. Virtually nothing is known about Namphamo of Numidia (the general region of St. Augustine's hometown of Hippo). Clearly, ben-Jochannan appears not to have checked the original sources, which are not cited.[44] If he had, he might have discovered that Namphamo was neither black nor the first African martyr. His name is Punic, as ben-Jochannan in fact notes: it means "man of good feet, i.e., bringer of good fortune."[45] Since he is mentioned along with three other persons with Punic names, he was probably a Carthaginian, in other words, a Semite. Furthermore, Namphamo was not a "first martyr" (*protomartyr*), but is called (somewhat sarcastically) an "important martyr" (*archimartyr*).[46] Perhaps he and his comrades were members of a heretical local sect that was suppressed by the Church.[47]

Such cults of martyrs were clearly important to the North African Christians in the first centuries A.D.[48] Saint Perpetua of Carthage, who was martyred in 203, appears to have come from a well-to-do family of Roman settlers in Carthage.[49] Felicity was a slave, but this tells us nothing about her ethnic origins; in the ancient world, anyone could become a slave. Since nothing is said about her being a foreigner, the presumption is that her background was unremarkable, that is, Roman or Carthaginian. The same presumption can be made about Tertullian of Carthage (ca. 160–240), who was the son of a Roman centurion and a Roman citizen. Cyprian of Carthage, who was martyred in 258, was a Roman citizen, and lived on his family estate.[50] St. Augustine was born in the North African town of Thagaste, now Souk Ahras in Algeria. His father appears to have been a property owner of Roman (that is, Italian) descent, but his mother may well have been a Berber, as her name Monnica (from the native god Mon) suggests.[51] The name of his son Adeodatus "by god given" is the Latin equivalent of the Punic (that is, Phoenician) name Iatanbaal, which was popular among Carthaginian Christians.[52] It is clear from his own writing that even though he thinks of himself as an "African" and writes in the distinctive style of a native of North Africa, he does not think of himself as a black or Ethiopian.[53]

WAS CLEOPATRA BLACK?

Until recently, no one ever asked whether Cleopatra might have had an African ancestor, because our surviving ancient sources identify her as a Macedonian Greek. Her ancestors, the Ptolemies, were descended from one of Alexander's generals. After Alexander's death in 323 B.C., these generals divided among themselves the territory in the Mediterranean that Alexander had conquered. The name Cleopatra was one of the names traditionally given to women in the royal family; officially, our Cleopatra (69–30 B.C.) was Cleopatra VII, the daughter of Ptolemy XII and his sister.[54] Cleopatra VII herself followed the family practice of marrying within the family. She married her two brothers (Ptolemy XIII and XIV) in succession (after the first died in suspicious circumstances, she had the second murdered). Her first language was Greek, but she was the first member of the Ptolemaic line who was able to speak Egyptian.[55] She also wore Egyptian dress, and the art of the time shows her wearing the dress of the goddess Isis. She chose to portray herself as an Egyptian not because she was Egyptian, but because she was ambitious to stay in power. In her surviving portraits on coins and in sculpture she appears to be impressive rather than beautiful, Mediterranean in appearance, with straight hair and a hooked nose.[56] Of course, these portraits on metal and stone give no indication of the color of her skin.

The only possibility that she might not have been a full-blooded Macedonian Greek arises from the fact that we do not know the precise identity of one member of her family tree: her grandmother on her father's side. Her grandmother was the mistress (not the wife) of her grandfather, Ptolemy IX. Because nothing is known about this person, the assumption has always been that she was a Macedonian Greek, like the other members of Ptolemy's court. Like other Greeks, the Ptolemies were wary of foreigners. They kept themselves apart from the native population, with brothers usually marrying sisters, or uncles marrying nieces, or in one case a father marrying his daughter (Ptolemy IX and Cleopatra Berenice III).[57] Because the Ptolemies seemed to prefer to marry among themselves, even incestuously, it has always been assumed that Cleopatra's grandmother was closely connected with the family. If she had been a foreigner, one of the Roman writers of the time would have mentioned it in an invective against Cleopatra as an enemy of the Roman state. These writers were supporters of Octavian (later known as Augustus), who defeated Cleopatra's forces in the battle of Actium in 31 B.C. (see figure 3).

Those are the known facts, but the question "was Cleopatra black?" has little to do with historical reality. If it did, the historians who thought that Cleopatra had an African ancestor would want to find out more about Cleopatra's father, Ptolemy XII, before they began to consider the question of Cleopatra. Ptolemy XII would have been more likely than Cleopatra to have learned Egyptian language and customs, if his mother had been an Egyptian. But the historians who claim that Cleopatra was black concentrate on Cleopatra, because she, and not her father or grandfather, is a legendary figure. Everybody knows her name, even if they know little or nothing else about ancient history.

Unfortunately, most of the writers who have raised and discussed the question about Cleopatra's ethnicity are not ancient historians. The first American writer to suggest that Cleopatra had a black ancestor was J. A. Rogers, in *World's Great Men of Color*. Rogers has several reasons for including Cleopatra along with Hannibal and Terence in his list of famous "black" Africans. One, of course, is the question about the identity of her grandmother. Here Rogers offers a garbled account: "Cleopatra's father, Ptolemy XIII, was the illegitimate offspring of Ptolemy XI" (actually her father was Ptolemy XII and her grandfather was Ptolemy IX); "her father, Ptolemy XIII, shows pronounced Negro traits."[58] In fact, Ptolemy XIII was Cleopatra's *brother* (and husband). Rogers appears to assume that if Cleopatra's father was illegitimate his mother must have been an African slave. But that is an assumption that is based on the recent past, not on the prac-

FIGURE 3

CLEOPATRA'S FAMILY TREE

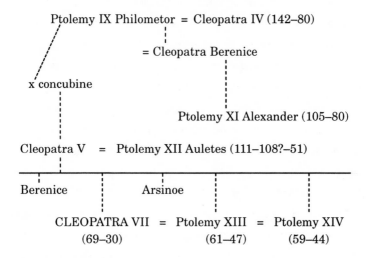

Ptolemy IX Philometor = Cleopatra IV (142–80)

= Cleopatra Berenice

x concubine

Ptolemy XI Alexander (105–80)

Cleopatra V = Ptolemy XII Auletes (111–108?–51)

Berenice   Arsinoe

CLEOPATRA VII = Ptolemy XIII = Ptolemy XIV
(69–30)   (61–47)   (59–44)

All dates are B.C.

tices of the Greco-Roman world. In the ancient world slavery was not based solely on skin type. Since most ancient slaves were war captives, they came from many ethnic backgrounds; Romans enslaved Greeks, and Greeks enslaved each other. But we do not even know that Cleopatra's grandmother was a slave. All we know about her is that she was not married to Cleopatra's grandfather. Rogers infers that she was black on the analogy of the practices of the slaveholding plantation owners in the nineteenth century. In support of his claims about Cleopatra's ancestry and the "Negroid" appearance of Ptolemy XIII, Rogers refers to the articles on Ptolemy XII, Ptolemy XIII, and Cleopatra in the *Encyclopaedia Britannica*, but nothing in these articles supports his statements.[59]

In support of his contention about Cleopatra's African ancestress, Rogers asserts that before the start of the slave trade even European writers thought of Cleopatra as a black woman: "until the rise of the doctrine of white superiority Cleopatra was generally pictured as colored." The "evidence" for this striking claim comes from Shakespeare. According to Rogers, "in the opening lines of his Antony and Cleopatra Shakespeare calls her 'tawny.'" This term, Rogers claims, was used in the seventeenth century to describe mulattoes; hence, he concludes, Shakespeare thought of Cleopatra as a mulatto. Rogers also cites a passage, where (as he puts it) Cleopatra speaks of herself as "'black,' made so by the sun."[60]

Here Rogers is on slightly firmer ground than in his account of Cleopatra's family tree; Shakespeare in fact does use the words *tawny* and *black* to describe Cleopatra. But in context neither adjective means what Rogers wants them to mean. The opening lines are in fact intended as a caricature of Cleopatra, not as an actual description of her appearance. The speaker, Antony's friend Philo, is describing how Antony has degenerated because of his love for Cleopatra, whom he compares to a gypsy woman: Antony's eyes that once "glow'd like plated Mars, now bend, now turn / The office and devotion of their view / Upon a tawny front," that is, a dark face; Antony's "captain's heart . . . is become the bellows and the fan / To cool a gipsy's lust" (I.i.2–9). Later in the play, when Antony realizes he has lost the war, he makes a similar attack on his lover: "O this false soul of Egypt! . . . like a right gipsy, hath at fast and loose / Beguil'd me to the very heart of loss" (IV.xii.25–29). Neither Philo nor Antony says that Cleopatra actually *was* a gipsy, which is to say an Egyptian, because that is what the word implied in Shakespeare's day. Shakespeare knew that she was a Ptolemy, as is clear from the words he gives to Charmian in the closing lines of the play: "it is well done, and fitting for a princess / Descended of so many royal kings" (V.ii.326–27). His source for the drama was a translation of an ancient Greek source, Plutarch's *Life of Antony*.

Nor does Shakespeare's reference to her as "black" indicate that he thought she had African ancestors. In his discussion of this passage Rogers seems to have missed the point of a clever joke: Cleopatra implies that while Antony is away she has taken the Sun God as a lover. She suggests that the god, whom she identifies with Phoebus Apollo, has bruised her with his pinches: "Think on me / that am with Phoebus' amorous pinches black / And wrinkled deep in time" because of Antony's long absence (I.v.27–29). In his eagerness to find references to Cleopatra's skin color, Rogers has misinterpreted Shakespeare's meaning.[61] She says only that her skin is bruised; if Shakespeare had meant to indicate that her skin color was black, he would have been more likely to have had her refer to herself as an "Ethiope."[62]

But evidently Rogers was not concerned with discovering what Shakespeare actually meant. He was interested in finding references and citations to "prove" his points; all his assertions are backed up by some sort of partial evidence. Selective use of evidence is a characteristic of propagandistic history; so is blinkered vision, the tendency simply to ignore or omit evidence that might contradict what the propagandist is trying to prove. Surviving portraits of Cleopatra do not suggest that she was a person of African descent. Rogers, however, says that there is no authentic portrait of Cleopatra in existence (there are in fact several). Instead he provides evidence from the modern popular writer Robert Ripley, author of *Believe It or Not*: "Robert Ripley, who says he has proof of all his facts, calls Cleopatra 'fat and black.'"[63] What sources did Ripley rely on? Rogers does not say.

I have gone into some detail about Rogers's *Great Men of Color* because despite its inaccuracies and insupportable claims, it was reprinted by Collier Books in 1972, and is still available, now in its nineteenth printing. Not only has this book been widely read; it is cited as the authority for discussions of Cleopatra by other Afrocentric writers. John Henrik Clarke, who was Professor and Chair of African History at Hunter College in New York, has a section about Cleopatra in his chapter on "African Warrior Queens" in *Black Women in Antiquity*. This book was originally an issue of the *Journal of African Civilizations*, but it was expanded in 1987 and reprinted in 1992.[64] Clarke's principal source is Rogers's *World's Great Men of Color*. He refers to no standard works on ancient history, but rather summarizes Rogers's discussion of the significance of Shakespeare's reference to her "tawny" skin—as if Shakespeare were an authority on Ptolemaic Egypt. He also cites the passage from Ripley's *Believe It or Not*. But he adds new supporting information of his own, such as a modern portrait by Earl Sweeney, showing Cleopatra with black skin and distinctively African features. He also states that "in the *Book of Acts* Cleopatra describes herself as 'black.'"[65] Clarke does not cite chapter and verse in the *Book of Acts*. This is not surprising, since Cleopatra is not mentioned in that work. It would indeed be miraculous if she had described herself there, because she died in 30 B.C., and the

Acts of the Apostles were written more than sixty years later, after the death of Jesus.

Clarke appears to be indifferent to problems of chronology and does not seem to have checked the ancient sources or standard works of reference. So it is no wonder that his account of Cleopatra's family is confused. He manages to identify her father correctly as Ptolemy XII. But then he states that Ptolemy XII was the son of Ptolemy XI (he was the son of Ptolemy IX). Ptolemy XI was in fact Ptolemy XII's first cousin. Like Rogers, Clarke insists on the importance of Ptolemy XII's illegitimacy, as if that proved anything about his ethnicity: "the legitimate line ended with Ptolemy XII. Those who say that Cleopatra was 'pure' Greek forget this fact."[66]

Clarke's account not only provides more misinformation than Rogers's; it is also further removed from the ancient sources. Rogers at least offered a detailed description of Cleopatra's character and actions, which he appears to have drawn directly or indirectly from ancient sources like Plutarch's *Life of Antony*. But Clarke offers only a brief account of Cleopatra's reliance on Caesar and Antony to keep Egypt from becoming a colony of Rome. For him, she is both an African and a victim of European oppression: "She was a shrewd politician and an Egyptian nationalist. She committed suicide when she lost control of Egypt."[67] This Cleopatra would not be out of place in a work of historical fiction that sought to provide an allegory of the social ills of the late twentieth century. But here she appears in a work that sets out to provide an account of "the historical status of African women and their contribution to the development of African societies."[68] She is the Cleopatra that schoolchildren are learning about, if they are being instructed by teachers who use the most wide-spread Afrocentric teaching resource, the African American Baseline Essays, developed for the school system in Portland, Oregon. From this text children are learning that "Cleopatra VII . . . was of mixed African and Greek parentage. . . . She was not fully a Greek."[69]

Some of my colleagues have argued that teaching that Cleopatra is black can do no harm, particularly if it helps to instill pride in students who have been mistreated by the majority society. It is, after all, only a "myth." The trouble is that a student who believes that such a myth is historically accurate will be reluctant to discuss or even unable to understand evidence to the contrary. In 1989 a Wellesley student wrote a letter to the college newspaper to complain that by showing the film *Cleopatra*, starring Elizabeth Taylor, my department had perpetuated a lie of "white supremacy." She repeated Rogers's basic arguments, and then added:

> By the time Cleopatra was born she was almost, if not all, Egyptian. . . . The theology [*sic*] behind the white Cleopatra is a clear reflection of the racial stereotypes that persist in this country. They believe that Africans and African Americans have made no significant contributions to history and that no prominent civilizations could be anything less than white.[70]

One of my classicist colleagues tried to discuss Cleopatra's genealogy with her, but she refused to believe what she was told because none of the surviving portraits of Cleopatra are in mediums that give an indication of her skin color. Apparently she still believes what she had learned about Cleopatra's African ancestry, because in May 1993 she wrote her instructor to complain about the "narrow minded 'scholars'" at Wellesley:

> I should have realized that once Wellesley professors openly supported the notion that Cleopatra was not a woman of color, that "education" is not always a measure of one's intelligence. It is shameful that those who appear to be so advanced, are actually far behind.[71]

Clearly she regards the notion of a black Cleopatra as an article of faith.

The myth seems to have an irresistible appeal. Dr. Shelley Haley, a professor of classics at Hamilton College, has written a vivid account of how she, a black woman, has come to believe in Cleopatra's African ancestry. When her grandmother insisted that Cleopatra was black, Haley replied that her own studies in the Classics had shown her that Cleopatra was Greek.[72] Some years later, Haley found herself teaching a class at Howard University that made the same assertions about Cleopatra that her grandmother had made. Some of her students insisted that she had "bought a lie." It was then that Haley said she "saw—for the first time—question marks where Cleopatra's grandmother ought to be." None of her instructors had pointed out that the identity of Cleopatra's grandmother was unknown. "I was shaken," she writes; "what did those question marks mean?"[73]

The traditional way to go about answering Haley's question would have been to ask how likely it was that the mistress of

Ptolemy IX could have been an Egyptian or Nubian, rather than a Greek. In favor of her being a Greek is (as I have pointed out) the fact that the Ptolemies tended whenever possible to marry each other (that is, other Greeks), and with one exception, took Greek mistresses. The one exception was Didyme, a woman who in the third century B.C. was one of the many mistresses of Ptolemy II Philadelphus (308–246 B.C.). Our information about Didyme comes from a memoir by this Ptolemy's son, Ptolemy III Euergetes (284–222 B.C.). A passage from this memoir is quoted by a later ancient writer, but the text of the memoir itself is lost. According to Ptolemy III, Didyme was "one of the native women."[74] Didyme, which in Greek means "Twin," along with its Egyptian equivalent *Hatre*, was a common name in Egypt, where there seems to have been a high proportion of twins.[75] If this Didyme is the same Didyme as a beautiful woman described in a contemporary poem by the Greek writer Asclepiades, she had the dark coloring of a Nubian.[76] I say "if," because Didyme was a common name. Of this Didyme the poet says, "When I gaze at her beauty I melt like wax before a fire; if she is dark [*melaina*], what of it? So are coals." The Greek word *melaina*, which I have translated as "dark" (our term *melanin* is of course derived from it), can simply describe the dark coloring of some Mediterranean faces. Aesop the Phrygian was "dark,"[77] and Sappho was described by one of her biographers as "dusky" (*phaiodes*).[78] But in the case of the "dark" Didyme described in the poem, "so are coals" suggests that she was black—Nubians lived in Egypt from the earliest times, and many adopted Egyptian customs and names.[79]

So Didyme, a mistress of Ptolemy II Philadelphus, was probably an African, and possibly even a Nubian. But it is important to remember that her son (if she ever had one) did not become king. It is also important to note that we know that Didyme was "one of the native women, of extraordinary beauty." The fact that she is so identified suggests that it was unusual for a Ptolemy to have a non-Greek mistress. No ancient writer has anything to say about the ethnicity or appearance of Ptolemy II's other mistresses: Bilistiche, Agathocleia, Stratonice, and Myrto—presumably because they were Greek.

Because the normal practice of ancient writers was to make as much as possible out of any anomaly or scandal, such as a love affair with or marriage to a foreigner, we can also presume that Cleopatra's grandmother and mother were Greek, because no ancient writer comments on them. Although the ancients were in general without color prejudice, they were sensitive to differences in appearance, background, and in language. They called foreigners *barbaroi* because what they said did not make sense—at least to Greek ears. So it is more likely that Cleopatra's grandmother was a Greek, and not a slave, because that would be the most unremarkable possible identity. Admittedly that is an argument from silence, but that is the only kind of argument we can make without specific factual information. Whoever her grandmother and mother were, Cleopatra regarded herself as a Greek. And what are the arguments in favor of the possibility that she was Egyptian? Only that she could have been an Egyptian, since the Ptolemies were based in Egypt. But she also could have been another type of foreigner, a Jew or a Persian, since Alexandria was at the time an unusually cosmopolitan place.

But Haley's answer to this question, if I understand it rightly, was to suppose that because no standard ancient history book had commented on the possible significance of the unknown grandmother, the white and mostly male authors of these books had concealed Cleopatra's true identity as a *black woman*: "I began to see and still am arriving at seeing that Cleopatra is the crystallization of the tension between my yearning to fit in among classicists and my identity politics."[80] This statement is remarkable because it suggests that the question of evidence one way or another can be decided by means of "identity politics." The purpose of "identity politics," or IDPOL, as Daphne Patai and Noretta Koertge characterize it, is to serve a political cause, or in this case two political causes.[81] Once IDPOL becomes a determining factor in history, present goals can be used to define what happened in the past, and Cleopatra's identity as a woman of African descent can be established with something like certainty:

> When we say, in general, that the ancient Egyptians were Black, and, more specifically, that Cleopatra was Black, we claim them as part of a culture and history that has known oppression and triumph, exploitation and survival. . . . Even as a "Greco-Egyptian," Cleopatra was a product of miscegenation. How is it she is not Black?[82]

But this assessment of Cleopatra's symbolic value is also inaccurate. In fact, Cleopatra's reign does not provide a good example of oppression and triumph, exploitation and survival. She did not triumph. She managed to stay in power until her forces were defeated at Actium, and she died because she did not wish to be led through the streets of Rome in the celebration of Octavian's triumph over Egypt.

In her treatment of Cleopatra, Haley tends to avoid direct discussion of the evidence. Instead, she characterizes the traditional notion of Cleopatra's identity as "a construction of classical scholars and the Greek and Roman authors they consulted." She presumes that because these writers were European, "they were willing—eager—to erase the Black ancestor and claim the beautiful Cleopatra for Europe."[83] But that claim seems unfair, for several reasons. Ancient writers would not have hesitated to record that Cleopatra had an African ancestor, if she had had one. Ptolemy III Euergetes called attention in his memoirs to Didyme's African background; there is no attempt on his part to conceal her identity. Also, the notion of a beautiful Cleopatra is not a construction of ancient historians, but of writers like Shakespeare. Plutarch (our principal ancient source) explicitly says that Cleopatra was not beautiful, nor is she shown with idealized features on ancient portrait coins.

The principal reason why classical scholars do not talk about Cleopatra's black ancestors is that no one knows that Cleopatra's grandmother was an Egyptian, or whether she was black, because *no one knows anything about Cleopatra's grandmother.* Haley avoids direct discussion of this key issue, adding in a footnote that "the Greeks took Egyptian and Ethiopian women as mistresses. . . . I think it is safe to say that Cleopatra had Black ancestors."[84] She offers two references in support of this claim.[85] But she does not point out that both of these references describe the same single instance of a Greek and Egyptian alliance: Didyme, the one non-Greek mistress among the "very many" mistresses of Ptolemy Philadelphus. Thus, statistically, since it is based on a sample of one, Haley's assertion can hardly be considered "safe." Now, it is not at all remarkable that Haley (or anyone) should come up with hypotheses about the past on the basis of insufficient evidence. But Haley's discussion appeared in a volume edited by classical scholars and published by a respected publisher, Routledge. Why didn't an expert reader or the volume's editors themselves ask her to state her claims about Cleopatra's "blackness" somewhat more tentatively?

Perhaps Haley's views were not subject to any searching critique because the editors of the book her essay appears in are themselves critical of traditional methodology and ideology.[86] The articles appear to have been included on the basis of the rightness of their ideology and motives, and these ends have been allowed to justify the authors' means. Nowadays such practices are not at all unusual. Instructors in universities now place less emphasis on the acquisition of factual information than they did a generation ago. They are suspicious of the value of facts, or to put it another way, they think that facts are meaningless because they can be manipulated and reinterpreted. If it is true (and I think it almost always is) that no historical work can be written without bias of some sort, it follows that no historian can be trusted to give an entirely accurate picture of what the writer is seeking to describe. Of course historians (and their readers) have always been aware that they can and do write with an evident bias—the Roman historian Tacitus tells us at the beginning of his *Annals* that he proposes to write the history of the emperors from Augustus to Nero *sine ira et studio*, "without anger or intensity," but his narrative shows that he did not mean what he said. But recently, many historians have been concentrating on another type of bias, this time unconscious: the blinkers put on everyone's vision by the values of their particular societies. These scholars insist that history is always composed in conformity or response to the values of the society in which it is produced, and for that reason can be regarded as a cultural projection of the values of that society, whether individual writers are aware of it or not.

Such beliefs, if carried to their logical extreme, make it possible to say that all history is by definition fiction. If history is fiction, it is natural to deny or to minimize the importance of all historical data (since it can be manipulated). Instead, these writers concentrate on cultural *motives*. Historians, in their view, write what they *are*. The debate has moved away from facts or evidence, to perceived motivations, and the quality of a discussion now depends on whether the participants in the discussion have good or beneficial motivations, as judged by themselves: if they believe that a person's motivations are good, then what they say will be right.

Concentrating on cultural motivations (however inaccurately defined or however irrelevant they may be to the past) allows us to form judgments without the careful amassing of details that characterizes traditional research, and without even learning foreign languages. It is also possible to ignore, or at least not to emphasize, questions of chronology. How reasonable is it to require the ancients to have shared our definitions of race or our concern with oppression of women and ethnic minorities?

The inevitable result of *cultural* history-writing, unless it is done with the greatest of caution, is a portrait of the past painted with broad strokes and bright colors of our own choosing. It is almost as if we removed all the Rembrandts from the museum and replaced them with Mondrians in order to study the history of the Renaissance. We are left with a vivid history of the concerns of our own society. We can now see in the past not the issues that the people living at that time considered important, whatever these might have been, but a biased history written to the dictates of dead white European males, and a literature largely insensitive to the needs and aspirations of women and cultural minorities. Academics ought to have seen right from the start that this "new historicism" has some serious shortcomings. But in fact most of us are just beginning to emerge from the fog far enough to see where history-without-facts can lead us, which is right back to fictive history of the kind developed to serve the Third Reich. It is not coincidental that ours is the era not just of Holocaust denial but of denial that the ancient Greeks were ancient Greeks and creators of their own intellectual heritage.

In traditional historical writing, arguments are based on the discussion of evidence. But in cultural history the quality of the argument depends upon its *cultural* merit. On these grounds (as opposed to traditional methods of proof), Haley's argument about Cleopatra's ethnicity seems eminently successful. Since her stated goal, which is shared by her editors, is to redress past oppression and to help establish a new social justice, she presents a portrait of Cleopatra as a woman (rather than as a Hellenistic despotic ruler), as a black (rather than a Macedonian Greek), and as a victim (rather than the loser in a closely matched struggle for power). It is not that there is no factual data to support some of these hypotheses; it is unquestionably true that we do not know the precise identity of Cleopatra's paternal grandmother, the mistress of Ptolemy IX. The problem lies in how the evidence is used. Surely it is misleading to suggest that the unique non-Greek mistress Didyme provides evidence of a common practice, or that Cleopatra was almost completely Egyptian. Possibility is not the same thing as probability. But people who want Cleopatra to be black tend to downplay the importance of *warranted* evidence in constructing their arguments. That is, in place of known historical fact, these writers prefer to substitute *acceptable* claims, simply because they are approved by their particular audiences.[87] Once the distinction between warranted fact and acceptable claim is collapsed, the way is open for daring new interpretations, and possibilities can easily be turned into probabilities. For example, because we know nothing about Cleopatra's grandmother, it is possible to conjecture that her identity was deliberately concealed. In the absence of any information about the reasons for the concealment, it is possible to hypothesize that the facts about her identity were suppressed because she was black, just as some people nowadays refuse to acknowledge their black ancestors. Therefore (to follow this line of argument to its logical conclusion), even though her portraits show her to have no characteristically African features, it becomes possible to conclude that she was black. The argument can then be judged to be successful because it is *culturally* plausible. No one seems to have pointed out that a generation ago, it would have been possible to argue on the same grounds that Cleopatra was Jewish.

Despite its anachronism, history based on *acceptable* (as opposed to warranted) proof has considerable appeal among American academics today. The best illustration of popularity of acceptable proof is the success enjoyed by Martin Bernal's multivolume project *Black Athena*, which is one of the few works about the ancient world (other than the Bible) that many modern nonclassicists have heard about, or have even tried to read. Its appeal derives from the cultural correctness of its author's motives: the explicit *political* purpose of Bernal's project is to "lessen European cultural arrogance."[88]

Bernal attempts to show that ancient historians have not acknowledged the full extent of Greece's debt to Egypt and the
Near East. He also seeks to establish that writers in the eighteenth and nineteenth centuries failed to give due credit to
the influence of Egypt and the Near East because of anti-Semitic and racist prejudice.

Evidently we have reached a point in historical study where
motive, however perceived, is more important than evidence.
Because questions like "Was Cleopatra black?" are asked for
cultural reasons, the only acceptable responses will be culturally rather than factually correct: "Yes, she was black because
she *might* possibly have had an Egyptian ancestor, and because as a black she *could* represent the fate of Africa under
European oppression." Myth has now taken precedence over
reality, even in the academy. Clearly the proponents of ethnic
history do not foresee what will happen if other groups, of
whom they do not approve, start writing their own histories
according to their own notions of ethnic correctness. When
someone argues, as Cheryl Johnson-Odim has done, that ancient Egypt should be allowed "to stand for the rest of Africa,"
since "what we are really talking about here is symbolism any-
way," she has made an argument that will find cultural accep-
tance.[89] But once symbolism is taken as a mode of historical
proof, the way is open for other groups, whose aims Johnson-
Odim might not support, to argue for a different symbolism.
Only a few of the people teaching in universities today seem to
have not forgotten that not long ago symbolic myths of ethnic
supremacy were responsible for the deaths of whole populations. One advantage (perhaps the only one) of being older
than most of my colleagues is that I do remember.

THREE

ANCIENT MYTHS
OF CULTURAL
DEPENDENCY

As we saw in the previous chapter, the "evidence" for the Greeks' Egyptian origins derives primarily from modern cultural aspirations and has virtually no foundation in historical fact. The question of Greek cultural dependency is more complicated, and in many ways more interesting. There is no doubt that Greeks were influenced by other neighboring cultures during the whole course of antiquity. The issue is rather: What is meant by influence? In what respects? And by which foreign cultures? How large a role did Egypt play in the development of Greek civilization?

Classicists have always been interested in these questions, and have pursued all possible links. In general, they believe that Greek sculpture was influenced by Egyptian sculpture, but that Greek language, poetry, myths, and other aspects of their art were influenced by Near Eastern civilizations, such as those of the Hittites and Phoenicians. On the basis of what is now known, classicists assume that foreign ideas and information came to the Greeks through nonviolent contact, especially trade. But Afrocentrist writers have rejected this complex model of influence because it assigns such a relatively modest role to the most prominent African civilization in the ancient Near East, that of Egypt. They argue that classicists have tended to overlook or to discount ancient accounts of the Egyptian legacy. Some even allege that the Greeks did not simply borrow, but actually stole their philosophy and science from Egypt. They argue that credit for this knowledge ought to be given back to Africa.

How accurate are these Afrocentrists' views about Greek cultural dependency? In this chapter and the next I shall show that the notion that Egyptian religion and philosophy had a significant influence on Greece is a cultural myth. It is no more likely to be historical than the notion that Egyptians "invaded" Greece in the seventeenth century B.C. or that Socrates had African ancestors. The idea that Greek religion and philosophy has Egyptian origins may appear at first sight to be more plausible, because it derives, at least in part, from the writings of ancient Greek historians. In the fifth century B.C. Herodotus was told by Egyptian priests that the Greeks owed many aspects of their culture to the older and vastly impressive civilization of the Egyptians. Egyptian priests told Diodorus some of the same stories four centuries later. The church fathers in the second and third centuries A.D. also were eager to emphasize the dependency of Greece on the earlier cultures of the Egyptians and the Hebrews.

Some Afrocentrists assume that the Greek historians had access to reliable information about ancient Egypt, and that the accounts of Greek writers can be regarded as literally true. But in this chapter I shall explain why in this matter the Greek writers are not as trustworthy as they claim to be. I will suggest instead that they were eager to establish direct links between their civilization and that of Egypt because Egypt was a vastly older culture, with elaborate religious customs and impressive monuments. But despite their enthusiasm for Egypt and its material culture (an enthusiasm that was later revived in eighteenth- and nineteenth-century Europe), they failed to understand Egyptian religion and the purpose of many Egyptian customs.

Classical scholars tend to be skeptical about the claims of the Greek historians because much of what these writers say does not conform to the facts as they are now known from recent scholarship on ancient Egypt. But Afrocentrists suggest that the classicists have de-emphasized the role of Egypt out of racist motives, because they want to minimize the importance of African civilization. It is alleged that before the nineteenth century, European scholars acknowledged the primacy of Egyptian civilization, but after that paid more attention to the influence on Greece from the Near East and from the Indian subcontinent. As Professor Molefi Kete Asante puts it, "The European construction of imperialism was accompanied by the European slave trade, cultural arrogance, anti-Semitism, anti-Africanism, and racist ideologies in science, literature, and history."[1]

This sweeping judgment has only a limited application to historical studies. Instances of active "cultural arrogance" can be found in eighteenth- and nineteenth-century European history writing, for example, in the work of men like the Baron Cuvier (1769–1832) and the Comte de Gobineau (1816–1882).[2] But their views could hardly be called representative among scholars.[3] In any case such racism had little demonstrable effect on the popular appreciation of Egypt. The information brought back to Europe as a consequence of Napoleon's invasion of Egypt (1798–1801) started a virtual craze. The more than seven thousand pages of illustrations, memoirs, descriptions and commentary contained in *La Déscription d'Égypte* (1809–28) inspired writers, artists, musicians, and artisans.[4] Egyptian themes were portrayed on dinnerware and in interior decoration. A range of skin color and facial characteristics were represented.[5]

The popularity of Egyptian themes in Europe is nowhere better illustrated than by opera. Mozart's operas *Thamos: King of Egypt* (completed 1779) and *The Magic Flute* (1791) are both set in ancient Egypt. Although the librettos were written by different authors, in each opera the civilization of Egypt is treated with reverence. The score for *Thamos* was never completed, but *The Magic Flute* almost immediately became a classic. The enthusiasm for new discoveries in Egypt inspired the sets for productions of *The Magic Flute* in 1815 in Vienna, 1816 in Milan, and 1818 in Munich. The tradition was continued in productions of Rossini's *Moïse* (1827), and act 4 of Gounod's *Faust* (1858). But the culminating tribute was probably Verdi's *Aïda* (1871), which was composed to celebrate the completion of the Suez Canal.[6] Aïda, the heroine of that opera, is herself an Ethiopian, who is loved by Radames, an Egyptian. As Richard Jenkyns observes, miscegenation between her and Radames is not an issue.[7] If Europeans placed less emphasis on the putative Egyptian origins of ancient Greek civilization in the nineteenth century, it was not because they lacked respect for Egypt.

Why, then, did European scholars stop taking at face value the accounts of Egyptian origins in Greek writers like Herodotus and Diodorus of Sicily? They had discovered that the Greek historians were less reliable than they had supposed. New empirical knowledge had enabled them to see how strikingly different ancient Greece was from Egypt. They ceased to emphasize the cultural debt of Greece to Egypt because it was no longer apparent. For centuries Europeans had believed that the ancient historians knew that certain Greek religious customs and philosophical interests derived from Egypt. But two major discoveries changed that view. The first concerned a group of ancient philosophical treatises attributed to Hermes Trismegistus; these had throughout the Middle Ages and into the Renaissance been thought of as Egyptian and early. But in 1614 the French scholar Isaac Casaubon demonstrated that the treatises were actually late and basically Greek. The second discovery was the decipherment of hieroglyphics, the official system of Egyptian writing, which was completed by 1836. Before decipherment, scholars had been compelled to rely on Greek sources for their understanding of Egyptian history and civilization. Once they were able to read real Egyptian texts, and could disregard the fanciful interpretations of hieroglyphics that had been circulating since late antiquity, it became clear to them that the relation of Egyptian to Greek

culture was less close than they had imagined. Egyptian be-
longed to the Afro-Asiatic language family, while Greek was an
Indo-European language, akin to Sanskrit and European languages like Latin.[8]

On the basis of these new discoveries, European scholars
realized that they could no longer take at face value what
Herodotus, Diodorus, and the church fathers had to say about
Greece's debt to Egypt. Once it was possible to read Egyptian
religious documents, and to see how the Egyptians themselves described their gods and told their myths, scholars
could see that the ancient Greeks' accounts of Egyptian religion were superficial, and even misleading. Apparently, Greek
writers, despite their great admiration for Egypt, looked at
Egyptian civilization through cultural blinkers that kept
them from understanding any practices or customs that were
significantly different from their own. The result was a portrait of Egypt that was both astigmatic and deeply Hellenized.
Greek writers operated under other handicaps as well. They
did not have access to records; there was no defined system of
chronology. They could not read Egyptian inscriptions or question a variety of witnesses because they did not know the language. Hence they were compelled to exaggerate the
importance of such resemblances as they could see or find.

Knowledge of Egypt from Egyptian sources revealed that
Herodotus's account of Egypt was off-the-mark in many particulars. The false information that he reports has led some modern scholars to suggest that Herodotus deliberately invented
some of the misinformation in his narrative.[9] But it is much
more likely that he and the Greek historians who literally followed in his footsteps reported what they did in good faith,

even when it turns out that they were confused or simply wrong. For that reason I shall speak of the misinformation they offer as historical myth rather than fiction or fantasy. We do not need to assume that Herodotus deliberately made up stories about Egypt, even when what he tells us is contradicted by known fact. The problem lies rather in his way of collecting his information.

Herodotus tells us very little about how he composed his history, but we can get an impression of some of the problems he encountered from his successor, the first-century Greek writer Diodorus of Sicily. Diodorus briefly describes some of the problems he encountered:

> We must make a distinction among historians, since many who have written about Egypt and Ethiopia have either believed false information or invented stories to attract readers, and thus may justifiably be distrusted. Most of what I have written has been taken from the accounts of Agatharchides of Cnidus in the second book of his history of Asia, and the compiler of geographies Artemidorus of Ephesus in his eighth book, and from some others who lived in Egypt— these have got it right in almost all respects. For when I was in Egypt myself, I met many priests, and I spoke with not a few emissaries from Ethiopia who were there at the time. I went over everything carefully with them, and tested what the historians told me, and wrote my account to conform with what most of them agreed on.[10]

Although the works of the historians Diodorus trusted are now lost, at least he tells us that he began by studying the work of Greek writers. Clearly he made an effort to distinguish fiction from history. But he was not prepared to engage in what we would now think of as historical research. He did not learn Egyptian and read Egyptian documents and consult archives. Instead, he relied on oral testimony from native informants. If what Greek writers like Agatharchides and Artemidorus said was corroborated by Egyptians or Ethiopians, Diodorus was ready to accept what they said. He does not ask where his native informants got their information, or say whether he heard it directly from them in Greek, or through interpreters. He does not inquire about their motives. He does not point out the dangers involved in this mode of inquiry: What if all his informants were relying on the same source, and that source was wrong? What if his informants wanted to prove something or to express their patriotism in some specific way? Another problem is that he has too high a regard for consensus: he accepts as true the account that most of his informants agree on. He does not ask if certain individuals, because of their intelligence or because they had special access to archives or records, might prove to be more reliable witnesses than others.

Diodorus's brief description of what we might call his "research methodology" helps to explain why he and other visitors to Egypt, including Herodotus, could have been misled by their native informants about the extent of Greek cultural dependency on Egypt. They placed too high a value on their informants' ethnicity, as if to be Egyptian implied an ability to know Egyptian history and to explain Egyptian customs. They imagined that the Egyptians would know about their own country, because they believed that only Greeks could understand about Greece. If an Egyptian or Phoenician could not be counted on to know much about Greece, how could Greeks be expected to know about the history of Egypt? Hence the importance of inquiry from indigenous informants, such as Egyptian priests, or emissaries from Ethiopia, men who would have been among the best educated, and who would have had the leisure to tell visitors about their history. The problem with this method is that some native informants will prove more reliable than others: not every modern pastor can be counted on to give an accurate account of the history of his church.

The need for such oral testimony explains why it was necessary for the historian himself to visit the country and inquire personally, a process known to the Greeks as *historia*. By relying on such inquiry the historians (or "inquirers") were able to bring back accounts of other countries that were more accurate and realistic than what poets or storytellers had been able to provide. But the process also had some significant limitations: to obtain accurate results the inquirer had to ask the right questions and receive well-informed answers.[11] But how likely was it that a foreigner would know what to ask, or that a native would be able to supply him with all the information he needed to understand a foreign practice or custom? It was inevitable that the process of inquiry worked best when the historian was investigating his own culture and his own time.

WHAT DID HERODOTUS KNOW ABOUT EGYPTIAN ORIGINS?

Even after Egyptian inscriptions could be read, and for the first time in thousands of years scholars could read what the Egyptians said about themselves, the second book of Herodotus's history still serves as an important source of information about ancient Egypt. Much of what he reports can be confirmed by comparison with Egyptian sources. Herodotus gives a generally accurate impression of the monuments he saw and the situation of the land and the river Nile. He reports much useful information about individual pharaohs. But his ideas about the relationship of Greece to Egypt are speculative, and often misleading. Apparently he was so impressed by the antiquity and complexity of Egyptian culture that he wanted to establish connections with Greek customs wherever he could. We need to consider the question of Herodotus's reliability on the subject of cultural dependency, because Herodotus is often cited as an authority for claims of Greek cultural dependency on Egypt. Not only was he an ancient witness; he was an eyewitness. Although few Greeks were able to travel there at the time because the country was occupied by their enemies, the Persians, Herodotus was technically a Persian subject. He visited Egypt sometime before 430 B.C.

Herodotus reported to his Greek audience that certain ritual and religious practices, which the Greeks had regarded as indigenous, in fact had their origin in Egypt, a country which few Greeks would have had an opportunity to see for themselves. Martin Bernal argues that Herodotus believed this information to be accurate and that "he was being relatively conventional in doing so."[12] But if we look closely at what Herodotus himself says, he makes it clear that he is putting forward his own interpretations and conjectures about what he saw and was told by native informants. If his ideas had been "conventional," as Bernal suggests, he would not have needed to explain to his listeners why he was making these assertions. To understand what Herodotus was trying to do, we need to examine each of his observations in its full context.

In a long and very interesting discussion of Egyptian religious practices, Herodotus suggests that the cult of Dionysus in Greece was inspired by the cult of Osiris in Egypt. He explains why he has associated the two gods with one another: in the ritual of Osiris, as in rituals of Dionysus in Greece, a phallus is carried in a procession by women. The only significant difference, in his view, is that the Greeks also had choral dances in honor of their god. "I will state that the resemblance cannot be accidental between what is done for the god in Egypt and in Greece." He reasons that the influence could not have gone the other way round in the case of these or any other customs. The Greek seer Melampus, he believes, learned them from the hero Cadmus in Phoenicia, before Cadmus came to Greece.[13] On the basis of this observation, Herodotus makes another conjecture:

> Roughly speaking, the names of all of the gods as well came to Greece from Egypt. For I made inquiries and found that it was true that the names came from the barbarians, and so I believe it is most likely that they came from Egypt.[14]

Through such expressions as "roughly speaking" (*schedon de*), Herodotus warns his audience that he is expressing an opinion, which may not be correct in all particulars.[15] By connecting this statement to his earlier discussion of ritual, he shows why he judges the connection with Egypt to be the "most likely": Egypt was one of the oldest civilizations.

Although Herodotus indicates that what he says about the

names of the gods is his own opinion, his speculation is taken more seriously than it should be by Afrocentrists and others who would like to think that there were close connections between Egyptian and Greek religion. In part, they are misled by the translations most of them depend on. The sentence I have quoted above is misconstrued in most translations. David Grene, for example, says "the names of nearly all the gods came from Egypt to Greece."[16] But if Herodotus had meant "nearly all," he would have put the words in the sentence in a different order. Also, Grene omits the connective "as well" (*kai*), which shows the train of Herodotus's thought. The connective also shows that he based his notion about the origins of the names of the Greek gods on the ritual similarities that he observed: women carry phalluses in processions to both Osiris and Dionysus. Omitting these nuances in translation makes Herodotus seem more certain of his material than he actually was.

How could Herodotus have imagined that the names of the gods of Greece resembled those of Egypt? He does not say, but possibly there were a few similarities in sound between some names.[17] The Greeks almost always used what we would now call puns to explain the etymology of words.[18] The poets derived the name of the god Zeus (which is based on the root *Di-*) from *dia*, "through," since all was accomplished *through* him.[19] Apparently, it did not occur to them that the root *Di-* is in fact cognate with the Greek word *dios*, "bright, shining"; Zeus was originally the god of the sky. But even though Herodotus did not have the means of knowing whether his guess about the names of the gods was right or wrong, modern linguists can make an informed judgment. None is persuaded that there is any connection between Egyptian and Greek names. A few names (like Zeus or Apollo) are clearly Indo-European, but most others are simply unknown. As the historian of Greek religion Walter Burkert has observed, in comparison with the gods of Near Eastern cultures "the names of the Greek gods are almost all impenetrable."[20] Linguists have not been convinced by modern attempts to find Egyptian etymologies for the names of the Greek gods. For example, in 1885 Gerard Manley Hopkins proposed (though no one seems to have believed him) that Aphrodite could be derived from the Egyptian name *Nefrat-isi*.[21] Bernal, with great ingenuity, argues that the name of the goddess Athena is derived from the Egyptian *Ḥt Nt*, "House of the goddess Neit," claiming that both the phonetic and semantic fit are perfect: Herodotus himself identified Athena with Neit.[22] But actually the semantic fit is not so close as Bernal suggests. Athena, daughter of Zeus and one of the most powerful Greek goddesses, is a virgin, and goddess of war and weaving; Neit, a relatively minor goddess, is the mother of the crocodile god and involved with hunting. Equally imaginative (and misguided) arguments could be made for deriving Athena's name from that of the Carthaginian goddess Tanit, or from that of the Hebrew Satan.[23]

Herodotus thought that the Greeks might have been influenced by Egyptian culture because the civilization of Egypt was more ancient than that of Greece. In logic, this type of argument is called *post hoc ergo propter hoc*, "after which means on account of which."[24] He does not seem to have reasoned that cultural exchange almost always works in both directions. Herodotus's explanation of the origins of the oracle

at Dodona provides an explicit illustration of after which / on
account of which reasoning. After discussing the founding of
the oracle of Zeus at Dodona in Greece, he observes:

> The oracles in Egyptian Thebes and in Dodona happen to be
> similar. Oracles from sacrifices also come from Egypt. The
> Egyptians were the first people to have festivals and proces-
> sions with cult statues or with offerings, and the Greeks
> learned them from the Egyptians. *In my opinion, the evi-
> dence for this is as follows: the Egyptian religious customs
> have been going on for a long time, and the Greek customs
> have been practiced only recently.*[25]

In a later passage, Herodotus again reasons that since Egypt
is the earlier civilization, any common practice must have
originated in that country. He says that the reason why the
rites the Greeks call Orphic and Bacchic are really Egyptian
and Pythagorean is that each forbids the wearing of woolen
garments.[26] For him, superficial resemblance, along with priority, is a sign of influence and even origin, and he simply ignores what we would now consider to be significant differences.
He does not point out that it is because linen is easier to clean
that Egyptian priests do not wear wool and are not buried in
woolen garments, whereas the Orphics and Pythagoreans have
a taboo against wool because it is an animal product.[27]

Once we understand why and how Herodotus makes these
comparisons between Egyptian and Greek culture, it is possible to see how, despite his best efforts to get at the truth, he
offers his audience misleading information about origins.
Unlike modern anthropologists, who approach new cultures

so far as possible with an open mind, and with the aid of a developed set of methodologies, Herodotus tended to construe whatever he saw by analogy with Greek practice, as if it were impossible for him to comprehend it in any other way.[28] It was inevitable that using Greece as a standard would cause considerable misunderstanding, especially in the case of Egyptian religion, which is both markedly different from Greek religion and extremely complex. The real and important distinctions are further obscured by the Greek practice of calling other peoples' gods by the names of Greek gods.[29] Herodotus regularly speaks of the Egyptian goddess Isis as Demeter, and her husband Osiris as Dionysus. These gods have some points in common: Isis searches for her husband, and Demeter travels to Eleusis in Greece for her daughter Persephone. Osiris and Dionysus both spend time in the Underworld, both are torn to pieces and reassembled. But they do not resemble one another in most other respects: Osiris is god of Duat, the Egyptian Underworld; Dionysus god of wine and the theater.

Because he tended to rely on such analogies as he could find, Herodotus inevitably made some false conjectures. Herodotus thought that Pythagoras learned about the transmigration of souls from Egypt, when in fact the Egyptians did not believe in the transmigration of souls, as their careful and elaborate burial procedures clearly indicate. Nonetheless, he insists that he is reporting what the Egyptians told him about their beliefs about life after death:

It is my practice in this entire account to write down what I have heard each of my informants say. The Egyptians say that Demeter and Dionysus rule in the world below. And the Egyptians are the first people who tell this story, that the human soul is deathless, and when the body dies the soul enters into another animal that is being born. Then when it has made the rounds of all animals on land, sea, and air, it returns again to the human body, and the soul's journey takes three thousand years. Greeks in the past, and more recently, have used this story [about the soul] as if it were their own. I know their names but I will not write them down.[30]

Herodotus tells us that he wrote down what the Egyptians told him; but when they spoke, what did he hear? Since he did not know Egyptian, his informants could have been Greeks living in the Greek colony of Naucratis in the Nile Delta, or Egyptians who knew some Greek. How well informed were his informants? On the question of origins, at least, it seems that neither group had any more than a superficial understanding of the other's culture.[31] Perhaps someone explained to him about the Egyptian "modes of existence," in which a human being could manifest itself both materially, or immaterially, as *ka* or *ba* or a name, and that death was not an end, but a threshold leading to a new form of life.[32] Belief in these varied modes of existence required that bodies be preserved after death, hence the Egyptian practice of mummification. Greeks, on the other hand, believed that the soul was separated from the body at death, and disposed of bodies either by burial or cremation. In any case, there is no reason to assume that Pythagoras or other Greeks who believed in transmigration, like the Orphics or the philosopher-poet Empedocles, got their ideas from anyone else: notions of transmigration have developed independently in other parts of the world.[33]

Another instance of such "translation" into Greek is Herodotus's account of the Egyptian festival of Khoiak, the Navigation of Osiris. It is from this, he suggests, that the daughters of Danaus brought the ritual of the Thesmophoria to Argos, but he is prevented by religious scruples from giving any particulars:

> On the temple lake [at Saïs] there is an exhibition by night of the god's sufferings, which the Egyptians call mysteries. I know more about every aspect of the festival, but let what I have said suffice. And as concerns the ritual of Demeter known to the Greeks as Thesmophoria, let what I have said also suffice, except for what it is permitted for me to say. It was the daughters of Danaus who brought this ritual from Egypt and who taught it to the Pelasgian women. The ritual was abandoned after the people of the Peloponnesus were driven out by the Dorians, but it was preserved by the Peloponnesians who remained and were not driven out [by the Dorian invasion], the Arcadians.[34]

Here Herodotus has made several assumptions. He thinks that the night ritual he saw enacted was a mystery or secret initiation rite, but in fact the depiction of Osiris's sufferings and the festival itself were open to the public.[35] It was a "mystery" only in the sense that he did not fully understand what was going on. Because he believes (although mistakenly) that the rites are secret, Herodotus refuses to name the god whose sufferings were enacted, but we know from Egyptian sources that the god was in fact Osiris.[36] Because Osiris's wife Isis was identified with Demeter by the Greeks, Herodotus associates the rites he saw with that goddess, and so deduces that one of her principal Greek rituals, the Thesmophoria, was of Egyptian origin. But he explicitly says that no close analogue to the Egyptian ritual survived in Argos. Instead, he suggests that the ritual was preserved in Arcadia, which the Greeks regarded as the most primitive and remote part of their country. In fact, there is no reason to believe that the Thesmophoria, which were celebrated by women throughout the Greek world from earliest times, were imported rather than indigenous.

His treatment of the Osiris festival shows how determined Herodotus was to find connections between Egyptian and Greek religious customs. In order to account for the generosity of the pharaoh Amasis to the temple of Athena at Lindos on the island of Rhodes in the sixth century, Herodotus reports a story that the temple at Lindos was founded by the daughters of Danaus on their way to Argos (Rhodes lay on an established trade route between Egypt and Greece).[37] Greeks often invented such stories of origins after the fact to explain curious customs and practices.

This same desire for antecedents led Herodotus to make a remarkable claim about the use of Egyptian material by the tragic poet Aeschylus. Aeschylus, he says, "stole" an unusual version of a myth from the Egyptians.[38] The Greeks believed that the goddess Leto was the mother of Apollo and Artemis, but according to the Egyptians, the goddess the Greeks associate with Demeter (Isis) is the mother of Apollo (Horus) and Artemis (Boubastis). The drama in which Aeschylus referred to the "Egyptian" version of the myth is now lost, so we do not know why Herodotus says that Aeschylus *stole* rather than simply *told* another version of the myth.[39] But since many different versions of the myths were in circulation at all times, and poets were free to choose from among them to suit particular occasions, it looks as if Herodotus was determined to say something provocative about the great poet to amuse (or tease) his Athenian audience.[40]

Since Herodotus is often skeptical and contemptuous of people who believe literally in myths, it is ironic that in the case of Egypt he is ready to believe almost everything that he is told, and on occasion, willing to supply plausible explanations of his own invention. But his deep respect for the antiquity of Egypt encouraged him to seek out possible connections.[41] Also, he was eager to show that Greece was linked to other countries by common bonds of humanity. He does not trace the development of customs or practices or point out the great differences between supposedly common beliefs. He simply assumes that similarity of any kind is "evidence" of Egyptian ancestry. Unfortunately, because his history was widely read and studied in antiquity, his "research methods" became the model for all subsequent Greek visitors to Egypt.

WHAT NEW INFORMATION COULD LATER GREEK WRITERS SUPPLY ABOUT THE GREEK DEBT TO EGYPT?

At the time when Herodotus visited Egypt, the country was under Persian domination, making it difficult for most Greeks to travel there. But after Egypt was conquered by Alexander in 333 B.C., it fell under the domination of his Macedonian

Greek successors. A Greek city, "Alexandria near Egypt," was founded near the coast on the Canobic branch of the Nile Delta. Once Greeks had settled in Alexandria, there was an opportunity for more cultural exchange than at any previous time. But on the whole the contact between the Greeks and the native population was limited. Regrettably—at least from the point of view of modern historians—the Greeks in Alexandria were not able to provide their visitors with as much real information about Egypt as might be supposed. Even though there was some intermarriage between Greeks and Egyptians and the large mercenary forces quartered in Alexandria, the Greek population remained fundamentally Greek.[42] Once outside of this Greek community, Greek travelers had to rely on interpreters. No works by third- or second-century writers survive, but we have extensive eyewitness accounts by two first-century writers, Strabo of Cappadocia (the area to the west and south of the Black Sea) and Diodorus of Sicily.

Like Herodotus before them, Strabo and Diodorus rely on what they themselves could see, what they could learn by inquiry, and what their predecessors had written. Since they also were interested in religious practices, they got much of their information from the Egyptian priests who tended the shrines and monuments that they sought to visit. These first-century priests seem to have been particularly eager to point out to visitors instances of what the Greeks had learned from Egypt.[43]

When the Greek historian Diodorus of Sicily visited Egypt in 60–56 B.C. during the reign of Cleopatra's father, Ptolemy XII,[44] Egyptian priests told him that they knew from accounts in their sacred books that the Greek wise men Orpheus,

Musaeus, Melampus, Daedalus, the poet Homer, the Spartan lawgiver Lycurgus, the Athenian lawgiver Solon, the philosopher Plato, Pythagoras, the mathematician Eudoxus, Democritus, and Oenopides had all come to their country. The priests showed Diodorus statues of these men, and buildings or places that were named for them. They brought exhibits of the course of study attempted by each man, and stated that "everything for which they were admired by the Greeks was brought from Egypt."[45]

Diodorus does not say he believed every word of what he was told. He does not say if he learned everything he reports from the priests or simply thought of some of the correspondences himself. But evidently he followed Herodotus's example in imagining that any similarity was proof of direct connection, rather than a sign of indirect influence, or simply a coincidental occurrence. Like Herodotus, he seems eager to discover correspondences, with such zeal that he takes the most superficial similarities as a sign of borrowing. To Diodorus, virtually any similarity was a sign of connection. Herodotus had remarked on some of the differences in Egyptian and Greek rituals for Osiris and Dionysus, but Diodorus ignores even these. He states that the rites of the Greek Dionysus and the Egyptian Osiris are the "same" (rather than similar), and that the rites of Isis are very similar to Demeter's—"only the names are changed." He says that Greek beliefs about the world of the dead (which Diodorus dismisses as fiction) were introduced by Orpheus in imitation of Egyptian burial rites.

In making these claims about cultural borrowing, Diodorus completely ignores significant differences in customs and

beliefs. Why not point out that in Egyptian myth Isis was married to her brother Osiris, whereas the Greek gods Demeter
and her nephew Dionysus are not connected with each other
in the same way in myth or in cult? Also, Diodorus never reck-
ons with the possibility of Greek influence on Egyptian religious practice. For example, Diodorus reports that Melampus
brought the worship of Dionysus from Egypt to Greece.
Herodotus, too, had conjectured that the worship of Dionysus
had been brought to Greece from abroad, but he thought that
Melampus learned about the rites from Cadmus, who came
from Phoenicia. Herodotus uses an analogy from Greek myth
to describe the complex of buildings at Lake Moeris, which he
refers to as a labyrinth. Diodorus turns the analogy into reality, and says explicitly that the Lake Moeris labyrinth was
built by Daedalus, who designed the labyrinth in Crete.[46]

Diodorus appears ready to believe the particularly absurd
notion that the Greek epic poet Homer studied in Egypt. The
"evidence" for this assertion derives from a few scattered and
vague similarities. In both religions Hermes brings the soul of
the dead to the lower world. He remarks that both Egyptians
and Greeks use the same word for boat, *baris* (it is indeed an
Egyptian loanword). Also, on the basis of some similarity in
sound, he connects the Greek mythological figure Charon and
the (unrelated) Egyptian word for ferryman, *kar;* but Homer
never mentions Charon. According to later tradition (although again Homer himself does not mention it) the daughters of Danaus are compelled in Hades to carry water in leaky
jars.[47] Egyptian priests carry water in a perforated jar to the
city of Acanthi.[48] In the *Odyssey* Homer mentions the healing
Egyptian drink *nepenthe*, a drug that is still used in Egyptian

Thebes.[49] Aphrodite is called "golden," and near Momemphis there is a plain of "golden Aphrodite." Homer tells in *Iliad* 14 how when Zeus slept with Hera on Mt. Ida he made grass and flowers grow on the ground beneath them, and in an Egyptian festival the shrines of Zeus and Hera (that is, Amun-Re and Mut) are carried up to a mountain that is strewn with flowers. At most, these correspondences suggest general cultural influence, in both directions.

The stories that the Greek lawgivers studied in Egypt seem also to be based primarily on inference. The priests told Diodorus that they "included many Egyptian customs in their laws."[50] He gives two examples; one is chronologically impossible, the other based on conjecture. The idea that early Greek law was inspired by Egyptian law is a historical fiction, designed to express the Greeks' mysterious faith in Egyptian wisdom. The legendary Spartan lawgiver Lycurgus may never have existed. But centuries later Plutarch reports that the Egyptians say that Lycurgus had admired the Egyptian way of separating the army from the rest of the population.[51] Had new records been discovered? Or (as is much more likely), had stories about their visits been developed and embellished because both the Egyptians and Greeks had laws, and Egypt was the earlier society?

The notion that Solon learned about law in Egypt follows the same pattern. Our earliest authority, Herodotus, says Solon went to visit the sixth-century pharaoh Amasis in Egypt *after* he established his laws in Athens.[52] The idea that he went there to study was invented by Plato, who tells how Solon went to Sais to consult with the priests, where he learned from an old priest about the history of the lost continent of Atlantis.

Plato indicates to his readers that the story is fictional, by citing as his authority a source that no living person could consult, and that he himself knows only by hearsay.[53] Over time, new details were added to the story; in the second-century A.D. the Greek writer Plutarch knows the names of Solon's Egyptian teachers: Psenophis of Heliopolis and Sonchis of Sais.[54] But such information, although it looks plausible enough, has no real historical value.

The priests were particularly eager to tell visitors about how the Greek philosophers studied in Egypt. They told Diodorus, as their counterparts centuries earlier had told Herodotus, that Pythagoras learned about the gods and the soul from the Egyptians. Now, however, they perceived a different kind of resemblance: this was that Pythagoras shared with the Egyptians the notion that animals had souls. The priests also assert that he learned about geometry in Egypt, although without mentioning any specifics. Once again the link appears to be that both Egyptians and Greeks were interested in geometry; the common interest is transformed into "evidence" of dependence by the principle of after which / on account of which. As in the cases of Solon and Lycurgus, more and more seems to be known about Pythagoras as time goes on. By the fourth century A.D. Pythagoras had become the model of the Greek savant who was schooled in Egypt. The Greek philosophical writer Iamblichus specifies that Pythagoras spent twenty-two years (547–525 B.C.) in Egypt. During that time he studied all aspects of Egyptian religion, was initiated into all the rites, and learned astronomy and geometry.[55] Like Diodorus, Iamblichus provides no specific information about what he actually learned. Rather, the point of the journey seems to be that he studied whatever it was he learned *abroad*. Before going to Egypt he visited Syria, and after Egypt he studied with the Magi in Babylon. As for Herodotus, foreign study seemed a natural way to account for the originality of Pythagoras's ideas.

By the time Diodorus consulted them, the priests had added other famous Greek philosophers to their lists. What they told him about these historical philosophers has no more substance than what they said about the legendary Pythagoras. They claimed that the fifth-century Greek philosopher Democritus of Abdera spent five years studying astrology in Egypt. This connection seems particularly tenuous, because in fact the Egyptians were interested in astronomy, that is, the motions of the stars, and not in astrology, the predictions about human fate that might be derived from astronomical observation.[56] Moreover, it would not have been easy for a student of philosophy to have undertaken such a journey in the fifth century, when Egypt was under Persian domination and effectively closed to the Greek world. Like many Greek writers, Democritus was interested in the causes of the inundation of the Nile, and his hypothesis of snow melted by south winds was not far from the truth.[57] But according to the second-century A.D. astronomer Ptolemy, Democritus did his research on weather indications in Macedonia and Thrace.[58] Certainly nothing that he is reported to have said suggests that he had a detailed personal knowledge of Egypt. Nonetheless, later biographers provide new information about what he learned abroad, as if to account for the wide range of his interests and the originality of his thought. According to these stories, Democritus learned geometry in Egypt; he studied with priests.[59]

Like Pythagoras, he is supposed to have traveled widely outside of Greece, going to Persia and India to study with wise men there.

In the case of the other Greek philosophers as well, interest in the Nile or in geometry seems to count as "evidence" of a visit to Egypt. The priests told Diodorus that the fifth-century B.C. Greek astronomer Oenopides of Chios learned from Egyptian priests about the obliquity of the ecliptic of the sun.[60] Diodorus does not point out (perhaps he did not know) that the Pythagoreans already knew about the ecliptic before Oenopides is supposed to have discovered it, or that it had been recognized by the Babylonians in 700 B.C.[61] Earlier in his account of Egypt, Diodorus gives Oenopides' explanation of the inundation of the Nile: Oenopides deduced from the temperature of well water, which feels warm in the winter and cold in the summer, that the subterranean waters that feed the Nile are warm in the winter, and cold in the summer, when there are no rains in Egypt.[62] But again, there is no reason to imagine that Oenopides needed to study in Egypt in order to form this false hypothesis; rather, his reliance on analogy (rather than on empirical evidence) seems characteristically Greek.

Diodorus reports that the fourth-century Greek philosopher Eudoxus of Cnidus, like Democritus, learned astrology from the Egyptian priests, even though it was the Alexandrian Greeks and not the Egyptians who were interested in that subject.[63] He also observes, more plausibly, that Eudoxus gave the Greeks much useful information about Egypt. Eudoxus explained the inundation of the Nile as a result of rains in Ethiopia, a theory that was adopted by Aristotle.[64] He was interested in Egyptian religion, mythology, and customs.[65]

Bernal suggests that Eudoxus might have learned geometry in Egypt. But surely it would have also been possible (and much easier) for him to have learned the theory of axiomatic mathematics from his teacher, the fifth-century Greek philosopher Archytas of Tarentum.[66] In fact, nothing in the surviving fragments suggests that Eudoxus had a highly specialized knowledge of Egypt, at least so far as we can judge from the fragments, since his original work is lost. He could have learned what he knew from Greek writers like Hecataeus and Herodotus, without ever having visited Egypt. Of course it is possible that Eudoxus could have traveled to Egypt, as Herodotus had done, even though the Persian domination might have presented serious difficulties. But it is still more likely that his interest in Egypt encouraged biographers to think that he actually studied there.

Again, as in the case of Solon, more is known about Eudoxus's travels as time goes on. The priests at Heliopolis showed Strabo statues of Plato and Eudoxus, and priests pointed out the places where they had studied. But no one was sure quite how long they stayed there. Strabo reports that "some say they spent thirteen years with the priests."[67] But in an ancient summary of Strabo the figure is given as "three," and according to the third-century A.D. Greek writer Diogenes Laertius, Eudoxus stayed there for a year and four months.[68] It is hard to account for the discrepancy in the numbers, except by assuming that there were several different versions of the story in existence. New details could be added to give verisimilitude. In his biography of Eudoxus, Diogenes supplies the name of Eudoxus's Egyptian teacher, Chonouphis of Heliopolis.[69] He says that while in Egypt Eudoxus shaved his beard and eyebrows (like an Egyptian priest) and that while he was there an Apis bull licked his cloak; the Egyptian priests understood this to be an omen that he would be famous, but short-lived.[70] These anecdotes tell us nothing about what Eudoxus studied or did in Egypt; instead, they portray him as a late antique holy man, like the Pythagoras described by Iamblichus.

Diogenes also says that according to some (not all) of his sources, Eudoxus translated "Dialogues of the Dogs" from Egyptian originals and published them in Greece. Since Eudoxus was associated with Plato and the Academics rather than with Diogenes and the Cynics (or "Dogs"), why would he write about *dogs?* The Greeks do not seem to have paid much attention to Egyptian literature until after they had settled in Alexandria, but it is at least theoretically possible that Eudoxus might have translated some Egyptian fables about dogs.[71] If that were the case, the content of these Dialogues would have been ethnological (rather than scientific), like the other information about Egypt in Eudoxus's surviving fragments. But in their zeal to confirm that Eudoxus studied in Egypt, other scholars have conjectured that Diogenes's text originally referred not to Dialogues of Dogs (*kyon*) but to Dialogues of the *Dead* (*nekron*); Bernal even suggests that some of his translations "may well have come from the [Egyptian] *Book of the Dead*."[72] Of course, that too is not impossible, but it is hardly very likely. Even assuming that he wrote about the dead, rather than about dogs, there is little appropriate subject matter for a Greek philosophical dialogue in the so-called *Book of the Dead*, an Egyptian collection of spells for the journey of the soul through the Duat, the Egyptian Underworld, to an afterlife of bliss in the field of reeds.[73]

DID PLATO STUDY IN EGYPT?

So much for the priests' claim that everything for which these Greeks were admired "was brought from Egypt."[74] Now we must ask if their assertions about Greek dependency could possibly apply to the most famous of these philosophers, Plato. We are in a better position to assess the accuracy of the priests' statement, because Plato's works have survived, and much more information is available about his life. Plato never says in any of his writings that he went to Egypt, and there is no reference to such a visit in the semibiographical Seventh Epistle.[75] But in his dialogues he refers to some Egyptian myths and customs. He speaks about tame fish in Nile aquariums, about the Egyptian love of money, about the Egyptian practice of mummification.[76] Socrates swears by the dog-god Anubis, and he tells the story of how the Egyptian god Theuth (or Thoth, who was identified by the Greeks with Hermes) invented numbers, writing, and so on.[77] Plato relates that Solon was told by an old Egyptian priest that the Greeks were mere children in the history of the world.[78] In his *Laws* Plato approves the Egyptian practice of forbidding change in traditional religious music.[79] None of these references shows a profound or first-hand knowledge of Egypt. Moreover, his chronology is shaky. Solon's travels may predate Amasis's reign by some thirty years.[80] Plato's genealogy of Solon's family is off by two generations.[81] The story of Solon's conversation with the priests bears a close resemblance to Herodotus's account of how the Greek visitor Hecataeus boasted to the priests in Thebes that he could trace his family back sixteen generations, and they countered with a family tree that went back 345 generations.[82] Plato, of course, was not a historian, and the rather superficial knowledge of Egypt displayed in his dialogues, along with vague chronology, is more characteristic of historical fiction than of history.

In fact, anecdotes about his visit to Egypt only turn up in writers of the later Hellenistic period. What better way to explain his several references to Egypt than to assume that the author had some first-hand knowledge of the customs he describes? For authors dating from the fourth century and earlier, ancient biographers were compelled to use as their principal source material the author's own works. In order to account for his knowledge of the topography of Ithaca, Homer's biographers assumed that he had traveled to Ithaca as a young man, and some even said that his father was Telemachus, son of Odysseus, so as to give him a direct connection to the principal characters of the *Odyssey*.[83]

Later biographers add details to the story of Plato's Egyptian travels in order to provide etiologies for the "Egyptian" reference in his writings. One such anecdote is attributed to the philosopher Crantor (ca. 300 B.C.). Crantor wrote that Plato's contemporaries, in fun, said that he had modeled the ideal state described in his *Republic* on Egypt, and that in response to this criticism Plato attributed to the Egyptians the story of Atlantis and Athens in his dialogue *Timaeus*.[84] Bernal would like to take the story of the Egyptian roots of the *Republic* at face value.[85] But the true origin of the anecdote was probably a joke in some comedy, which was later taken seriously. Ancient biographers like to connect specific works with an event in a writer's life.[86] Another anecdote relates how Plato (presumably as a very young man) traveled to Egypt with the tragic poet Euripides. Biographers imagined that Euripides had gone to Egypt because his drama *Helen* is set in Egypt.[87] Another reason for thinking he went to Egypt is that in the prologue to his now lost drama *Archelaus* he alludes to Anaxagoras's theory of the inundation of the Nile.[88] The anecdote about Plato and Euripides provides a setting where one of Euripides' most famous sayings can be used as the punch line. While in Egypt, Euripides fell ill and was cured by Egyptian priests with seawater; that explains why he said "the sea washes away all human ills."[89]

Later biographers were even more inventive. In a letter that purports to have been sent by Phaedrus to Plato in Sais, Plato is studying the question of the "all" and Phaedrus asks for information about the pyramids and unusual Egyptian animals.[90] But the most ironic anecdote of all is preserved by the church father Tertullian (160–240 A.D.). Plato studied in Egypt with Hermes the "Thrice Great" (Trismegistus). This is tantamount to saying that Plato studied with himself *after his death*. Hermes Trismegistus was thought to have been the grandson of the god Hermes, the god identified by the Greeks with the Egyptian god Thoth. According to the story, Hermes Trismegistus transferred the writings of Thoth from stelae to books, which were then translated into Greek. But in chapter 4 I shall explain why the works of Hermes could not have been written without the conceptual vocabulary developed by Plato and Aristotle; it is deeply influenced not just by Plato but by the writings of Neoplatonist philosophers in the early centuries A.D.[91] But the zeal to discover cultural dependency was so great that any inconsistencies were overlooked.

Biographers offered several different accounts of Plato's studies in Egypt. In the *Timaeus* Plato tells how the god taught mankind to reckon by the stars and calculate the length of a year.[92] Centuries after his death, writers assumed that he acquired this interest in mathematics (even though Plato says nothing specific about it in the dialogue) in Egypt. When Strabo visited Heliopolis in the first century B.C. he was shown the houses where Eudoxus and Plato lived during the thirteen years they spent with the Egyptian priests. They had come there (so Strabo was told) to learn about the heavens from the priests, but the priests concealed most of what they knew, and told them only some of their theories, though they taught them how to calculate accurately the number of days in a year.[93] Later writers are even more specific: Plato is said to have heard specifically from one Sechnupis of Heliopolis the story of Theuth that he tells in the *Phaedrus*.[94] According to Diogenes Laertius, in the third century A.D. Plato went to Egypt to study with Egyptian seers.[95] But whoever his teachers were supposed to be, Plato seems never to have learned from them anything that is characteristically Egyptian, at least so far as we know about Egyptian theology from Egyptian sources. Instead, Plato's notion of the Egyptians remains similar to that of other Athenians; he did not so much change the Athenian notion of Egyptian culture as enrich and idealize it, so that it could provide a dramatic and instructive contrast with Athenian customs in his dialogues.[96]

WHY SHOULD GREEKS HAVE STUDIED IN EGYPT?

The Greeks, as we have seen, were eager to connect themselves in whatever way they could to Egypt. If any vague possibility suggested itself, biographers quickly turned it into "evidence" of contact or influence. The process is well illustrated by case of the sixth-century B.C. philosopher Thales, about whom little was known until many centuries after his death. Both Diogenes Laertius in the third century and Plutarch in the second century A.D. assume that Thales studied in Egypt. The reason? Thales had a theory about the inundation of the Nile, and he was interested in geometry.[97] He also said that water was the first principle, and the Egyptians believed that the earth floated on water. The same type of "evidence" explains why the poet Homer would have studied in Egypt: he calls Ocean, the mythical stream that surrounds the earth, the origin of the gods.[98] Why insist that it was in *Egypt* that Thales and Homer learned about the importance of water, when the idea is inherent also in Babylonian mythology? The Greeks had such a high regard for Egyptian religion and laws, because they understood so little about them; quite unrealistically, they thought of the country as a utopia.

The Greeks respected Egypt for the great antiquity of its civilization, but the Egyptians had a more urgent reason for wanting to assert their priority over the Greeks.[99] Because in Herodotus's day the country was under Persian domination, and then was ruled by Greeks after Alexander's conquest, one of the few remaining ways for them to maintain national pride was through their history. Unfortunately we have no direct information about what the Egyptians said; all we know is what Greek visitors reported. But we can get a sense of why they asserted the priority of their own ideas from the literature of another ethnic group who lived in Alexandria during the last three centuries B.C. The Jews shared the Egyptians' patronizing attitude toward the dominant Greek culture. Jewish historians were determined to show that although the Jewish people were now subject to Greeks, they not only understood Greek culture but had themselves provided the inspiration for the authors of the sacred writings and cherished literature of their conquerors' civilization. They sought both to instill pride and to encourage Hellenized Jews to return to the faith of their fathers.[100] Although the works of these writers are now lost, we know something about what they wrote from citations and quotations in Christian authors.

Wherever possible, these writers sought to show that Greek religion and philosophy had been inspired by Hebrew ideas. The mythical Greek singer Musaeus was none other than Moses.[101] This identification of the two disparate figures of Moses and Musaeus would almost certainly have seemed less farfetched to an ancient audience than it does to us. The ancients would have been impressed by the similarities in the sound of the two names, since etymologies in the ancient world were not at all scientific but often based simply on similarity of sound. Furthermore, both Musaeus and Moses could be considered as founders of their respective civilizations.[102]

But an even more definitive assertion of the derivative nature of Greek culture was made by an Alexandrian Jew called Aristobulus in the second century B.C.[103] Aristobulus did not hesitate to invent information, or to report information invented by others. He even made up verses that he attributed to the famous Greek writers, in order to "prove" that these famous Greeks had believed in a single male deity (in reality, of course, they were resolutely polytheistic).[104] Although the Greeks believed that the Goddess Earth was the ancestor of all the gods and in effect the mother of the universe as we know it, according to Aristobulus (or some other Jewish forger) Sophocles said "God is one in very truth, who fashioned

heaven and broad earth."[105] Most Greeks thought that pun-
ishment after death had been meted out only to the great sinners of mythology, but according to the Jewish verse-writers,
Euripides in the fifth century B.C. advised the sinners in his
audience, "Give heed, you who think there is no God" because
they would in time come to pay the penalty.[106]

Aristobulus also claimed that Pythagoras, Socrates, and
Plato had "heard the voice of God," that is, the God of the Hebrews, and that they had believed that the universe was sustained by him.[107] He said that the Greek philosophers
Pythagoras, Socrates, and Plato knew and studied the books
of Moses, that is, the Torah or Pentateuch, the first five books
of the Bible: "Plato followed our system of law, and clearly
worked out every detail in it."[108] In order to explain how Plato
had access to Jewish wisdom, Aristobulus said that Plato was
able to consult a Greek translation of the Bible. This translation would have had to be available several centuries before
the composition of the Septuagint, which is of course the only
Greek translation of the Old Testament that anyone else
knows about.[109] "It is evident," Aristobulus wrote, "that Plato
took many ideas from it—for he was very learned, and so did
Pythagoras who imported many of our [i.e., Jewish] ideas into
his philosophical writings."[110]

Of course no scholar today would take seriously the claim
that Plato's philosophy derives from Moses, because in his surviving works Plato, like most Greeks of his day, does not refer
to any Hebrew writings or writers and cannot possibly have
known the language. In fact, nothing in his surviving works
suggests that he even knew who Moses was, much less read
what Aristobulus and Jews of his era would have regarded as

his "works," that is, the Torah. Nonetheless some influential members of the Jewish community in second-century Alexandria were prepared to believe that Plato derived his ideas about the law from Moses, and that Moses was the same person as Musaeus. As a result, by the first century A.D., some people believed that Plato, while in Egypt, studied with Moses. The Jewish philosopher Philo of Alexandria and the Jewish historian Josephus both speak of Moses' influence on Plato.[111] But perhaps the most forceful contention about Plato's dependency was made by a pagan philosopher, the second-century A.D. neo-Pythagorean Numenius of Apamea in Syria, who simply asked, "For what is Plato other than Moses in Attic Greek?"[112] We have no idea of the context in which Numenius made this (to us) bizarre assertion, but no clearer evidence survives to show how at that time even pagan philosophers were eager to point out all possible similarities between pagan and Jewish thought.

So far as we can tell, these Jewish historians sought only to show that the famous Greek philosophers were dependent on Hebrew thought, not that the Greeks were lacking in ideas of their own or in any way reluctant to acknowledge their debt to the Jews. Evidently Greeks and Jews in second-century Alexandria communicated more effectively with each other than either did with the natives of the country they inhabited.[113] But later church fathers like Clement of Alexandria (150–215 A.D.) and Eusebius (ca. 260–340 A.D.) took a decidedly more hostile line.[114] Clement, for example, accused the Greeks of theft and plagiarism: "They not only stole their religious doctrines from the barbarians, but they also imitated our [that is, Jewish] doctrines."[115] He also reiterated

Herodotus's mistaken claim that the Greeks took from the Egyptians the doctrine of transmigration of the soul.

The determination of both Jews and Christians to assert the priority of Hebrew culture over the Greeks helps to explain why the Egyptians were eager to point out to Greek visitors that the famous Greeks had been inspired by Egyptian learning. It was a way of asserting the importance of their culture, especially in a time when they had little or no political powers. The Greeks were willing to listen to what they were told because of their respect for the antiquity of Egyptian religion and civilization, and a desire somehow to be connected with it. But as we have seen, there is no reason to believe that Greeks derived their philosophy or learning from Egypt, despite their great (and wholly justified) respect for Egyptian piety and knowledge.[116] Both Egyptians and Greeks liked to believe that famous Greeks had studied there, but the evidence that they did so is both inconsistent and late.

Because of the Egyptians' sophistication in geometry and astronomy, it is tempting to speculate about possible Greek borrowings.[117] But as Robert Palter has observed in his important study of Greek science, "influence tracing requires care." Borrowing is not the only possible explanation for similar practices, because even complex ideas can be developed independently.[118] There was considerable cultural interchange throughout the Mediterranean in the eighth and seventh centuries B.C., which affected both scientific thought and artistic style.[119] But even if the Greeks had been able to take advantage of Egyptian expertise in certain areas, that would not mean that they had "robbed" Egypt of her knowledge, because knowledge (and culture) cannot be "stolen" like *objets d'art*.[120]

The priests' assertions to Diodorus that "everything for which [the famous Greeks] were admired by the Greeks was transferred from Egypt" no doubt had a direct emotional appeal.[121] But the fate of Jewish ethnic historians like Aristobulus offer a warning to modern advocates of Greek cultural dependency. How many people have ever heard of Aristobulus? And, more importantly, who believes him?

FOUR

THE MYTH OF THE EGYPTIAN MYSTERY SYSTEM

Even after nineteenth-century scholars showed that the reports of Greek visitors to Egypt misunderstood and misrepresented what they saw, the myth that Greek philosophy derived from Egypt is still in circulation. The myth is not only believed, but is being taught as if it were the truth, and as if no progress had been made in our knowledge of Egypt since the eighteenth century. How the myth has managed to survive, despite all evidence and scholarship that demonstrates its falsity, is a fascinating story. In this chapter, I will describe how the notion of an Egyptian legacy was preserved

91

in the literature and ritual of Freemasonry. It was from that source that Afrocentrists learned about it, and then sought to find confirmation for the primacy of Egypt over Greece in the fantasies of ancient writers, like Herodotus and Diodorus. In the next chapter, I will discuss how and why in this century Afrocentrist writers went beyond the claims of the Freemasons, who speak only of Egyptian *origins* and not of deliberate theft on the part of the ancient Greeks.

In order to show that Greek philosophy is in reality stolen Egyptian philosophy, Afrocentrist writers assume that there was in existence from earliest times an "Egyptian Mystery System," which was copied by the Greeks. The existence of this "Mystery System" is integral to the notion that Greek philosophy was stolen, because it provides a basis for assuming that Greek philosophers had a particular reason for studying in Egypt, and for claiming that what they later wrote about in Greek was originally Egyptian philosophy.

The most elaborate account of the alleged theft and plagiarism is given in *Stolen Legacy* (1954). Its author, George G. M. James, taught Greek and mathematics at several colleges in Arkansas. Although the foundation on which his thesis rests is the notion of the Egyptian Mystery System, James does not supply an account of its origins and development. Rather, he treats the notion of Egyptian mysteries, temples, and schools as if their existence were an established fact. But in reality, the notion of an Egyptian Mystery System is a relatively modern fiction, based on ancient sources that are distinctively Greek, or Greco-Roman, and from the early centuries A.D. How did these fundamentally Greek practices come to be understood as originally Egyptian?

WHY GREEKS THOUGHT EGYPTIANS
CELEBRATED MYSTERIES

The notion that the Egyptian religion involved mysteries originated with the Greeks who visited Egypt and had difficulty
understanding what they were shown.[1] Throughout the Greek
world, there were from earliest times cults that required special rituals of admission. These were known as mystery or initiation cults (from the Greek word *myeisthai*, to be initiated).
The modern term *mystery* cult can be misleading, because
many of these rituals were not completely secret; also, the initiation rites were usually relatively brief, lasting no longer
than a few days or the duration of a festival. But initiates into
Greek mystery or initiation cults regarded themselves as spe-
cially privileged, because they had access to information and
practices which were not revealed to non-initiates.

The Greeks who visited Egypt thought of Egyptian cults as
having mystery rites because they were carried out by a spe-
cially consecrated priesthood. The notion of a consecrated
priesthood was foreign to Greece, where most priests and
priestesses served their gods on a part-time or temporary basis, and lived like other civilians. Egyptian priests were per-
manently attached to each temple, where they tended the
statue of the god where the god was believed to reside. They
distinguished themselves from the rest of the population by
their religious learning, as well as by their costume, eating,
and living habits. Because the Egyptian priests had access to
special knowledge, and lived differently from the rest of the
population, the Greeks imagined that they had been initiated
into something like their own mystery cults. But in reality the

festivals of the Egyptian gods were open to the public and not restricted to special groups of initiates.[2]

If there were no mystery cults in Egypt, where did the idea of an Egyptian Mystery System come from? George G. M. James, the author of *Stolen Legacy*, appears to have been misled by relying on Masonic literature, rather than standard histories of religion. As his principal source of information about the Egyptian mysteries, James cites a book written in 1909 by the Reverend Charles H. Vail, a thirty-second degree Mason, called *The Ancient Mysteries and Modern Masonry*.[3] In this book Vail speaks of public mysteries, such as those celebrated by Egyptian priests in the rites of the god Osiris and in the schools founded in Greece by Initiates. He quotes directly from only one ancient source: Plutarch's *On Isis and Osiris*, which he claims is a description of the "mysteries" of Isis. Vail speaks of "Initiates," but in fact Plutarch is not describing a special ritual of initiation for laypeople, he is discussing the training of the priests who are the bearers of Isis's sacred objects (*hieraphori*) and the wearers of her special vestments (*hierostoloi*), and who know the sacred story (*hieron logon*).[4] None of the passages from *On Isis and Osiris* that Vail cites describes what the ancients would have regarded as a mystery or initiation cult; rather, Vail seems to have confused the ancient and modern meanings of *mystery*. Plutarch does not use the term *mysterion* in connection with special arcane learning of the priests.[5]

In practice, mystery cults only came to Egypt after the third century B.C., as Greeks began to settle in the newly founded Greek city of Alexandria. These mystery rites were observed by Greeks living in Egypt, rather than by native Egyptians. Pagan writers were reluctant to describe exactly what went on in mystery cults, because the experience was supposed to be secret. But Christian writers were restrained by no such scruples, and it is from them that much of our knowledge of these cults is derived. A description of such a mystery cult is preserved by the fourth-century A.D. monk Epiphanius. It is a ritual which took place on January 6 at the temple of the Maiden (the *Koreion*) in Alexandria. After an all-night vigil, the celebrants descended into a cave with torches and brought up a wooden statue. They then carried the statue seven times around the inner sanctuary of the temple. Epiphanius observes that "when asked what the initiation (*mysterion*) was, they replied that the Maiden (*Kore*) at this hour, on this day, had given birth to a son, Eternity (*Aion*)."[6] Vail seems to think the cult has something to do with Isis, but the Maiden of the ritual is not Isis but Persephone, the Greek goddess of the Underworld, and the ritual is similar to the famous mysteries at Eleusis in Athens, where the birth of her child was celebrated.[7] Yet Vail offers this distinctively Greek cult as an example of an "Egyptian Mystery."

Only one Egyptian ritual had some of the characteristics of a Greek mystery cult, and that is the procession of priests in honor of Isis, as we know about it from the second-century A.D. Latin writer Apuleius, who was born in Madaura in North Africa. Apuleius provides a vivid description of a priest's initiation in his novel *Metamorphoses*, better known as *The Golden Ass*. In his book, the cult of Isis appears to be international: the hero Lucius is initiated as a priest of Isis in Greece, and then moves to Rome.[8]

The ritual of Isis that Apuleius describes is a trial of abstinence and obedience. Lucius, the candidate, must avoid forbidden food, and wait patiently until summoned to the initiation;

in this case the sign comes to Lucius in a dream. He is then led to the temple by the high priest of Isis, and instructed from sacred books written in "indecipherable letters."[9] He buys special clothes, and goes to the baths, where he is sprinkled by the high priest with pure water. He fasts for ten days, forbidden to eat meat and drink wine. Then, toward evening, he goes to the temple and receives gifts while sitting at the feet of the goddess's statue. He puts on a new linen gown and is admitted by the high priest to the innermost recesses of the sanctuary. Lucius refuses to tell the reader exactly what he saw and did there, except in the most general terms:

> Hear then and believe; what I tell you is true. I arrived at the boundary of death. After I had stepped on the threshold of Proserpina, I was carried through all the elements and returned. I saw the sun shining with brilliant light in the middle of the night. I came face to face with the gods of the lower world and the gods of the upper world and worshipped them from close at hand. Behold, I have told you everything, but although you have heard it, you must be ignorant of what I have said.[10]

The next day he wears the twelve stoles that mark him as an initiate. He is then dressed in vestments with elaborate designs; he holds a torch in his right hand and wears a crown of palm leaves. He is shown to the crowd, and then allowed to celebrate the conclusion of his initiation with a feast.[11]

This ritual conflates Greco-Roman ideas with Egyptian practices. The distinctive costume of the priests, their asceticism, and the "secret" hieroglyphic books are clearly Egyptian. The twelve stoles worn by the candidate may represent the hours of the sun god's journey through the day; in Egyptian mythology the soul of the dead man is united with the sun god by day, and then returns to be united by night with Osiris, the god of the Underworld.[12] But other elements of the ceremony are clearly non-Egyptian. The notion that the initiate travels through the elements (earth, air, fire, water) comes from Mithraism. The cult of Mithras, which the Greeks imagined to be an import from Persia, was popular in second-century Italy, and Mithras himself was associated with the sun god. Alternation of light and darkness are common to Mithraism and to various Greek cults, such as the Mysteries at Eleusis.[13]

The Egyptian myths describe the journey of a dead man's soul and the travels of the sun god. But there is one important respect in which Lucius's initiation differs from these narratives: he is a *living man*, who will not travel to the world of the blest, but will return to human life.[14] This aspect of Lucius's initiation is fundamentally Greco-Roman. It is the ancient story of the hero who descends to the world of the Dead before his time and returns a wiser man, to tell his story to others who have not shared and cannot really understand the nature of his experience.[15] Apuleius was of course familiar with Homer's *Odyssey*. In this epic, which was a basic text in schools in the Greek-speaking world, the hero Odysseus goes to the edge of the earth to talk to the shades of the dead and to learn what will happen to him in the future.[16] In Virgil's *Aeneid*, the first-century B.C. Roman national epic that makes deliberate reference to the *Odyssey*, Aeneas goes to the Lower World to see what happens to people who disobey the gods, and to learn from his father why he must carry out the task, despite all the pain it has cost him, of founding the city of Rome.[17] Virgil describes the descent as a kind of initiation.

Aeneas must find and carry a special talisman, the golden bough. He must make special sacrifices. None but he can accompany the Sibyl of Cumae, who will serve as his guide to the underworld: "Stay back, stay back, you who are not initiated (*profani*), leave this grove; and you, Aeneas, take your sword from its sheath! Now is the time for courage and a firm heart."[18] When Lucius tells his Latin-speaking readers that he has stepped on the threshold of Proserpina and approached the boundaries of death, the image of Aeneas descending to the Lower World would surely have come to mind.

But it is this hybrid ceremony, with its long preparation, special learning, journeys, and trials, and not an indigenous Egyptian rite, that became known in Europe as the example par excellence of an "Egyptian" initiation.[19] The fourth-century A.D. pagan philosopher Iamblichus imagines that Pythagoras underwent many such initiations during the twenty-two years that he spent in Egypt, studying Egyptian religion, astronomy, and geometry.[20] Adding to the confusion is Apuleius's reference to the priest's special books,[21] which are written in indecipherable letters. Some of these books indicated through various forms of animals condensed versions of liturgical learning; others were shielded from being read by the curiosity of the uninitiated (*profani*) because their extremities were knotted, curved like wheels, or twisted like vines.

These books were papyrus rolls, written in hieratic script.[22] We know from other sources that Egyptian priests used such books. A first-century A.D. temple scribe and Stoic philosopher Chaeremon (an Egyptian who wrote in Greek) describes the priests' piety and their knowledge of astronomy, arithmetic, and geometry; this learning was recorded in sacred books.[23]

Clement of Alexandria preserves a description of a procession of Egyptian priests carrying forty-two treatises containing what he calls "all of Egyptian philosophy." First comes a Chanter, with some symbols of music; he must learn two books of Hermes, which are hymns to the gods and regulations for the life of the king. Then comes an Astrologer, with the symbols of his subject; he must know the four astrological books of Hermes, which deal with the stars, and the movements of the sun and the moon. Then comes the Scribe, who knows hieroglyphics, cosmography, geography, and all about the equipment of the priests and their ceremony. After him comes the Stole-keeper, who knows about the training of priests and about sacrifices; there are ten books which deal with details of worship. The last in the procession is the Prophet, who carries a special vase of Nile water,[24] and after him come attendants with loaves of bread. The Prophet is the governor of the Temple, and he must learn the ten books that deal with the laws, the gods, and the training of the priests; he also supervises the distribution of the temple revenues. These priests among them know the contents of thirty-six books. But the *Pastophoroi*, or image-bearers, must know six other books of Hermes that deal with the body, diseases, instruments, medicines, the eyes, and women.[25]

This passage helps to explain why James thinks that there was a corpus of Egyptian philosophy available for the Greeks to plagiarize. James discusses the procession of Egyptian priests twice in his book, first as a description of Egyptian priestly orders, and then as evidence for the priestly "curriculum" in the Egyptian Mystery System.[26] But in order to show that the Greeks "stole" their philosophy from these books, or others like them, James is compelled to assume that the works Clement lists in the second century A.D. are copies of much more ancient writings. Although that is possible, even if we ignore the problem of chronology, the forty-two books of Hermes in Clement's list do not seem to be concerned with the kind of abstract problems that the Greeks dealt with in their philosophical writings.[27] Rather, the forty-two books of Hermes seem to contain practical information and regulations, specific to Egyptian religion; Clement's general topic is in fact the debt of Greco-Roman religion to other cultures. When Clement speaks of them as containing "all of Egyptian philosophy (*philosophia*)," he is referring to learning or knowledge of the occult, to spells and magic.[28]

Although James concentrates on the forty-two books of "philosophy" catalogued by Clement, the principal source of the notion that there was a corpus of Egyptian philosophy derives from yet another, and even later source, the so-called Hermetica or discourses of Hermes. These are writings that were supposed to have been composed at the beginning of time by Hermes the Thrice-great (*trismegistos*), grandson of the god Hermes, who was identified with the Egyptian god Thoth.[29] The pagan writer Iamblichus (ca. 250–326 A.D.), who believed that these discourses were authentic, says that one of the authors he consulted knew of 20,000, and another 36,525 such treatises.[30] But the two dozen discourses attributed to Hermes that have come down to us are not Egyptian at all. Rather, they are treatises written in Greek centuries after the deaths of the famous Greek philosophers they purport to have inspired. As Isaac Casaubon showed in 1614, this small collection of writings could not be as early as Iamblichus and other ancient writers thought, because its author or authors were much influenced by the very writers that Hermes the Thrice-great was supposed to have inspired, especially Plato, and his much later followers the Neoplatonists, not to mention the Hellenistic Hebrew writers known as Gnostics. There is no record of any Egyptian-language original from which they were derived, and it is clear from both their style and their vocabulary that they could not have been composed without the conceptual vocabulary and rhetoric developed by the Greek philosophers in the fourth century B.C.

Why did the Greek author or authors of the discourses of Hermes pretend that their writings were written by Egyptians at the dawn of time? It would be wrong to imagine that these writings were forgeries in the modern sense. Rather, the Greek authors were following the standard conventions of a type of historical fiction that was popular in antiquity among both the Greeks and the Hebrews. In order to make their work seem more impressive, ancient writers concealed their real names and pretended to be famous historical figures and to have been living in earlier times. Often ancient writers of historical fiction claim to have found a hidden document, or to have translated a text from an ancient language.[31] The story of the "discovery" of the discourses of Hermes follows that established pattern. In the fourth century Iamblichus explains that an otherwise unknown "prophet" Bitys had found Hermes' teaching inscribed in hieroglyphics in the inner sanctuary of the temple at Sais and translated (!) them for "king Ammon," by whom he meant the god Amun or Amun-Re.[32] Iamblichus accounts for the presence of the technical vocabulary of Greek philosophy in these "early" Egyptian texts by insisting that the texts have been translated skillfully: "The books of Hermes contain Hermetic thought, even though they employ philosophical language. They were translated from the Egyptian language by men who knew philosophy."[33]

Similarly, the author of a Hermetic treatise addressed to "king Ammon" pretends that his discourse has been translated from Egyptian into Greek, and warns that the god's philosophy will suffer in translation. His characterization of Egyptian must be intended for an audience ignorant of that language, because what he says about it could be applied to any language, including Greek itself. The writer of the treatise puts his discourse into the mouth of the god Asclepius. Asclepius begs the god Amun to prevent his words from being translated into Greek, because Egyptian is more powerful and onomatopoeic than Greek:

> Therefore, my king, so far as it is within your power, and you can do anything, keep this discourse untranslated, and do not let mysteries this great come to the Greeks, and do not let the extravagant, verbose, and (as it were) dandified phrasing of the Greek make the solemnity and solidity, and the energetic phrasing of our words disappear. For the Greeks compose discourses that are empty of effective proofs, and the philosophy of the Greeks is philopsophy [that is, not love of wisdom but love of noise], but we do not use empty discourses, but sounds full of action.[34]

One imagines that this gentle mockery of their rhetoric gave his Greek-speaking audience some pleasure. It is of course flattery in disguise, since it makes the Greeks seem artful and sophisticated, while the Egyptians are direct, sincere, and closer to nature.

Why did the Greek author of this treatise want to pretend that he was an Egyptian? Probably because, like other Greeks who had some acquaintance with Egypt, he admired the antiquity of Egypt and its religion.[35] Like Iamblichus, he had some knowledge of Egyptian theology, and of the Egyptian creator-god who made the universe.[36] But in this and in the other treatises of the surviving books of Hermes, he seeks to defend Egyptian religion not so much by explaining it on its own terms, but by making it appear to resemble the Greek philosophy of his time, Neoplatonism. Unlike modern anthropologists, who seek to represent foreign cultures so far as possible on their own terms, the ancient Greeks judged other civilizations by comparison with themselves. Hence the highest compliment that they could pay to another civilization was to show that it had in some way inspired the Greek ideas and practices that they admired. In particular, they seemed to prefer to believe that this wisdom, although actually Greek, in fact derived from or was dependent upon barbarian sources. Thus forgeries like the Hermetica had the distinct advantage of providing proof positive of the theory to which they owed their existence.[37] Iamblichus, the fourth-century pagan philosopher, uses the Hermetic writings to defend the Egyptians against another Greek who regarded their religion as less philosophical than his own. The Greek philosopher Porphyry had argued that the Egyptians believed only in corporeal beings, and not in incorporeal essences.[38] But on the basis of the Hermetic writings Iamblichus can claim that Egyptian philosophy is like Neoplatonic philosophy, with its ideal forms and notion of a god who founded the universe. He insists that Pythagoras and Plato read the writings of Hermes on old stelae in hieroglyphics.[39] On that basis he concludes that the Egyptian priests had access to a special body of knowledge inaccessible to ordinary persons. Hence he characterized Egyptian theology as a mystery that could be understood only by those who are initiated into its secrets.[40] He imagined that hieroglyphics were symbols and secret signs, though as we now know they were used primarily to represent specific sounds, like an alphabet.

If the books that were supposed to have contained Egyptian philosophy either did not refer to philosophy at all or were Greek philosophical treatises written by Greeks, and if the Egyptians themselves had no special mysteries or initiations, other than in the Greco-Roman version of the cult of Isis, is there any ancient support for James's notion that there was a universalized "Egyptian Mystery System"? The only possible ancient analogue was the cult of Isis. By the second century A.D. the worship of Isis had been imported into most major settlements. A first-century B.C. hymn claims that she is worshipped throughout the Mediterranean world.[41] A hymn to Isis on second-century A.D. papyrus lists sixty-seven towns in the Nile Delta (the section that dealt with upper Egypt is lost), and fifty-five places outside Egypt, in Greece, the Greek islands, Asia Minor, Syria, Arabia, Rome, and Italy.[42] The hymn writer's claims may be exaggerated. Also, he includes among the nations where Isis is worshipped places about which he could have had little or no real information: he lists the Amazons (who exist only in myth), the Indians, the Persians, and the Magi. But in any case only the Greeks and Romans would have understood the special training of the priests as initiations or mysteries. In Egypt, and presumably in any other place where Isis was worshipped, the rites would have had a different, and indeed more traditional, significance.

James, however, does not discuss the cult of Isis, but instead speaks of a "Grand Lodge" in Egypt, known as the Osiriaca. According to James, the Grand Lodge always met in the temple at Luxor, and all lodges in the rest of the world are modeled on this temple.[43] James does not explain why the alleged site of this Grand Lodge should be called the Osiriaca. The choice of name is curious, because the god worshipped there by the Egyptians was not Osiris, but Amun-Re. Amun-Re's Luxor temple was known as his "harem," and the god was closely associated in the temple cult with the fertility god Min.[44] As the authority for his account of the Grand Lodge, James once again cites Vail's *Ancient Myths and Modern Masonry*, but there is nothing about the Luxor temple on the pages he refers to. Vail in fact does not say that there was a Grand Lodge in Egypt which met in the temple of Luxor.[45] According to Vail (and this is the usual Masonic view) Masonic temples in modern times are all modeled on the Temple of Solomon in Jerusalem:

> The Lodge represents King Solomon's Temple. The Temple is a symbolic image of the universe, and as such is symbolic in all its parts and arrangements, therefore, the temple of Solomon resembles all the temples of antiquity that practiced the Mysteries.[46]

James appears to have transferred the archetypal Grand Lodge to Egypt in order to lend greater credibility to the alleged Egyptian origins of his "Mystery System."[47]

HOW DID THE MYTH OF AN EGYPTIAN MYS-
TERY SYSTEM COME TO BE PRESERVED IN
FREEMASONRY?

We now need to account for the long life of the strange and fundamentally Greek myths about a secret Egyptian "philoso-phy" and special "Egyptian mysteries." James's insistence on the importance of lodges in the Egyptian Mystery System pro-vides the basic clue to the reason for the myth's survival, de-spite all the real knowledge about Egyptian thought and cult that has been amassed by scholars in the last few centuries. In modern Europe and the European diaspora, lodges are the designated meeting-places of Freemasons and groups in-spired by them. In reality, the Freemasonic movement in its present form is relatively modern, and has its origins in the seventeenth century A.D.[48] But it is an article of faith in nine-teenth-century accounts of the origins of Masonry.[49] Their rites and mythology preserve the essence of "Egyptian" mys-teries and "philosophy" prevalent in late antiquity, but in a new and even more characteristically European form than anything we have seen so far.

A striking quality of Freemasonry is its "imaginative at-tachment to the religion and symbolism of the Egyptians."[50] The Egypt to which the Masons refer is of course an imaginary one, but this was the Egypt that was rediscovered in the Re-naissance: for convenience, I shall call it *Mystical Egypt* (to distinguish it from the historical Egypt that was first explored scientifically and understood only in the nineteenth century). European writers learned about Mystical Egypt from the writings of the church fathers. They knew the Hermetic treatise known as *Asclepius* because it had survived in a Latin version, and they supposed that it was one of the books of Hermes to which Clement of Alexandria referred in his description of the procession of Egyptian priests. So around 1460, when a Greek manuscript containing most of the Hermetic treatises was brought to Florence, Cosimo de'Medici thought that it was more important to translate them than the works of Plato, because "Egypt was before Greece; Hermes was earlier than Plato."[51] As a result of this "huge historical error," the Hermetic corpus was given serious attention, and its fictions were widely accepted as truth.[52] Although the theology of the Hermetica had been criticized by the church fathers for its "idolatry," the writings found a sympathetic new home in the greater religious tolerance of fifteenth-century Europe. Their first translator, Marsilio Ficino (1433–1499), thought that Hermes Trismegistus had foretold the coming of Christ and the birth of Christianity.[53]

Hermeticism, in this updated form, became in itself a new religion. The key figure in the new movement, Giordano Bruno (1548–1600), was burned at the stake for his heretical beliefs. Bruno had joined the church as a Dominican monk but had been expelled for his unorthodoxy. He then became in effect the high priest of Mystical Egyptian Hermeticism. He taught that Christianity was a corruption of Hermeticism. He advocated the knowledge of alchemy, astrology, and Mystical Egyptian magic, and he taught the art of memory, the technique of which was based on building, and hence of particular interest to masons: a speaker, when memorizing a speech, would imagine himself walking through a particular structure. In that way, he would be reminded of the topics of his speech as he recalled specific features of the building. Since Hermes was also the patron of Masons, the Freemasons became interested in the learning and magic arts associated with his name.[54]

Among the magic arts was the mastery of the "symbolism" of hieroglyphics. Even in antiquity, most educated Greeks and Romans thought that hieroglyphs were used primarily as symbolic representations, rather than as representations of specific sounds or things, as is usually the case. Diodorus, for example, believes that the hieroglyph of the hawk or falcon represented swiftness. (In fact, it represents the god Horus).[55] He explains that "the idea is transferred through appropriate metaphors to everything swift and to everything similar, as if they had been named."[56] Plutarch thought that hieroglyphics were like pictorial allegories.[57] He "translates" an inscription with a child, an aged man, a hawk, a fish, and a hippopotamus, as "you who are being born and you who are dying, the god hates shamelessness." But in fact this symbolical explanation cannot be derived from those particular signs. The first two signs could be understood to mean "children of the great ones," but the rest does not make sense.[58] Apuleius, in his description of the priest's sacred books, speaks of "indecipherable letters," some of which were animal forms that represented "condensed versions of liturgical learning."[59]

A few Greeks and Romans seem to have had a limited knowledge of the hieroglyphics that are used as ideograms, that is, which represent a particular concept such as a verb or a noun rather than a letter, and in those cases their allegorical explanations were closer to the truth. Some of these less fanciful interpretations are preserved by the first-century A.D.

temple scribe Chaeremon, who presumably knew the language. His definition of the hieroglyph of a hawk was "soul, and also sun and god," which is a reasonable inference from its actual meaning, the god Horus.[60]

But unfortunately, in the only surviving Greek treatise on hieroglyphics, many explanations are still more complicated and fanciful. This is a treatise that purports to have been translated into Greek from the Egyptian of an otherwise unknown scholar, Horapollo (his name is a combination of the Egyptian and Greek names for the same god). The style of the Greek suggests that the treatise was written around the fourth century A.D. Sometimes "Horapollo" bases his interpretations on the actual meanings of the Egyptian, but he never explains that hieroglyphics can be combined to form words and sentences. Often his interpretations are misleading. For example, he explains the hieroglyph of a hawk (the god Horus) as a symbol of sublimity or baseness, or blood or victory, or of a god like Ares or Aphrodite; and it is also a symbol of the sun, because the hawk among all the birds flies straight up, or of something lowly, because he flies straight down.[61] Because they relied on these elaborate and idiosyncratic definitions, rather than on something closer to the actual meaning of the signs, Horapollo's readers, both in antiquity and in the Renaissance, came away with the impression that hieroglyphs were not ideograms but complex abstract symbols that were little "mysteries" in themselves.

Although after 1614 it became known that the books of Hermes were not what they appeared to be, and some two hundred years after that it was shown definitively that Horapollo's interpretations of hieroglyphics were wrong, the fundamental

notions of Egypt expressed in these works and in the Renaissance philosophy connected with them were preserved in
Freemasonry.[62] The Masons believed that their initiation ritual was dated from earliest times, and that it was modeled on
the mysteries of Egypt and of other ancient countries.[63] They
preserved as part of their own secret symbolism alchemical
signs and hieroglyphics, that is, hieroglyphs as interpreted by
Horapollo. One of these is familiar to everyone in this country.
It is the Great Seal of the United States, the unfinished pyramid, whose detached top is an eye surrounded by brilliant
rays. Some of our founding fathers were Freemasons, including George Washington himself. The Treasury Department
now explains that the pyramid is unfinished because the government is new, and that "a sunburst and eye are above the
pyramid standing for the Deity."[64] Why did they choose these
particular symbols? As Masons, they wished to emphasize
their connection with the great civilization of Egypt. The explanation of the eye surrounded by a sunburst can be found in
Horapollo. The eye of the hawk symbolizes sublimity and divinity, and it is associated with the sun, because of the sharp-
sighted rays of its vision. In Masonic symbolism an eye in a
triangle radiating rays of light stands for the Grand Architect
of the Universe.[65]

The Masons also preserve in their rituals and lore the notion that the Egyptian mysteries were connected with a
larger system of moral education. Here again, we are dealing
with a historical fiction that has been accepted as reality. In
their original form, ancient mysteries had nothing to do with
schools or particular courses of study; rather, the ritual was
intended to put the initiate into contact with the divinity, and

if special preparation or rituals were involved, it was to familiarize the initiate with the practices and liturgy of that particular cult. The connection of mysteries to education in fact dates only to the eighteenth century. It derives from a particular work of European fiction, published in 1731. This was the three-volume work *Sethos, a History or Biography, based on Unpublished Memoirs of Ancient Egypt*, by the Abbé Jean Terrasson (1670–1750), a French priest who was Professor of Greek at the Collège de France.[66] Although now completely forgotten, the novel was widely read in the eighteenth century; English and German versions appeared in 1732, and an Italian version in 1734.[67] Of course, Terrasson did not have access to any Egyptian information about Egypt, since hieroglyphics were not to be deciphered until more than a century later. He was dependent on the notion of Mystical Egypt preserved in Greek and Latin sources. But he had read widely in that literature, and during the years 1737–44 he published a translation of Diodorus of Sicily, one of the principal sources of the ancient idea that Greek religion and customs derived from Egypt.[68]

Terrasson's *Sethos* purports to be a translation of an ancient manuscript found in the library of an unnamed foreign nation that is "extremely jealous of this sort of treasure." The author is said to have been an anonymous Greek in the second century A.D. Here Terrasson is following the conventions of ancient writers of historical fictions, such as the author of the Hermetica, who pretend that their works are translations of ancient writings that no one but themselves has seen. But Terrasson is careful not to deceive his readers completely: he assures them that the work he has "translated" for them is a fiction; he acknowledges that his work is a narrative of education or *Bildungsroman*, like *The Education of Cyrus*, by the fourth-century B.C. Xenophon, and like *Télémaque* (1699), by the French Archbishop François Fénelon.[69] He assures them that although fictional, the story keeps close to ancient sources, which, for the reader's convenience, he cites throughout the text. But he also says that "it is natural to suppose" that his author had access to original sources (now lost), such as memoirs available in the sacred archives of Egypt, written by unknown priests who accompanied Sethos on his travels.[70] The sophisticated reader would be amused by the notion that the anonymous author had consulted these otherwise unknown documents, but Terrasson gives no warning to less well-educated readers that there is in fact no reason to "suppose" that these documents ever existed.

Sethos, the hero of this long "biography," is supposed to have lived in the thirteenth century B.C., a century before the Trojan war. The story begins at Memphis, where Sethos's father is king. Thirteenth-century Memphis, as Terrasson imagines it, has many of the features of an idealized French university. The temple of Isis, Osiris, and Horus serves as the theater of arts and sciences. There are beautiful gardens, maintained by the priests, an art gallery, and a natural history museum with specimens, medicines, and chemical preparations. The chemical gallery leads to the galleries of anatomy and embalming, and there is a large outdoor zoo. There is also a gallery of mathematics (the author assures us that the study of geometry originated in Egypt), agricultural machines, and hydraulic lifts. Beneath the buildings there were underground passages. These, Terrasson tells us, had been built at the beginning of time by Hermes Trismegistus, with hieroglyphs and stone symbols. It was here, he says, that Pythagoras studied hieroglyphics and geometry, and astronomy, together with Thales. But no other Greeks were initiated, because the whole complex was destroyed by the Persian king Cambyses in 525 B.C.[71]

Terrasson also describes a university complex in Thebes. Here was a great library, with "Food for the Mind" inscribed on its gate, though the books for priests were not available to the public. Priests also served as judges of the law, and it was with them, Terrasson states, that the Greeks Solon and Lycurgus studied. There were art galleries with statues and paintings, and a music gallery. For the benefit of his French readers Terrasson points out that these academies were supported by the kings, and young noblemen studied there.[72] The result, from Terrasson's point of view, was a system of education that was far better than anything produced in ancient Athens.[73]

Sethos goes to Memphis to study, but while there he is also initiated.[74] The initiation takes place in the recesses of a pyramid—before serious archaeological work was done in Egypt in the nineteenth century it was not known that pyramids were used exclusively as tombs.[75] An inscription over the entrance explains to the candidate the significance of the ordeal he is about to undergo:

> Whoever goes thro' this passage alone, and without looking behind him, shall be purify'd by fire, by water, and by air; and if he can vanquish the fears of death, he shall return from the bowels of the earth, he shall see light again, and he shall be intitled to the privilege of preparing his mind for the revelation of the mysteries of the great goddess Isis.[76]

Terrasson's basic model for the initiation is the ritual allusively described by the narrator Lucius in Apuleius's *The Golden Ass*.[77] Again, the presiding goddess is Isis, and the hero must descend to the world of the dead and return. But Terrasson has added mythical elements from ancient Greek sources. The idea that the hero cannot look behind him during his journey to and from the Lower World derives from the myth of Orpheus and Eurydice.[78] The notion that the soul must be purified in fire, water, and air was well known to the Neoplatonists, but ultimately derives from the fifth-century B.C. Greek philosopher Empedocles.[79] Although most candidates (including Orpheus himself, we are told) are frightened off by the threatening inscription, Sethos descends into the pyramid. Three men warn him that they will block his way if he tries to return. He is led to a place where he must endure the purification of fire, water, and air: he crosses between red-hot iron bars; then he must swim across a canal, and subsequently cross a drawbridge, which hurls him through the air. He emerges from behind a triple statue of Osiris, Isis, and Horus; then he is given canal water to make him forget what he has seen, and a special barley mixture to drink. These elements of the rite also come from Greek sources. In the myth of Er in Plato's *Republic* the souls of the dead must drink the water of Forgetfulness (Lethe) before they can enter new bodies, and the barley mixture called *kykeon* was given to initiates into the Eleusinian mysteries.[80] The initiation described above, however, was only preliminary. Other physical trials await him during a final period of twelve days, including fasting, silence, and a course of lectures on morality. Terrasson concludes his account of the preliminary mysteries by stating

that the similarities between the "Egyptian" and Greek practices show that the Eleusinian mysteries were based on the
cult of Isis.[81] The reverse, of course, is true, but evidently
some of his readers were prepared to take him at his word.

In order to become a priest, candidates who completed the
preliminary tests successfully underwent a final twelve-day
initiation.[82] They began by taking an oath at the triple statue
of Isis, Osiris, and Horus not to reveal what they had seen.
Terrasson interrupts the narrative here to invoke the poets
who described the descent of the heroes to the Lower World.[83]
But what he describes is not a further ordeal, but a system of
education. The candidates are shown the subterranean city in
which the priests live, and the schools in which they acquire
vast knowledge. Terrasson assures us that a vague and distorted picture of this secret world survives in the Greek
myths about the afterlife. After the candidates have seen the
subterranean city, they march in a final triumphal parade
with the priests, modeled on the Egyptian procession described by Clement.

In addition to these final rites of initiation at Memphis, Terrasson describes other mysteries at Thebes, again educational
in nature. There is a college at Thebes specializing in astronomy: its equipment includes an observatory, globes, and three
or four hundred priests employed in calculations.[84] Mysteries
are an important theme also in the second volume of *Sethos*, in
which Terrasson describes his hero's travels around the continent of Africa. Sethos discovers a debased version of the Egyptian mysteries in Guinea, and he establishes a sacerdotal college
there, with initiation rites and lectures, and instruction in
virtue.[85] The book ends with the initiation of the Egyptian

princess Mnevia, Sethos's intended bride, into the mysteries at
Memphis. But Sethos elects to remain celibate. He renounces
the kingdom, and devotes himself to his priesthood and his
studies.[86]

It is not easy to understand why this long and tendentious
account was so inspiring to several generations of European
readers. Stories of tests and trials were popular in the eighteenth century.[87] But Terrasson also was (so to speak) user-
friendly. His Egypt was almost completely Europeanized, and
therefore accessible. A portrait of real Egypt, even when based
on such sources as were then available, would have been too
foreign. Instead, Terrasson, using Greek and Roman sources as
a starting point, offered an Egypt that his contemporaries
could readily imagine, and presented it in familiar terms. There
was, first of all, the anachronistic but vivid account of the ancient Egyptian schools and university. Throughout Sethos's ad-
ventures there are references to Greek and Roman myths. The
initiations follow the pattern of the hero's descent to Hades,
which all educated men would have studied in school. Even
though the novel is supposed to be about ancient Egypt, its
ethics are distinctly Christian. At the end of all his trials, and
his extensive travels, having endured everything and achieved
everything, Sethos rejects all he has won (including a beautiful
prospective bride, who has been initiated in the mysteries) for a
quiet and celibate life, to be lived among the priests.[88] It is no
accident that the principal deities in this narrative are Osiris,
his wife Isis, and their son Horus, because they offer the closest
ancient analogy to the Christian Holy Family.

Whatever the other reasons for its success, Terrasson's
description of the "Egyptian" initiation rites appears to have

been one of the most influential passages in the book.

A verse tragedy based on it was produced in 1739; it provided the inspiration for a ballet, Jean-Philippe Rameau's *The Birth of Osiris* (1751) and an opera, Johann Gottlieb Naumann's *Osiris* (1781).[89] The French Freemasons used it as the basis of their initiation rites.[90] Because the book was quickly translated into English, German, and Italian, features of Sethos's initiation were adopted in the rituals of other countries. Freemasonry was particularly active in Vienna in the 1780s.[91] In 1783 the Masonic Lodge of Doing Good initiated one of its most enthusiastic members, the composer Wolfgang Amadé Mozart (1756–1791).[92] Mozart was also introduced to the Lodge of Crowned Hope. The master of this lodge, Ignaz von Born (1742–1791), wrote a treatise, "About the Mysteries of Egypt," for the first issue in 1784 of a new *Journal for Freemasons*.

In his treatise, von Born set out to write the history of Egypt. He cites ancient sources, but his notion of mysteries was based on the elaborate portrait of the educational system described by Terrasson.[93] One of von Born's explicit aims was to show that the Egyptians had been wrongly characterized in historical writing; instead, he argued, their mysteries showed them to be a highly civilized people, and demonstrated that many features of their rites were preserved in Freemasonry.[94] Toward the end of the treatise he lists some of the general similarities between Masonic rites and the Egyptian mysteries. Among these are killing the serpent that threatens the life of Horus; the importance of the number three, geographical orientation, the symbols of hieroglyphs, the hierarchical order of the priests, the four elements, the Sun and the symbolism of light and dark. He concludes that "the goal of the Egyptian Mysteries was truth and wisdom and the good of mankind."[95] According to von Born, that goal was shared by Freemasonry.[96]

Mozart had read Terrasson, and to him his ideas about the importance of the mysteries were not only credible but inspiring. In *Thamos, King of Egypt* (1773) and the opera *The Magic Flute* (1791), Mozart portrays "Egyptian" religion with deep respect, but as if it were an ancient version of Christianity. In *Thamos*, the worship of a supreme being (the sun god) in an Egyptian setting is portrayed with dignified choruses that would have been equally appropriate in the mouths of a church choir.[97] In the first chorus, contrasting major and minor keys emphasize the contrast between light and darkness.[98] The high priest, whose name (not coincidentally) is Sethos, alludes to an initiation ceremony, speaking of the education the hero Thamos has received and the burden that that places upon him.[99]

But it is from *The Magic Flute*, where the reminiscences of *Sethos* are even more obvious, that we can get some sense of the continuing appeal of Terrasson's novel in the eighteenth century. Mozart's librettist was a fellow Mason, Johann Emanuel Schikaneder. Schikaneder had also read Terrasson in Matthias Claudius's newly published German translation (1777–78).[100] The influence of Terrasson helps explain many curious features of the opera, such as its being set in Egypt, rather than somewhere in Europe. Isis and Osiris are the principal gods of the opera, as of the novel. In the first scene the life of the opera's hero, Tamino, is threatened by a snake; Sethos also sets out to kill a serpent. He brings it back alive;

but Tamino, a less idealized character than Sethos, is rescued by the Three Ladies. Tamino, like Sethos, is impressed with the grandeur of the pyramids. Tamino enters the sacred precinct of the pyramid from the north, like Sethos; like him he is watched by priests and confronted by men in armor. In the opera, Sarastro offers a prayer to Isis that is taken almost directly from Terrasson.[101] Papageno, who has been accompanying Tamino, is too frightened by the thunder (another legacy from *Sethos*) to continue the ordeal, but Tamino is able to proceed to a second stage of the initiation.[102] The men in armor sing a duet. The tune is from the chorale of Luther's versification of the twelfth psalm.[103] But their words echo the words of the inscription over the entrance to the pyramid in Terrasson's novel:

Whoever travels on this road full of difficulties, will become purified through fire, water, air, and earth. And if he can overcome the fear of death, he can raise himself from earth to heaven, and when he stands illuminated on this level, he will devote himself completely to the Mysteries of Isis.[104]

The text of Terrasson's "inscription" cataloguing the dangers of the initiation was apparently read out in certain Masonic ceremonies, and the ritual of purification through the four elements is acted out in several different ways in *The Magic Flute*.[105] In the Masonic initiation that Mozart himself underwent, the liturgy emphasizes the ability to face and so to triumph over death.[106] Masonic initiates must triumph over the serpent, who represents temptation, as he does in the Bible.[107] There are many other specific allusions to Masonic ritual in the opera: in the progression of chords, for example, and in the frequent use of the numbers three, five, and six. Both Sarastro's second aria and the final chorus of act 2 express the benevolent humanism of the Order.[108] The opera celebrates the triumph of reason and wisdom over the irrational.[109] In that respect particularly it remains faithful not only to Terrasson but also to his classical sources, Virgil and Apuleius.

But the portrait of the "Egyptian mysteries" in Terrasson's novel, even though fictional, was understood to represent the truth. Terrasson was a highly regarded scholar in his day, and his research for the novel seems to have been regarded as "state-of-the-art." For example, in 1814 the French art historian Alexandre Lenoir (1761–1839) published a book defending the notion that the origins of Freemasonry were ancient. In this work he drew on *Sethos* as the authority for his claim that the rituals of Freemasonry preserved the form of ancient Egyptian rites.[110] He did not realize—in fact, no one at the time seemed to realize—that his reasoning was completely circular, and that in effect he was only proving that rites based on *Sethos* were based on *Sethos*.[111] Like Terrasson, Lenoir insisted that the Eleusinian mysteries in Greece were only another version of the mysteries of Isis and Osiris celebrated at Memphis.[112] He did not, and perhaps could not, suspect that the sources on which Terrasson relied produced a portrait of Egypt that would soon be proved to be unreliable, and that what he thought was "Egyptian" was actually not only Greco-Roman, but in character a distinctive product of the French Enlightenment. Serious scholars soon forgot about the idea of Egyptian mysteries, but meanwhile, the Masons continued to believe in this essentially fictitious account of their ancient origins.[113] And, understandably, it was this Masonic view of Mystical Egypt, and not the Egyptologists' view of Egypt, which was celebrated in the rituals adopted by black Masons in the West Indies and in this country.

FIVE

THE MYTH OF THE
STOLEN LEGACY

In Lenoir's book about the origins of Freemasonry, there is a striking illustration of the ordeal of the Four Elements in the Mysteries at Memphis. The artist suggests that the relevance of the trial is timeless; the setting, which is based directly on a scene in Terrasson's *Sethos,* looks less like a subterranean chamber in a pyramid than a fantastic prison designed by Piranesi in the eighteenth century A.D.[1] (see figure 4). The Masons believed that the Memphis ritual had served as the model for all other initiations throughout the world. As they saw it, the influence of the Egyptian mysteries spread throughout the world by a natural process of imitation, the ancient Greeks being early and fortunate beneficiaries of the

FIGURE 4

THE ORDEAL OF THE FOUR ELEMENTS

Egyptian legacy, and the Masons themselves being only the latest practitioners of the ancient and virtually universal rite.

But this idealistic vision of a world unified through the legacy of the Egyptian mysteries underwent a drastic change in the twentieth century. From the older Masonic notion of gradual evolution a new myth developed that ceased to portray the Greeks simply as inheritors of more ancient traditions. Now, for the first time, the Greeks were the villains in the story, who stole the Egyptian legacy and passed it off as their own achievement.

The idea that the most characteristic of all ancient Greek inventions, philosophy, was literally stolen or plagiarized goes beyond any claim of cultural dependency made by Terrasson or Lenoir in their portrayals of the Egyptian mysteries. Not even the church fathers were so hostile to the Greeks, when they tried to prove that the Greeks had no original ideas of their own. When a writer such as Clement of Alexandria accused the Greeks of imitating Jewish religious thought, his primary intention was to praise the Hebrews, by showing that the great pagan writers had been inspired by Hebrew writers and shared many of their important ideas.[2] Clement wrote in Greek; he had studied and read many pagan Greek authors and frequently quoted passages from their works. He was well aware of their importance and their genius, even when he was prepared to mock them. He was less interested in disparaging the Greeks than in promoting his new religion.

In this chapter I will show how and why the older notion of benign Egyptian influence was replaced by the idea of a deliberate and ruthless conspiracy. I will also explain why I believe that these new charges against the Greeks are false. Not only was there never such a thing as an Egyptian Mystery System; there was never an organized educational program or established canon of books of Egyptian philosophy that the Greeks could steal or plagiarize. Although Greeks who went to Egypt learned something about Egyptian mythology, Greek philosophy as it was developed in the fifth and fourth centuries B.C. is fundamentally a Greek invention. It could not have been devised without the ability of the Greek language to express impersonal abstractions, or without the strong rationalism that characterizes Greek thought. I shall discuss the work of the Afrocentrist writers, who, in the hope of promoting their own culture, disparage the ancient Greeks and encourage their readers to distrust those of us who believe that Greeks were the inventors of what has always been thought to be Greek philosophy.

Perhaps the most influential Afrocentrist text is *Stolen Legacy*, a work that has been in wide circulation since its publication in 1954. Its author, George G. M. James, writes that "the term Greek philosophy, to begin with is a misnomer, for

there is no such philosophy in existence." He argues that the
Greeks "did not possess the native ability essential to the development of philosophy." Rather, he states that "the Greeks
were not the authors of Greek philosophy, but the Black people of North Africa, The Egyptians."[3] In making this assertion, James's motives resemble those of the Hellenistic Jewish
writers Artapanus and Aristobulus, who insisted that Plato's
laws were directly inspired by Moses. But where the Hellenistic Jews simply wished to show that their culture had priority
over that of their conquerors, James wants to assert both
African priority and Greek inferiority.

It is not hard to understand why James wishes to give credit
for the Greek achievement to the Egyptians, even if there is little or no historical foundation for his claims. Like the other na-
tionalistic myths, the story of a "Stolen Legacy" both offers an
explanation for past suffering and provides a source of ethnic
pride. Halford Fairchild, a professor of psychology and black
studies at Pitzer College in California, speaks of the "trans-
forming effect" the story of the Stolen Legacy has on African-
American audiences, not least because most black Americans
have been raised in a culture that disparages or neglects the
contributions of black people. According to Fairchild, learning
that the early Greek philosophers did their "most important research" in Africa "empowers black people to reclaim their right-
ful place as equal players in contemporary society."[4]

But although the myth may encourage and perhaps even
"empower" African-Americans, its use has a destructive side,
which cannot and should not be overlooked. First of all, it offers them a "story" instead of history. It also suggests that
African-Americans need to learn only what they choose to

believe about the past. But in so doing, the Afrocentric myth seeks to shelter them from learning what all other ethnic groups must learn, and indeed, face up to, namely the full scope of their history.[5]

What people on earth have had a completely glorious history? While we point to the great achievements of the Greeks, anyone who has studied ancient Greek civilization knows that they also made terrible and foolish mistakes. Isn't treating African-Americans differently from the rest of humankind just another form of segregation and condescension? Such implied discrimination is the most destructive aspect of Afrocentrism, but there are other serious problems as well. Teaching the myth of the Stolen Legacy as if it were history robs the ancient Greeks and their modern descendants of a heritage that rightly belongs to them. Why discriminate against them when discrimination is the issue? In addition, the myth deprives the ancient Egyptians of their proper history and robs them of their actual legacy. The Egypt of the myth of the Stolen Legacy is a wholly European Egypt, as imagined by Greek and Roman writers, and further elaborated in eighteenth-century France. Ancient Egyptian civilization deserves to be remembered (and respected) for what it was, and not for what Europeans, ancient and modern, have imagined it to be.

WHAT IS THE ORIGIN OF THE STOLEN LEGACY?

In *Sethos*, Terrasson imagined that the Egyptians were white, and racially distinct from the population of the rest of Africa. But in the nineteenth century, educated blacks realized that Herodotus had described the ancient Egyptians as dark-skinned and woolly-haired, that is, as blacks according to the definition of their own (and our) times. One of the first writers to call attention to the fact that Egyptians were Africans was the American writer Frederick Douglass (1817–1895). In 1854 Douglass argued that the study of Egyptian civilization got less attention than it deserved because it was in Africa, rather than in Europe, Asia, or America:

> Another unhappy circumstance is, that the ancient Egyptians were not white people, but were, undoubtedly, just about as dark in complexion as many in this country who are considered genuine Negroes; and that is not all, their hair was far from being of that graceful lankness which adorns the fair Anglo-Saxon head.[6]

He also observed, with restrained irony, the lengths white writers of his day were prepared to go in order to ignore the physical affinities of the ancient Egyptians to the peoples of Africa.[7]

Similar arguments were put forward by Edward Wilmot Blyden (1832–1912), a native of St. Thomas who emigrated back to Africa. Blyden, a prolific and accomplished writer, knew the Greek and Latin classics well, but he brought to his learning the distinctive viewpoint of an African; as one obituary writer observed, "Dr. Blyden is the only man we have ever known, or heard of, that has thoroughly mastered the Arts, Science, Philosophy, and Literature of the European, and still remained a Negro."[8] In 1887 Blyden observed that

> a superficial criticism, guided by local and temporary prejudices, has attempted to deny the intimate relations of the

Negro with the great historic races of Egypt and Ethiopia. But no one who has travelled in North-eastern Africa, or among the ruins on the banks of the Nile, will for a moment doubt that there was the connection, not of accident or of adventitious circumstances, but of consanguinity between the races of inner Africa of the present day, and the ancient Egyptians and Ethiopians.[9]

Blyden, like Douglass, had read Herodotus on the racial characteristics of the Egyptians. But Blyden took the argument a step further. He was familiar with the reflections of the French traveler Count Volney (1757–1820) about the accomplishments of the black peoples of Egypt.[10] When he visited Egypt sometime during the years 1783–85, Volney was amazed to discover that the population of that country resembled the mulattoes he had seen in Europe. This discovery caused him to reflect: "Just think that this race of black men, today our slave and the object of our scorn, is the very race to which we owe our arts, sciences, and even the use of speech!"[11]

Blyden likewise insisted that all Africans were the true heirs of the great civilization of ancient Egypt. After he visited Egypt in 1866, he concluded that the Pyramids had been built by blacks:

This, thought I, was the work of my African progenitors. . . . Feelings came over me far different from those I have ever felt when looking at the mighty works of European genius. I felt that I had a peculiar heritage in the Great Pyramid built . . . by the enterprising sons of Ham, from which I descended. The blood seemed to flow faster through my veins. I seemed to hear the echo of those illustrious Africans.

I seemed to feel the impulse from those stirring characters who sent civilization to Greece. . . . Could my voice have reached out to every African in the world, I would have earnestly addressed him . . . : "Retake your Fame."[12]

The call to reclaim the Egyptian heritage resounds throughout modern Afrocentric writings. But it is important to note that the Egyptian civilization Blyden had in mind is not the true history of ancient Egypt, which was still being written during his lifetime. Rather, it is the "Egypt" invented by the writers of late antiquity, and preserved by Terrasson and the Masonic mythology.

The notion of such a specifically black Egyptian heritage appears to have been well established by the turn of the century.[13] It was taken up by the historian W. E. B. Du Bois (1868–1963).[14] It also was adopted by black Masons.[15] The anonymous writer of an article published in 1903 in *The Colored American Magazine* claims that the first Mason was a black man, because the first Masons were Egyptians. For that reason, if for no other, white Masons were not justified in refusing to include blacks in their lodges. The writer makes it clear that in ancient times black civilization was far more advanced than that of any Europeans at the time:

When the ancestors of the present haughty Saxons—the Gauls, the Normans, and the Celts—were naked barbarians, living in grottoes and dropping [*sic*] caves, slinging stones at wild animals for food, and eating that food uncooked, there was on Africa's soil, in Egypt, the land of the black man, a civilization resting on the "pinnacle of national splendor" far exceeding that of Greece or Rome today. On the great Oasis in the desert of antiquity blossomed the golden deeds of the world's first Masonry. Here mind was the standard of the man, and natural ability ranked above birth. Every woman was educated. . . . Here the landmarks of Masonry were born.[16]

This writer's Egypt is even more idealized than Terrasson's, and more liberal in its treatment of women than eighteenth-century Masonry, from which they were generally excluded. Even though an "official" history of black Masonry published in 1903 makes no reference to it,[17] the notion that the first Masons were black Egyptians seems to have become an article of faith in twentieth-century black Masonry:

So out of Egypt and through the black man, the world gains its first knowledge of the worship of the deity and the cultivation of science. . . . The Negroes [were] the founders of arts, sciences, and other forms of culture instead of being only hewers of wood and drawers of water.[18]

It was this utopian vision of black Egypt as the cradle of civilization that inspired one of the most important black leaders of the twentieth century, Marcus Mosiah Garvey (1887–1940).

Garvey joined the Masons, but he was too busy to attend meetings and eventually dropped out. Instead he founded his own organization, the Universal Negro Improvement Association (UNIA).[19] Fraternal societies played an important role in the West African countries from which most slaves had been taken. They continued to serve many useful purposes among the peoples of the African diaspora, especially since blacks were excluded from most white societies.[20] To a large extent, the UNIA was organized along Masonic lines: it had a significant benevolent function; it had a constitution based on the Masons'; it also had a "potentate," analogous to the "imperial potentate" of the black Masonic Ancient Egyptian Arabic Order of the Nobles of the Mystic Shrine. Both organizations favored large-scale public displays, and the UNIA potentate's helmet closely resembled the ceremonial hat worn by Masons in special parades.[21]

Garvey also appears to have taken from black Masonry its distinctively utopian idea of Egypt's superiority to ancient European civilizations. As a young man he became interested in the history both of Africa and famous Caribbean islanders of African descent. He also knew that history could be used to serve a purpose. In his case, the purpose was to instill in black people of the African diaspora pride in their own race and resentment of their white oppressors.[22] In "African Fundamentalism" he wrote:

The time has come for the Blackman to forget and cast behind him his hero worship and adoration of other races, and to start out immediately to create and emulate heroes of his own. We must canonize our own saints, create our own martyrs, and elevate to positions of fame and honor Black men and women who have made their distinct contributions to our racial history.[23]

Evidently he was prepared to rewrite ancient history along these lines. In keeping with his determination to prove the superiority of the black race, he added a new calumny against

Europeans. Not only had they derived their civilization from Egypt; they had in fact *stolen* it. In "Who and What Is a Negro?" (1923) Garvey claimed that

> every student of history, of impartial mind, knows that the Negro ruled the world, when white men were savages and barbarians living in caves; that thousands of Negro professors at that time taught in the universities in Alexandria, then the seat of learning; that ancient Egypt gave to the world civilization and that Greece and Rome have robbed Egypt of her arts and letters, and taken all the credit to themselves. It is not surprising, however, that white men should resort to every means to keep Negroes in ignorance of their history, it would be a great shock to their pride to admit to the world today that 3,000 years ago black men excelled in government and were the founders and teachers of art, science and literature.[24]

Garvey developed these ideas as time went on. In 1935 he published a poem and essay, "The Tragedy of White Injustice." In the poem he reiterated the idea that when the civilization of Egypt was flourishing, white men were living in a morally degraded and primitive state. He also sought to justify his claim that white men have concealed the important role played by people of African descent in European history:

> Out of cold old Europe these white men came,
> From caves, dens and holes, without any fame,
> Eating their dead's flesh and sucking their blood,
> Relics of the Mediterranean flood;

Literature, science and art they stole,
After Africa had measured each pole . . .

Cleopatra, Empress Josephine,
Were black mongrels like that of the Philippine:—
Mixtures from black and other races they,—
Yet, "true," the white man's history will not say
To those who seek the light of pure knowledge
In the inquiring world, school or college.
Napoleon fell for a Negro woman;
So did the Caesars, and the Great Roman.[25]

In the essay accompanying the poem Garvey told his audience
not to believe what white historians told them, and he explicitly stated that ancient peoples of North Africa were black:

> The educational system of today hides the truth as far as
> the Negro is concerned. . . . As for instance, you will read
> that the Egyptians were a great people, the Carthagenians
> [sic], the Libyans, etc., but you will not be told that they
> were black people or Negroes. You should, therefore, go be-
> yond the mere statement of these events to discover the
> truth that will be creditable to your race.[26]

I do not know if Garvey was the originator of the idea that
Europeans had deliberately concealed the truth from blacks,
but wherever the idea came from, it was not inconsistent with
his philosophy of racial purity and separation.[27] He believed
that one reason why whites had reached "such a height in civilizations" was that they had been taught that they were
superior: "the white race has a system, a method, a code of

ethics laid down for the white child to go by," and that black children needed to have a similar creed.[28] In any case, his idea that all education was fundamentally racist was widely influential, and his notion that blacks were the victim of a conspiracy has had a lasting emotional appeal.

IS THERE ANY HISTORICAL EVIDENCE FOR A STOLEN LEGACY?

In his speeches Garvey did not discuss in detail how the Europeans "stole" literature, science, and art from Africa. But in *Stolen Legacy*, George G. M. James offers an extended account of the conspiracy. The new details appear to be James's own contribution to the story. As we have seen, he had learned the basic outline of the myth of cultural dependency from the Masons. From them he got the idea that there had been a Mystery System in Egypt from earliest times, which formed the basis of an educational system distributed throughout Egypt in Lodges. Like Garvey, he takes it for granted that all the peoples of North Africa were black, including the Carthaginians and Cyreneans. He follows Diodorus in claiming that Greece was colonized from Egypt. These are the basic premises from which he is prepared to reconstruct Greek history. Since these premises, as we have seen, are demonstrably false, James's work has virtually no historical value. But the book is interesting nonetheless, as an example of how and why mythic or propagandistic "histories" come to be written.

According to James, although the Greeks began to study in Egypt when that country was occupied by the Persians, the main transfer of knowledge was accomplished when Alexander, accompanied by Aristotle, looted the library of Alexandria in 333 B.C. Then the School of Aristotle converted the stolen Alexandrian library into a research center and university. Finally, the Romans in the fourth century A.D. suppressed the Egyptian Mystery System in favor of Christianity.[29] James augments his claim that Greek philosophy was stolen by ingenious arguments. He adds new details to the basic description of the Egyptian educational "system." He attempts to show by means of summaries that the basic tenets of Greek philosophy have analogues in Egyptian thought. He asserts that the intellectual climate of Greece was hostile to philosophy, and that Greeks were naturally incapable of it. He provides what appears to be extensive documentation for each of these claims.

James's book has been reprinted many times since it was first published forty years ago, and many otherwise well-educated people believe that what he claims is true. Because his thesis has been more widely credited than it deserves to be, I believe that it is appropriate here to explain in some detail why virtually none of his assertions is supported by the available evidence. To learn about Africa we must look where the Afrocentrists fail to look, that is, to the historical Egypt described by the ancient Egyptians themselves, and to the important cultural links to neighboring parts of Africa. For example, the idea of a semidivine ruler king like the Egyptian pharaoh has analogues in East Africa.[30] The practice of elaborate rhythmic hand-clapping at festivals, which Herodotus observed during his visit to Egypt, also has parallels elsewhere in Africa.[31] But James says nothing about such truly African features of Egyptian culture, because the Egypt that he offers to his readers is not African. It is (as we have seen) fundamentally Greco-Roman.

There are many indications throughout the book that James's idea of ancient Egypt is fundamentally the imaginary Mystical Egypt of Freemasonry. He speaks of grades of initiation.[32] In these Mysteries, as the Freemasons imagined them, Neophyte initiates must learn self-control and self-knowledge.[33] He believes that Moses was an initiate into the Egyptian mysteries, and that Socrates reached the grade of Master Mason.[34] In his description of Greek philosophy, he emphasizes the Four Elements that play such a key role in Terrasson's Memphis and Masonic initiation ceremonies.[35] He speaks of the Masonic symbol of the Open Eye, which as we have seen is based on an Egyptian hieroglyph but in Masonry has come specifically to represent the Master Mind.[36] As in the University/Mystery system invented by Terrasson, Egyptian temples are used as libraries and observatories.[37] Like the Freemasons, James regards the Egyptian Mystery System as the basis for all other mystery cults, in Greece and elsewhere.[38] The Grand Lodge at Luxor had branches throughout the world, including "Lodges" among the native populations of the Americas, such as the Mayas, Aztecs, and Incas.[39]

As we saw in chapter 4, the Mystery System that James describes never existed, and its connection to an educational system is purely imaginary. What then are the Greeks supposed to have stolen from the Egyptians? Are there any texts in existence that can verify the claim that Greek philosophy was stolen from Egypt? How was the "transfer" of Egyptian materials to Greece accomplished? If we examine what James says about the way in which the "transfer" was supposed to have been carried out, we will find that little or no historical data can be summoned to support it. In fact, in order to construct his argument, James overlooked or ignored much existing evidence.

To begin with, no ancient source says that Alexander and Aristotle raided the library at Alexandria. That they do not do so is not surprising, because it is unlikely that Aristotle ever went there. Aristotle was Alexander's tutor when Alexander was young, but he did not accompany him on his military campaign. Even if he had gone to Alexandria, it is hard to see how he could have stolen books from the library there. Although Alexandria was founded in 331 B.C., it did not begin to function as a city until after 323. Aristotle died in 322. The library was assembled around 297 under the direction of Demetrius of Phaleron, a pupil of Aristotle's. Most of the books it contained were in Greek.[40]

James makes no reference to these problems. Instead he explains the silence of history as an example of the European conspiracy against Egypt. If ancient accounts of Aristotle's life say nothing about his having visited Egypt, that is because Aristotle and his contemporaries deliberately attempted to suppress all knowledge of his visit, so that no one would know that Egypt (rather than Greece) was the true source of his so-called original philosophy: "This silence of history at once throws doubt upon the life and achievement of Aristotle."[41] But this convenient line of argument could also be used to "prove" that Aristotle went to India with Alexander, and had borrowed (or taken) ideas from the Indian Gymnosophists.[42] James also relies on the "silence of history" to explain why all traces of the educational program of the Egyptian Mystery System have disappeared. The System was abolished by the

Romans, who could not comprehend the "higher metaphysical doctrines" of the Mysteries, and were envious of the "lofty culture system of the Black people."[43] He does not mention the other, and more obvious reason why no ancient Egyptian records of the Mystery System survived antiquity: that no such System ever existed.

James's other charges against Aristotle are equally insubstantial. If Aristotle had stolen his ideas from the Egyptians, as James asserts, James should be able to provide parallel Egyptian and Greek texts showing frequent verbal correspondences. As it is, he can only come up with a vague similarity between two titles. One is Aristotle's treatise *On the Soul*, and the other is the modern English name of a collection of Egyptian texts, *The Book of the Dead*.[44] These funerary texts, which the Egyptians themselves called the *Book of Coming Forth by Day*, are designed to protect the soul during its dangerous journey through Duat, the Egyptian underworld, on its way to life of bliss in the Field of Reeds.[45] Both Aristotle and the Egyptians believed in the notion of a "soul." But there the similarity ends. Even a cursory glance at a translation of *The Book of the Dead* reveals that it is not a philosophical treatise but rather a series of ritual prescriptions to ensure the soul's passage to the next world. It is completely different from Aristotle's abstract consideration of the nature of the soul.

James fails to mention that the two texts cannot be profitably compared, because their aims and methods are so different. Instead, he accounts for the discrepancy by claiming that Aristotle's theory is only a "very small portion" of the Egyptian "philosophy" of the soul, as described in the Egyptian *Book of the Dead*.[46] On that basis, one could claim that any later writer plagiarized from any earlier writer who touched on the same subject. But why not assume instead that the later writer was influenced by the earlier writer, or even came up with some of the same ideas independently, especially if those ideas are widespread, like the notion that human beings have souls? James does not discuss these other obvious possibilities but rather supplies further ingenious arguments to account for the lack of written evidence. Some of Aristotle's surviving works are thought to have been notes, rather than the full form of his treatises. James argues that the use of notes indicates that Aristotle wrote in haste, "while doing his research at the great Egyptian library." But since the ancient method of teaching was oral, Aristotle would not have needed to take notes during lectures or in discussions with his Greek instructors.[47]

James also asserts that since Aristotle could not have learned everything he is said to have known from his teacher, Plato, Aristotle stole his information from Egypt. He does not mention the other—and infinitely more likely—explanation of why Aristotle's work differed from his predecessors': he was a great original thinker, who naturally was able to go beyond what he had learned from his teachers. Instead, James insists that Aristotle's own categories of scientific knowledge, practical, poetical, and theoretical, are comparable to those of the curriculum of the Egyptian Mystery System.[48] What curriculum? James can only supply a summary description, based on the forty-two books carried by Egyptian priests in the procession described by Clement of Alexandria in the second century A.D., five centuries after Aristotle's death. These books contained "all of Greek philosophy," but as we have seen, by "philosophy" Clement meant simply learning, and the priests' books were accounts of practical information and regulations completely different in character from the abstract considerations discussed in Aristotle's works.[49]

James also alleges that Aristotle's theory of matter was taken from the so-called Memphite Theology. The Memphite Theology is a religious document inscribed on a stone tablet by Egyptian priests in the eighth century B.C., but said to have been copied from an ancient papyrus. The archaic language of the text suggests that the original dates from sometime in the second millennium B.C.[50] According to James, Aristotle took from the Memphite Theology his doctrine that matter, motion, and time are eternal, along with the principle of opposites, and the concept of the unmoved mover.[51] James does not say how Aristotle would have known about this inscription, which was at the time located in Memphis and not in the Library of Alexandria, or explain how he would have been able to read it. But even if Aristotle had had some way of finding out about it, he would have had no use for it in his philosophical writings. The Memphis text, like the Egyptian *Book of the Dead*, is a work of a totally different character from any of Aristotle's treatises.

The Memphite text describes the creation of the world as then known (that is, Upper and Lower Egypt). One section presents a theological argument that all the gods "came into being in," that is, are manifestations of the god Ptah, the creator god of Memphis, who was identified by the Greeks with their god Hephaestus. The Memphite inscription relates how Ptah's mind (or "heart") and thought (or "tongue") created the universe and all living creatures in it: "for every word of the god came about through what the heart devised and the tongue commanded." From one of his manifestations, the primordial waters of chaos, the sun-god Atum was born. When Ptah has finished creating the universe, he rests from his labors: "Ptah was satisfied after he had made all things and all divine words."[52]

In form and in substance this account has virtually nothing in common with Aristotle's abstract theology. In fact, in *Metaphysics* Book 11, Aristotle discards the traditional notion of a universe that is created by a divinity or divinities, in favor of a metaphysical argument. If there is eternal motion, there is eternal substance, and behind that, an immaterial and eternal source of activity, whose existence can be deduced from the eternal circular motion of the heavens. The source of this activity is what is called in English translation the "unmoved mover." The Greek itself is more abstract and impersonal than the translation suggests: "something that moves, itself being unmoved" (*ti kinoun auto akinēton on*).[53] This force is completely different in character from the anthropomorphic creator god Ptah of the Memphite Theology. All that the two texts have in common is a concern with creation of the universe. On the same insubstantial basis, it would be possible to argue that Aristotle stole his philosophy from the story of creation in the first book of Genesis.

The final "proof" that Aristotle stole his philosophy from Egypt is, according to James, that ancient writers give widely divergent totals of the number of his collected works. Such inconsistency, he suggests, is grounds for considering that many of them were plagiarized. "If Aristotle in 200 B.C. had only 400 books, by what miracle did they increase to 1,000 in the Second Century A.D.? Or was it forgery?"[54] In fact Aristotle's works would have filled 106 book rolls, and we know of 19 spurious works.[55] These forgeries were written by later Greek writers and have no particular connection with Egypt. Such discrepancies as there are in the three surviving ancient catalogues resulted from the use of differing methods of classification. For example, the catalogues seem to be lists of manuscripts rather than complete works; sometimes related treatises are collected under one title, at others they appear as separate entries.[56] There are analogous discrepancies in the lists of works attributed to other prolific ancient writers, such as the Greek tragic poets, where the same work might be listed twice under two alternative titles. Where did James get his figures of 400 and 1,000? One ancient source says that Ptolemy, the first-century A.D. biographer of Aristotle, listed a thousand works, but a list attributed to Ptolemy by an Arabic source lists only ninety-two titles.[57] The number 400 appears to have come out of thin air.

James is also determined to show that the other Greek philosophers plagiarized from Egyptian sources and "did not teach anything new."[58] First James discusses "similarities" between the doctrines of the early Greek philosophers and Egyptian "philosophy." Again, he insists that their theories of creation ultimately derive from the Memphite Theology. The creation story in the first book of Genesis is the source of Thales's idea about everything coming from water, Anaximander's idea of the boundless, and Anaximenes' notion that all creatures get their life from air. Since the author of Genesis, Moses, was an initiate into the Egyptian Mysteries, James states that the Hebrew creation story is "clearly of Egyptian origin," and that "the early Ionic Philosophers drew their teachings from Egyptian sources."[59] The Memphite Theology is also the source of the theory of opposites expounded by Zeno, Parmenides, and Democritus. It also inspired Heraclitus's notion that the origin of the cosmos was fire, Anaxagoras's concept of a controlling Mind, and Democritus's theory of Atoms.[60] Such an argument can be sustained only if one is prepared to ignore any or all significant differences among the texts discussed, and overlooks any inconsistencies, such as the notion that the Greeks stole from the same Egyptian source the contradictory ideas that the universe was created from water and from fire.

According to James, the other key document used by the Greeks was once again the Egyptian *Book of the Dead*. We have seen how James, by failing to describe accurately the widely different character of the two texts, insists that the *Book of the Dead* is the source of Aristotle's treatise *On the Soul*. He also believes that Pythagoras's theory of transmigration derives from it, and likewise Plato's theory of recollection. Like Herodotus, James seems unaware that the Egyptians did not believe in the transmigration of souls.[61] Other important Greek doctrines were taken directly from the Egyptian Mysteries. These include the notion of the Summum Bonum in Pythagoras, Socrates, Plato, and, of course, Aristotle.[62] He relies on Freemasonic literature to claim that the theory of the Four Elements originated in Egypt in 5000 B.C.[63] Its real source, as we have seen, is the initiation ritual invented by the Abbé Terrasson.

James also asserts that Democritus's theory of Atoms, in addition to being derived from the Memphite Theology, was in-

spired by the magical doctrines of the Egyptian Mysteries.
James seems to think that Democritus learned about magic on
his visit to Egypt; but according to Diogenes Laertius in his
sketch of Democritus's life, Democritus went to Egypt to learn
geometry, and to Persia to learn about magic.[64] He never explains just how Democritus was supposed to have learned
about atomism from the Egyptian *magic*. But James apparently is prepared to use any argument that can be made to
seem plausible. He asserts that Democritus, like Aristotle,
could not possibly have written all the books attributed to him,
and therefore he must have taken them from the Mystery System. He even suggests a scenario for the transfer of information: Egyptian Mystery System books were sold to Democritus
by Anaxarchus, who accompanied Alexander in his invasion of
Egypt. He does not point out that it is chronologically impossible for Democritus to have received Egyptian books from
Anaxarchus. Alexander and Anaxarchus went to Egypt in 332
B.C., at least forty years after Democritus's death (ca. 380–370).
Again, as in the case of Aristotle and the Library of Alexandria,
James is prepared to overlook even such significant chronologi-
cal problems in order to drive home his central points.

James's treatment of Socrates is even more irresponsible.
Once again, James uses the "silence of history" as a reason to
suppose that Socrates studied in Egypt and was initiated as a
Master Mason.[65] James believes that Socrates' sense of justice,
self-control, and perfect honesty show that he was an initiate.
He presumes that Socrates was initiated into a higher degree
of Masonry than Anaxagoras, Plato, and Aristotle, because he
did not go into exile in order to avoid being tried and con-
demned to death.[66] He claims that while in Egypt Socrates

studied astrology and geology, and also learned about the doctrine of self-knowledge, where the phrase "Man, know thyself" was written on all the temples.[67]

But again, James's hypothesis about Socrates works only if we are prepared to ignore significant evidence to the contrary. Why doesn't James mention that during his trial for impiety Socrates explicitly states that he knows absolutely nothing about astrology and geology?[68] Why doesn't he point out that the motto "know thyself," so far as anyone else knows, is Greek in origin? It was inscribed on the entrance to the temple of Apollo at Delphi.[69] And finally, why doesn't he point out that in reality history is *not* silent on the subject of Socrates' life? We know much more about him than about many famous Greeks, from the writings of his pupils Plato and Xenophon. Plato, in particular, specifies that Socrates never left Athens except on military campaigns elsewhere in Greece.[70] If no ancient writer says that Socrates studied in Egypt, there is a natural and evident explanation: he never left Greece at all during his lifetime. He did not learn about justice and self-control from the Egyptian Mysteries; rather, his conduct in life provided the inspiration for Plato's notion of a philosophical training. Plato's writings, in turn, inspired the Neoplatonists and writers like Iamblichus, and ultimately the elaborate portrait of Sethos's initiation in Terrasson's novel.

The charges that James makes against Plato are virtually the same as those he made against the pre-Socratic philosophers and against Socrates himself. From the Memphite Theology Plato took the doctrine of opposites, and the notion of the demiurge responsible for creation. The All-Seeing Eye of the Mystery System suggested Plato's doctrine of the Mind. The initiation ritual inspired Plato's doctrine of the good and of virtue. The Judgment drama in the Egyptian *Book of the Dead* provided the model for the ideal state in Plato's *Republic*.

But James is not content with asserting that Plato took his ideas from Egypt. He also seeks to show that Plato, like Aristotle, was not the author of the works traditionally assigned to him. Although no responsible ancient or modern scholar has ever questioned the authenticity of Plato's dialogues *Republic* and *Timaeus*, James mentions two obscure ancient anecdotes that raise doubts about their authorship. These are the stories recorded by Diogenes Laertius that Plato based his *Republic* on Protagoras's *Controversies*, and transcribed his *Timaeus* from a copy of a work (now lost) on necessity and harmony by Philolaus of Croton in Italy.[71] Even if those anecdotes had come from a more reliable source than the undiscriminating biographer Diogenes Laertius, it would be unwise to take such stories of dependency literally. In ancient biography, a claim that one writer took something from another usually means only that they both wrote on the same kinds of subject.[72] Often such tales are based on jokes in comedy.[73]

James's attempt to prove that Plato stole his philosophy is particularly easy to discount. He insists that Plato could not have learned about chariots from any Greek source, "for nowhere in their brief military history (i.e., up to the time of Plato) do we find the use of such a war machine by the Greeks." Therefore, James asserts, Plato's use of the metaphor of the chariot and winged steeds must have been plagiarized. He identifies Egypt as Plato's source, because they used chariots, as, for example, in the case of Pharaoh's pursuit of the Israelites in the Bible.[74] But why couldn't the idea have come from Assyria or Persia or China, or, for that matter, from Greece itself? James seems to believe that the Greeks did not know about chariots because they did not use them in the wars they fought during the fifth century B.C. But that does not mean they did not have them. Once again James has overlooked significant and obvious evidence. Chariots are mentioned frequently in the great Greek national epic, Homer's *Iliad*, where they were used to bring warriors into battle. By the fifth century, that type of warfare was technologically out of date, but the Greeks still used chariots in ceremonial functions. There were chariot races at many of the competitions regularly held at religious festivals, such as the Olympic and Pythian games. Plato would have had many opportunities both to read about chariots and to see them portrayed in art, and to watch them in action.

Such eagerness to find fault with the Greeks, even where none exists, is characteristic of *Stolen Legacy*. James alleges that the intellectual climate of Greece was hostile to philosophy and that the Greeks had no creative powers.[75] He attempts to show that the Greeks were by nature a contentious and noncontemplative people.[76] He does not give them credit for any success. He asserts that their battles against the Persians were indecisive, even though all surviving historical evidence indicates that they won decisive victories at Marathon, Plataea, and Salamis.[77] He argues that it would have been impossible for Aristotle to write on all the different subjects attributed to him.[78] He refers to Socrates as the "alleged teacher of Plato."[79] By frequently making and often repeating disparaging remarks such as these, James attempts to create a fantasy world in which his theory of the Stolen Legacy becomes ever more plausible, even though, as we have seen, he can muster no real evidence to support it.

Did James believe that he was offering his readers a true account of the history of Greek philosophy? Probably he did, since he started from the false premise that there was such a thing as an Egyptian Mystery System. Clearly he was committed to a noble goal, that of liberating black peoples and promoting a new formulation of race relations.[80] Perhaps he thought that this end justified any means at his disposal. Otherwise he would not have been prepared to suppress contradictory evidence, or to make claims about the Greeks that could immediately be discounted by anyone with even a superficial knowledge of Greek history.

Perhaps also, if James had been less committed to his cause, he would have been more straightforward in the way he supplies documentation for his arguments. As it stands, he presents citations of both primary and secondary source materials in a particularly misleading way. There are no footnotes. Instead, he lists the sources he has consulted only at the end of individual sections, so that it is impossible to know which claim is supposed to be supported by any particular citation.[81] As a result, the reader is left with the impression that some of James's more extravagant claims about the Greeks are supported in some of the standard authorities he cites, and that *Stolen Legacy* is a bona fide work of scholarship. But in fact no authorization for the notion of a "stolen legacy" can be found in books like Zeller's *History of Greek Philosophy* (1881), or Turner's general *History of Philosophy* (1903), or Sanford's textbook *The Mediterranean World in Ancient Times* (1938).[82] Readers who try to find the passages cited will often discover that references to both ancient and modern texts are incomplete or simply wrong.[83]

But historical accuracy was not James's primary concern. Some of his assertions are purely fanciful, such as the idea that the Egyptian sun-god Atum is connected with the Greek concept of the atom.[84] The word *atom* is Greek, from *a-* ("not") and *temnein* ("cut"). It is not true that "it was a habit of the Greeks to Hellenize Egyptian words by transliterating them and adding them to the Greek vocabulary." James cites only one example of this alleged practice: the name *Io*, which James believes to be Coptic. If that were true, it would prove little or nothing, since Coptic was the form of Egyptian used after the Greek conquest. But in fact, the real etymology of Io's name is unknown, like that of many mythological proper names.[85] James insists that the Greek word *Aigyptos* means "black," but it too is another proper name of uncertain origin. James appears to have invented the notion that Simeon "who was called black" (Acts of the Apostles 13.1) was "an Egyptian professor attached to the Church of Rome."[86] But all we know about this obscure person is that his Latin nickname, *niger* (that is, "black"), may suggest that he was of Ethiopian descent.[87] The pyramids were not so called because the Egyptians were worshippers of fire (Greek *pyr*).[88] The name derives from the Greek cakes they were thought to resemble, and which were made of wheat (*pyros*).[89] And why does James persist in saying that hieroglyphs were secret symbols, when since the time of decipherment it has been known that they were used primarily as letters?

Because of all these inaccuracies, and the many fundamental flaws in his argument and documentation, no one who has seriously studied the ancient world has found James's arguments persuasive. Nonetheless, in 1987 Martin Bernal complained that the Cornell University Library did not contain a copy of *Stolen Legacy*, because it was "not recognized as a proper book," or known outside of the black community.[90] Bernal is certainly justified in insisting that the book belongs in university libraries, even though it has virtually no academic value. The book has a place in research libraries because of the wide influence it has had within the black community, and the significant role it has played in the history of ideas. I believe that all ancient historians ought to be aware of the book's existence, and of the importance it seems to have even in intellectual circles.

But that does not mean that James's conclusions must be accepted or that his work can be regarded as a form of scholarship. It cannot and should not be forgotten that all of his most dramatic contentions are simply untrue. Aristotle did not steal books from the library at Alexandria and try to pass them off as his own. Nor did any of the other Greek philosophers learn their ideas in Egypt, because even if they went there (and not all of them did), they would not have been able to study with priests in the Egyptian Mystery System. The existence of a few common themes does not prove or even suggest that Greek writers plagiarized from the *Book of the Dead*, the Memphite Theology, or any other Egyptian source. The ancient Greeks were completely capable of inventing the literature that has always been attributed to them. Despite its many political controversies, the intellectual climate of ancient Athens encouraged discussion, argument, and inquiry. The general account of the development of Greek thought to be found in conventional history books is basically true.

Not only does *Stolen Legacy* not add to knowledge, it has inspired other writers and teachers to make misleading and extravagant claims about ancient history. In his book *Africa, Mother of Western Civilization*, James's pupil Yosef A. A. ben-Jochannan describes how the Greeks began "their major efforts in copying and otherwise plagiarizing Kimit's [that is, Egypt's] and other Nile Valley High-Cultures' concepts" and speaks of how "Western Educators" have concealed from the world the true extent of the Greek debt to Egypt.[91] Aristotle, he claims, "sacked" the Library of Alexandria, in 332 B.C., when he "had full run of all educational institutions in Egypt."[92] He removed the names of African authors from the books in the Library and put his name "on African works that predated his own birth by thousands of years."[93]

Ben-Jochannan seems more concerned about the alleged sacking of the library than interested in the materials Aristotle was supposed to have taken. For a detailed account of the university "curriculum" from which Greek philosophy was supposed to have been derived, it is necessary to turn to the Senegalese scholar Cheikh Anta Diop. In his principal work, *Civilization or Barbarism*, Diop assures us that "every Greek initiate or pupil had to write a final paper on Egyptian cosmogony and the mysteries, irrespective of the curriculum that he had followed."[94] With much ingenuity, Diop attempts to show that Plato's *Timaeus* is heavily dependent on Egyptian ideas, which Plato learned during his thirteen-year visit to Heliopolis. The "proof" that Plato is transmitting Egyptian ideas is that in the *Timaeus* Plato says the world was created by a demiurge, and that Ra, the god of Heliopolis, was also said to have created the world. Like James, Diop assumes that the existence of common themes is a proof of dependency. According to Diop, another notable sign of Egyptian inspiration is Plato's optimism, which must be "a heritage of the African school" because Indo-Europeans are generally pessimistic(!). Also Plato, like the Egyptians, emphasizes the role of order and laws.[95] Plato's astronomy, Diop claims, is an integral copy of Egyptian theory, but he does not supply details. Instead, he argues that since Plato offers only a "mediocre, degraded and mystical" account of Egyptian learning, the resemblance is obscured.[96] Like James (whose book is listed in his bibliography), Diop assumes that most of the other Greek philosophers studied in Egypt. Like James, he claims that the theory of opposites was of Egyptian origin, because in Hermopolitan cosmogony the gods are paired as opposites, for example, the hidden and visible, night and day.

One therefore sees how abusive it is to credit Heraclitus alone with the theory of opposites: this was a commonplace to all those Greek scholars who had studied under the Egyptian priests and who were using almost word for word the "laws of opposites" of the Hermopolitan cosmogony, or who were contenting themselves with making variations on the same theme.[97]

Diop does not point out that there is a considerable difference between the complex relationships between Egyptian deities, who can and do assume many different forms and identities, and the impersonal and abstract formulations of Heraclitus and Aristotle. Nor does he observe that the notion of opposites can be found in virtually any religious text, because it is a fundamental mode of human thought.

Diop also accuses the Greek mathematician Archimedes of being "faithful" to a Greek tradition of plagiarism. He states that Archimedes' favorite discovery was a sphere inscribed in a cylinder equal to the height of the cylinder, and states that the Egyptians already knew how to determine the area of both spheres and cylinders. The Egyptians knew how to determine the area of spheres, but that was not what Archimedes claimed to have discovered. Archimedes determined that the volume of the cylinder was 3/2 the area of the sphere, and that its surface (sides and bases) is 3/2 the surface of the sphere. No comparable formulation exists in Egyptian mathematics.[98]

James introduced a new school of historical research, by demonstrating in *Stolen Legacy* that anyone can claim anything about the past.[99] The first step is to downplay contradictory evidence; then to deduce from the limited facts one has assembled only those conclusions that support one's central thesis, or (if necessary) to invent evidence that suits one's own particular purposes. In order to establish similarity, one needs to begin from the assumption of a direct connection, and then make the evidence fit the facts, by omitting details and by overlooking significant differences. The only problem is that the result of such efforts is not history, but rather a kind of hybrid between myth and history, a myth about history.

In *Nineteen Eighty-Four* George Orwell described a nightmare world in which "all history was a palimpsest, scraped clean and reinscribed exactly as often as was necessary."[100] A little later in the book Winston Smith, the book's hero, is told by a colleague in the Records Department of the Ministry of Truth,

> "By 2050—earlier probably—all real knowledge of Old-speak [that is, standard English] will have disappeared. The whole literature of the past will have been destroyed. Chaucer, Shakespeare, Milton, Byron—they'll exist only in Newspeak versions, not merely changed into something different, but actually changed into something contradictory of what they used to be."[101]

What Orwell predicted for 2050 actually happened a century earlier, with the publication of *Stolen Legacy* in 1954. For in that book George G. M. James rewrote ancient history so drastically that it became both different from and contradictory to what it had previously been.

SIX

CONCLUSION

If the notion of a Stolen Legacy is a myth, and has virtually no historical value, why should it be taught in schools and universities as history? It should not, especially since study of the myth replaces real learning about the ancient Mediterranean world and about Africa. Extreme Afrocentric "ancient history" has no place in the curriculum of schools or of universities. Appealing mythologies about the past bring satisfaction in the short run, but in the end they damage the very cause they are intended to promote. The events of this century have shown that it is dangerous to allow propaganda to usurp historical truth. Even if the group sponsoring the propaganda feels their intentions to be noble, by substituting myth for history they open the way for other groups to invent their own

155

histories. Some of these new mythologies could harm African-Americans far more than Afrocentrist mythology could ever help them.

In the particular case of the Afrocentric myth of antiquity, not only is the myth unhistorical, it is essentially not African. As we have seen, it is a product of the same Eurocentric culture that the Afrocentrists seek to blame for the eclipse of African civilization, and for world problems generally. Most ironically, by claiming as African a myth that is fundamentally European, the Afrocentrists make Africa the source of the culture that they blame for their own troubles. Another Eurocentric feature of Afrocentrism is its concentration on Egypt. By failing to pay equal regard to other African civilizations, such as that of Nubia, the Afrocentrists appear to be judging African cultures by European standards. Egypt has always been admired by Europeans for the antiquity of its civilization and for its artistic and architectural remains. Why focus on one African nation which has won European admiration for its achievements?

Extreme Afrocentrism prevents students from learning about real ancient African civilizations. But that is just one of the dangers involved in Afrocentric myth. The notion of a Stolen Legacy is destructive in other ways as well. First of all, it teaches young students to distrust all Europeans, past and present. That is a racist approach, and like all forms of racism, both morally wrong and intellectually misleading. Are all Europeans alike? Are they one single race, and all Africans another? Anyone who has so much as glanced at a map realizes that neither Europe nor Africa is composed of one ethnicity or nation.

Another limitation of Afrocentric ancient history is that while pretending to be scholarly, it is often completely unscientific. As we have seen, there is little or no historical substance to many of the Afrocentrists' most striking claims about the ancient world. There is no evidence that Socrates, Hannibal, and Cleopatra had African ancestors. There is no archaeological data to support the notion that Egyptians migrated to Greece during the second millennium B.C. (or before that). There is no reason to think that Greek religious practices originated in Egypt. Even if the Greek philosophers actually went to Egypt, they did not steal their philosophy during their visits there. The important Egyptian religious texts share only a few general common themes with the Greek philosophical writings, most of which can be found in the religious works of other ancient Mediterranean peoples.

Other assertions are not merely unscientific; they are false. Democritus could not have copied his philosophy from books stolen from Egypt by Anaxarchus, because he had died many years before Alexander's invasion. Aristotle could not have stolen his philosophy from books in the library at Alexandria, because the library was not built until after his death. There never was such a thing as an Egyptian Mystery System. The notion of mysteries, or rituals of initiation, is fundamentally Greek, and such information as we have about Egyptian mysteries dates from a period when Egypt had been occupied and influenced by both Greeks and Romans. The Egyptian universities described by James and Diop never existed, except in their own imaginations, and in that of the French scholar-priest Jean Terrasson.

Because of all these inaccuracies, Afrocentrism not only

teaches what is untrue; it encourages students to ignore known chronology, to forget about looking for material evidence, to select only those facts that are convenient, and to invent facts whenever useful or necessary. It does not warn students that nations do not borrow (or steal) cultures from one another in the way that neighbors borrow cups of sugar. If the Greeks had learned their philosophy from a large theoretical literature produced by Egyptian writers, surely some trace of that literature would have remained in Egypt, and we would know the names or schools that produced it. We have a detailed knowledge of Greek literature, even though the Romans used it as the model for their own original literary creations.

In short, the Afrocentric myth of antiquity does not educate its adherents. Instead, it keeps them in a state of illusion, both about the true course of history and also of the ways in which people have always been able learn from cultures other than their own.

IS AFROCENTRISM A NEW
HISTORICAL METHODOLOGY?

As I observed in chapter 2, it has become fashionable to assume that history is culturally determined, and that each culture or ethnic group can write its own history differently. In particular, cultural relativism has offered an intellectual justification for Afrocentric history. "This is the age of Diop," Molefi Kete Asante assures us in *Kemet, Afrocentricity, and Knowledge* (1990). In Asante's view, Diop's achievement was to free people of African descent from their dependence on Eurocentric frames of reference, by arguing that "the objectivity of knowledge referred to by European scholars could not be separated from the consciousness of the social-cultural world and that Europeans brought that consciousness with them whenever they discussed Africa."[1] Asante appears to be saying that no one need believe anything that any European says about Africa. That declaration is indeed liberating, at least to Afrocentrists. Anyone who accepts Asante's formulation need not trust a word I have said in this book, or that anyone has said or will ever say in criticism of Afrocentrism.

This line of reasoning requires us to assume that invariably and without exception the character of a person's motivations is predetermined by his culture or ethnicity, instead of by individual volition. Isn't that virtually the same as saying that it is not I who speak, but my skin that speaks for me? To return for a moment to the question of Socrates' ancestry that I raised in the first chapter: if Professor Asante says there is no evidence that Socrates is black, should he be trusted because he himself is black, but if I say exactly the same thing, no one need believe me, because I am a person of European descent, and a classicist, and for that reason motivated by self-interest, self-promotion, or inherent prejudice? Is the remark more true because he said it, but less true because I said it? Leaving aside for the moment the question of historical reality, whatever happened to the notion that individuals could think for themselves, and break beyond the bounds of their culture, nationality, race, or ethnicity? Diop's historicism is not so liberating as it first may seem, because it requires its adherents to confine their thinking to rigid ethnic categories that have little demonstrable connection with practical reality.

We come now to the other flaw in Diop's methodology. As we saw in the last chapter, his mode of history writing allows him to disregard historical evidence, especially if it comes from European sources. But does being an African enable one to know about the particulars of African history, simply by intuition or osmosis? Asante seems to think so. But what about the revisionist ancient "history" that he has offered to his readers? The Egyptian Mystery System that he imagines to be African is in reality actually European in origin, as we saw in chapter 4. So African intuition is not a more reliable guide to the truth about Africa than European or Asian intuition, whatever those might be supposed to be.

Instead of relying on such extra-rational devices as cultural motivation or intuition, surely everyone will be better served by paying attention to history rather than to the historian. What is the quality of the evidence? Does it stand up to scrutiny? Discussions about evidence is what scholarship used to be about, and I would argue that we must return to debates about the evidence. When Professor Asante and I debated the issue of Egyptian influence on Greece on a radio program in May 1993, we agreed about many issues. As I recall, we discussed the evidence and agreed that the Egyptians were an African people, and that the Greeks did not steal their philosophy from Egypt. It is possible to say that some things are true, and others are not, and some things are more likely to be true than others, at least on the basis of what is now known. Rather than assume that each race, or each ethnic group, or each nation, should write its own versions of history, I would like to join David Hollinger in calling for a wider cosmopolitanism, which seeks to be sensitive to different points of view, and which can represent a diversity of viewpoints.[2]

IS THERE A DIVERSITY OF TRUTHS?

There are of course many possible interpretations of the truth, but some things are simply not true. It is not true that there was no Holocaust. There was a Holocaust, although we may disagree about the numbers of people killed. Likewise, it is not true that the Greeks stole their philosophy from Egypt; rather, it is true that the Greeks were influenced in various ways over a long period of time by their contact with the Egyptians. But then, what culture at any time has not been influenced by other cultures, and what exactly do we mean by "influence"? If we talk about Greek philosophy as a "Stolen Legacy," which the Greeks swiped from Egyptian universities, we are not telling the truth, but relating a story, or a myth, or a tall tale. But if we talk about Egyptian *influence* on Greece, we are discussing a historical issue.

In historical and scientific discussions it is possible to distinguish degrees, and to be more or less accurate. As a classicist, I may overemphasize the achievement of the Greeks because I do not know enough about the rest of the Mediterranean world; Egyptologists may be inclined to make the same mistake in the opposite direction. We recognize that no historian can write without some amount of bias; that is why history must always be rewritten. But not all bias amounts to distortion or is equivalent to indoctrination. If I am aware that I am likely to be biased for any number of reasons, and try to compensate for my bias, the result should be very different in quality and character from what I would say if I were consciously setting about to achieve a particular political goal.

Drawing a clear distinction between motivations and evidence has a direct bearing on the question of academic freedom. When it comes to deciding what one can or cannot say in class, the question of ethnicity or of motivations, whether personal or cultural, is or ought to be irrelevant. What matters is whether what one says is supported by facts and evidence, texts or formulae. The purpose of diversity, at least in academe, is to ensure that instruction does not become a vehicle for indoctrinating students in the values of the majority culture, or for limiting the curriculum to the study of the history and literature of the majority culture. That means that it is essential for a university to consider developments outside of Europe and North America, and to assess the achievements of non-European cultures with respect and sympathy.

It is another question whether or not diversity should be applied to the truth. Are there, can there be, multiple, diverse "truths?" If there are, which "truth" should win? The one that is most loudly argued, or most persuasively phrased? Diverse "truths" are possible only if "truth" is understood to mean something like "point of view." But even then not every point of view, no matter how persuasively it is put across, or with what intensity it is argued, can be equally valid. I may sincerely believe that Plato studied with Moses (like the Jews in Alexandria in the second and first centuries B.C.) and speak eloquently about all that Plato learned from him, but that will not mean that what I say corresponds to any known facts. Moses lived (if indeed he lived at all) centuries before Plato; they spoke different languages, and the Torah (or Pentateuch), even though it contains admonitions and legislation, has little in common with Plato's Laws. In order to be *true*, my assertion about Plato would need to be supported by warranted evidence. And it cannot be. The notion of diversity does not extend to truth.

If it is not possible for the same thing to be at once false and true, there is a means of judging what should be taught in a university. Should we offer (and use university money to staff) a course in which the instructor contends that ancient Greek philosophy was stolen from ancient Hebrew philosophy? For convenience, let's call this course "The Hebraic Laws of Plato." In favor of such a course, it might be argued that there is some limited historical support for contending that the Greeks were inspired by the Jews. As we have seen, in the second and third centuries A.D. Clement and some other church fathers took the idea seriously. Another argument in favor of the course is its potential appeal to Jewish students, who would be "empowered" or at least be made to feel less culturally isolated by what they learned in it.

Now suppose that our primary goal were to "empower" Jewish students. If the course empowered them, would it really matter if its content were manifestly untrue? In some universities today, it appears that the answer to this question would be no, it does not matter whether what is taught is true, or is supported by warranted evidence, because a diverse point of view, with a laudable social goal, has been presented. Moreover (so the argument goes) it would be wrong for the university administration to interfere in any way, because the academic freedom of the instructor should be protected.

Those who believe that the primary purpose of the university is to promote particular social goals may be willing to include courses like "The Hebraic Laws of Plato" in the curriculum. But I believe that we would be better advised to think of social justice as an important, perhaps even the most important by-product of education. If the real purpose of universities has been, and should remain, the dissemination of knowledge, then we need to be concerned with the quality of "knowledge" on offer. If we do not, there will be irreversible damage, far greater than if we abandoned all notions of trying to teach social justice in our courses.

ARE THERE ANY LIMITS TO ACADEMIC FREEDOM?

If diversity does not apply to truth, then there are limits to academic freedom. That does not mean that we should try to keep students from knowing about erroneous theories or hypothetical possibilities, or from reading works like Hitler's *Mein Kampf*, the Nation of Islam's *Secret Relationship between Blacks and Jews*, or James's *Stolen Legacy*. In my own case I would never teach Plato again without mentioning the Afrocentrist theory that Socrates was of African descent, and in all my courses I discuss the question of Egyptian influence on Greece. But I also point out why I believe that the allegations made by Afrocentric writers such as James and ben-Jochannan are wrong, and I give the students access to all the information they need to make up their own minds about Socrates' ancestry, and the extent to which Greek culture was borrowed from earlier civilizations.

But courses that are designed to conceal a considerable body of evidence, or that are intended to instill resentment and distrust in place of open discussion, have no place in the curriculum. We do not need a course on "The Hebraic Laws of Plato," even if someone wants to teach such a course and some students are willing and even eager to take it. Even as recently as thirty years ago it would not have seemed unreasonable to ask faculty members at least to explain why particular courses needed to be offered. But now the raising of such questions seems to many people a violation of the basic principles of university life. When I suggested that Afrocentrists discuss the evidence for their claims about the past, one critic complained that my viewpoint was "McCarthyite in its intolerance."[3] Why "McCarthyite?" In the essay I said nothing about taking disciplinary action of any kind against instructors who teach what is manifestly untrue. Rather, I was trying to draw attention to the differences between freedom of speech and academic freedom. Freedom of speech gives me the right to say that Aristotle stole his philosophy from Egypt, provided that it is clear that what I am expressing is my opinion, and that I do not pretend or assert that it is factually accurate and true in every respect. One can say many outrageous, untrue, and cruel things in this country, and on the whole it is better to have such license than to restrict free expression.

Whether freedom of speech extends to the classroom is another question. Academic freedom and tenure are not intended to protect the expression of uninformed or frivolous opinions. Implicit restrictions are already in place, even though they may not be stated in college catalogues. One such restriction is competence within a field. Faculty are appointed as instructors in particular subjects, not as generalists. For example, I was hired to teach Greek and Latin; not Egyptian. I should not be allowed to teach Egyptian because I have no credentials in Egyptian; another reason is that I know only a few words of Egyptian, even though I can read a Coptic dictionary because the Coptic alphabet is based on Greek. This does not mean that if I chose to learn Egyptian and acquire an advanced degree in the subject, I should not be allowed to teach it. Until I acquire such credentials no one, not even the most avid partisans of the subject, should want me to do so, because I do not have the necessary competence.

The question of competence in language study is relatively easy to determine, because it is possible for many people to agree about what it means to be fluent in or knowledgeable about any given language, its literature, and culture. For the same reason, it is relatively easy to determine who is competent in scientific subjects. We do not hire geographers who teach that the world is flat, because there is a considerable body of evidence that shows that flat-earth theory is false, even though for many centuries it was universally regarded as true.

It is much more difficult to identify competence in subjects where there is no established body of evidence or where there is more than one possible methodology. There are many valid ways to read a literary text, although here again one expects instructors to have professional credentials, to be able to provide an argument for their way of reading the works of literature that they profess, and to show that they know its basic content (Hamlet is not the hero of *Macbeth*, for example).

But in certain subject areas motivation and identity have been taken as the equivalent of professional credentials. For example, does being a woman automatically guarantee knowledge of Women's Studies? I would argue that being a woman may make me or someone else aware of women's problems, but not necessarily of their extent or of their solutions. In the case of the study of the ancient world, being female encouraged some of us to take a particular interest in the status of women in Greece and Rome. But being female did not help us interpret ancient documents and archaeological data; for that we needed to have professional training in ancient languages and civilization. Similarly, a person of African descent may be more curious about the civilization of ancient Egypt than someone from another ethnic background. But African ancestry alone will not help him understand ancient Egyptian religion or enable him to read hieroglyphics. As we have seen, it did not prevent Diop from imagining that Mystical Egypt was a reality.

The reason why we require competence and certification is that we are hired to teach people who want to learn about our subjects. We will not be serving our students well if we insist on teaching them what is factually incorrect, even if we imagine that it would be better for them if we did do so. If some students were comforted by being taught that the world was flat, would that justify the inclusion of Flat Earth Theory in the curriculum? Shouldn't we object if a geographer repeatedly taught that the world was flat, and did not mention that most other geographers happened to disagree with her, or describe fairly the reasons why they did so?

WHAT CAN BE DONE, IF ANYTHING?

One strategy is to ignore the geographer who teaches that the earth is flat. Akin to this principle of turning a blind eye is the notion of minimizing damage: if only a few students are affected by flat-earth theory, why make a big fuss about it? With any luck they will never be in a position to drive their cars off the face of the earth. But even though ignoring the problem is the least difficult option, it is important to remember that it does not really solve the problem. Some students, even if only a few, will be learning nonsense. What happens if a student who thinks that the earth is flat becomes an engineer? It is our responsibility as educators to see that all our students get the best possible education.

Of course, teaching false information about Socrates and Aristotle will not put anyone in immediate physical danger. But nonetheless these untruths do injustice, not only to the ancient Greeks who have been falsely maligned, but to their descendants. Why deprive the Greeks of their heritage, particularly if the charges against the ancient Greeks can decisively be shown to be wrong? Why encourage hostility toward any ethnic group? Haven't we seen enough examples in this century of the horrific results of teaching hostile propaganda?

If we can bring ourselves not automatically to accept the first and easiest option of putting our heads in the sand and pretending that nothing is wrong, what ought to be done instead? I think the very least we can do is to complain and call attention to what is wrong. Certainly pointing out why flat-earth theory is wrong involves publicizing the inadequacies of both instructor and university, and that will cause a certain amount of pain. Bringing problems to light will lead (at the very least) to arguments and name-calling. But it is the better of the two options from an educational point of view, because it guarantees that at least some of our students have the opportunity to know that there are or have been opposing viewpoints, thereby enabling them to make their own decisions. In order to learn and teach, we must ask tough questions. As

Plato points out in the *Republic*, the search for the truth inevitably causes pain to those who search for it.[4]

Some of my colleagues have suggested that it is the responsibility of students (rather than of faculty) to point out that flat-earth theory is wrong, and vote against it, in effect, by not attending the lecture or taking the course. But that assumes that students will always be capable of knowing about the subject in question. Presumably all our students know that the earth is not flat, because they have seen photos of the (round) earth taken from cameras in space. But do all of them know that Aristotle could not possibly have stolen his philosophy from Egypt, and why it is possible to say so? Even though some students do know something about Aristotle, the main responsibility for determining the competence and contents of university instruction belongs and must belong to the faculty.

There is another reason why we should not insist that our students decide about the quality of course offerings. The students who are in the best position to know about the quality or nature of a course are the students who are presently taking that course. But these students are being graded by the instructor whose methods or information they have reason to question. They may not be free to comment until they are no longer in a position of being judged, or of needing letters of recommendation from that particular instructor, and it is unfair to ask them to put their grade-point average in jeopardy.

For these reasons, we cannot leave it up to students to determine whether what they are being taught is reasonably accurate and/or represents all responsible viewpoints fairly. Why do we even need faculties if students are capable of making such determinations without their expert and informed assistance?

We consider ourselves to be capable of judging faculty competence when we make new appointments to our faculties, and when these faculty members are considered for promotion and tenure. The trouble is that after a certain point in a person's career, we virtually suspend judgment.

Suspending judgment might seem to serve effectively the interests of the senior faculty, if those interests consist in being allowed to do whatever they think best, provided that they either persuade their colleagues to let them do it, or that they behave in so obstructive a way that their colleagues will allow them to do whatever they wish, in return for noninterference with their own work. But it is questionable whether such protective behavior, as it has long been practiced in this country, offers much benefit to the students or to the institution. Who has not had at least one instructor who had not kept up with developments in his or her field? And who has not resented the fact, and wished that the university had offered something better?

When as an undergraduate I complained of such substandard instruction, I was told, as students are still being told, that the person in question had tenure. Tenure, in effect, has become a kind of carte blanche to do whatever one wants, once one is lucky enough to get it. That may be what we have turned it into, but that was not its original purpose. Tenure was designed to allow faculty academic freedom. Initially, that meant that faculty should be allowed to teach theories and subjects that trustees and parents might not approve of. But it did not guarantee and could not guarantee complete autonomy, for the simple reason that no one can competently teach anything and everything.

Academic freedom is the right to profess a discipline according to its recognized content and procedures, free from constraints and considerations extraneous to that discipline. I do not believe that academic freedom (whatever it has come to mean since) includes the right simply to cease to be an active member of the intellectual community, since that hardly serves the purposes of the university or its students. Nor do I believe that it can or should guarantee anyone the privilege of teaching what is beyond his or her range of proven competence, even when such teaching is fully acceptable to students, or at least not questioned by them. Academic freedom does not include the right to teach in a way that prevents students from being able to learn. A university may want to keep a poor teacher who is a brilliant scholar on its staff, but it should not allow him to teach beginners. Similarly, instructors should not use their classrooms systematically to arouse hatred of particular ethnicities or genders or individuals, because only people who subscribe to these same prejudices or orthodoxies can be comfortable in such an atmosphere.

What (if anything) should be done about the instructors who go beyond even our vaguely defined limits? I have suggested that we begin by debating all these issues, even if the debates are painful, because that way will be most educational for most people, both faculty and students. These debates will take time, because people are never eager to relinquish cherished views and established practices, especially when their egos are involved. Specifically, I think universities should not be quick to discipline instructors who insist on substituting false information for true, even if some individuals or groups have been injured by them. The issue is not whether someone's feelings have been hurt. Rather, it is the quality of instruction at our universities. So the first line of defense should be words, and, when appropriate, even ridicule of the theories that have been shown to be contrafactual.

Can, or should, anything else be done about courses used for dissemination of false information or for purposes of indoctrination? The issue has received considerable public attention in the last few years as the result of the lawsuit against the City University of New York by Professor Leonard Jeffries. Jeffries teaches the Afrocentric theories of antiquity that I have described in this book. But the University did not attempt to remove him from the chairmanship of his department or discipline him in any other way because of the quality of his teaching. Rather, they were concerned about a speech he made in 1991, which was thought to be anti-Semitic. The lower court reinstated Jeffries. But in his opinion ordering the reinstatement, Judge Conboy made a useful distinction between freedom of speech and academic freedom. He observed that there was no reason why City University should "continue to disserve its own students by subjecting them in class to the bigoted statements and absurd theories of any of its professors."[5]

Conboy observed that the issues being litigated in the Jeffries case were basically irrelevant, and that the real question is about standards, about what Jeffries teaches in the classroom. In effect, he said that it was the University's business, and not the Court's, to deal with academic questions. Surely he was right, because if these problems are left to the courts, academic freedom will be restricted in ways that affect even faculty with tenure.

The problem is illustrated by the 1995 decision of the U.S. Appeals Court for the Second Circuit (New York) reversing and remanding its prior decision to allow Jeffries's reinstatement.[6] The court had been asked to reconsider its decision based upon *Waters v. Churchill*, a Supreme Court decision which held that a government employer could fire an employee for making a disruptive speech (in this case a nurse had complained about a department in the hospital where she was employed).[7] In the light of the *Waters* decision, the Second Circuit court found that the City University was justified in disciplining Jeffries, because what he said in 1991 in a speech off campus was likely to be disruptive to the University. This potential disruptiveness was enough to outweigh whatever First Amendment value Jeffries's speech might have had.

The court also concluded that the decision did not infringe his academic freedom as a faculty member, because he still had tenure and "the defendants have not sought to silence him or otherwise limit his access to the 'marketplace of ideas' in the classroom." Presumably he (or anyone) can go on saying whatever he wants so long as he has tenure and as a department chair has only ministerial functions. The court did not specify whether they thought Jeffries's 1991 speech was disruptive because of its anti-Semitism, or because what he said showed that the university tolerated and employed in a position of some authority a person who was apparently willing repeatedly to profess as true information that is known to be false.

From the university's point of view, the charge of academic incompetence is the more serious charge. Anti-Semitism is obnoxious and reprehensible (like any other form of racism),

but what is even more disruptive to the university is a reluctance to marshal evidence fairly, and a refusal to present to
students a complete and balanced view of the subject. Should
a professor at a university speak as if scientific research had
confirmed "melanin theory," which contends that skin pigmen-
tation has a direct relation to intelligence, or state, as if it
were a historical fact, that "ice is a key factor in the development of Europeans culturally, economically, socially?"[8] In the
context of academe it matters whether a faculty member's
contentions are reasonable and made on the basis of all
known evidence. The problem with saying that Aristotle stole
his philosophy from Egypt is not that modern Greeks and
classicists will be offended; what's wrong with the statement
is that it is untrue.

The ambiguities in this decision suggest why it is not a good
idea to count on the courts to clean house for us. As Nathan
Glazer has observed, academics now tend to abdicate responsibility for the quality of instruction at their universities, with
the result that many decisions that ought to be made by university administrations and faculties are now being made by
the courts. Because courts can only wield the "clubs of free
speech and nondiscrimination," they will ignore what ought to
be the prime aim of the university, dissemination of knowledge. So far as the courts are concerned, "truth and nonsense,
competence and incompetence, will hold the same position."[9]

Because of the confusion about the purpose of the university (do we enforce social justice, or do we disseminate knowledge?), we have reached the point where academic discourse
is impossible, at least in certain quarters, because the achievement of social goals, such as diversity, has been allowed to

transcend the need for valid evidence. But once we accept the idea that instead of truth, there are many truths, or different ethnic truths, we cannot hope to have an intellectual community. This is why we cannot each remain in our own separate enclaves without talking with colleagues who share similar interests and concerns.

University administrators ought to ask whether we need courses in flat-earth theory—or Afrocentric ancient history—even if someone is prepared to teach them. Ideally, those discussions should take place within departments.[10] But in most universities academic deans and curriculum committees also have the authority to ask why a course needs to be offered, and to request an explanation of why instructors choose to ignore and/or suppress evidence. At the very least they could insist that the departments provide accurate descriptions of such courses in the catalogue: *caveat emptor.*

Students of the modern world may think it is a matter of indifference whether or not Aristotle stole his philosophy from Egypt. They may believe that even if the story is not true, it can be used to serve a positive purpose. But the question, and many others like it, should be a matter of serious concern to everyone, because if you assert that he did steal his philosophy, you are prepared to ignore or to conceal a substantial body of historical evidence that proves the contrary. Once you start doing that, you can have no scientific or even social-scientific discourse, nor can you have a community, or a university.

EPILOGUE

*N*ot *Out of Africa* appeared in bookstores in February 1996. During the next few months it was widely reviewed, in the national newspapers and weekly magazines as well as in many local papers. I was interviewed on radio and television and in the *Chronicle of Higher Education, The Boston Globe, The Washington Post, The International Herald Tribune,* and *The Times* of London. Basic Books sponsored an internet debate between Martin Bernal and myself, one of the first of its kind in the history of scholarship.[1] It is of course unusual for a book about ancient history to get so much, or indeed any, public attention, but this book raises issues that continue to be the subject of national debate, at least in this country. Why is history taught? Is it to record as accurately as possible what happened in the past, or is it rather to instill confidence and pride in the young people to whom it is taught? Do we study the ancient Greeks in order to learn about the origins of modern civilization or to remind ourselves of the glories of past European achievements? Does the dominant culture, however that may be defined, use school and university curricula to enforce a set of values, and if so, shouldn't the views of minority cultures also be represented?

I tried to answer these questions in *Not Out of Africa*. I argued that the purpose of teaching history is to try to understand the past and that present-day academicians owe it to the people of the past to preserve the memory of their accomplishments as accurately as we can. I do not imagine that we can ever know all that we want to know, but I believe that some things in the past can be shown to have happened, on the basis of existing evidence, and that other things (even though plausible) cannot be assumed to have happened just because they might have happened. I also know that on occasion historians can and do give disproportionate emphasis to certain aspects of a subject, and I am no exception to the working of this rule. This book is not the last word on the extent of the debt of ancient Greece to ancient Egypt, nor does it pretend to be. But I hope at least that I have shown which lines of inquiry are not worth pursuing and that I have suggested areas in which more research is needed by scholars qualified to undertake it. In this epilogue to the paperback edition, I discuss some of the issues raised by reviewers and, in the course of doing so, remind my readers of what the book is really about. I also want to take this opportunity to clarify some of key issues discussed in the book.

NOT OUT OF AFRICA AND ITS CRITICS

When I finished writing *Not Out of Africa*, I hoped that because I had written about the facts in a rational manner, my critics would be able to respond in kind and that the discussion would concentrate on issues that ought still to be debated.[2] How can we measure, on the basis of existing evidence, the exact degree of Egyptian influence on Greek thought? Which aspects of the second-century A.D. initiation described by the Latin writer Apuleius in his novel *The Golden Ass* come directly from Egypt? What characteristics of the treatises in the Hermetic corpus are specifically Egyptian? Although most reviews so far have been favorable, including those by classicists and Egyptologists, in order to encourage further discussion I shall comment here on my critics' response to the issues raised in the book.

It is not surprising that so far none of my reviewers or critics has been able to offer a persuasive challenge to the central thesis of this book: that the Greeks did not steal or even borrow their philosophy from Egypt, that Egyptian influence on Greek philosophical thought was not extensive, and that the idea that scholars have ignored the Greeks' Egyptian origins has its foundation in Masonic myth rather than in historical fact. It is from Masonic myth that the notion arose that there was such a thing as an Egyptian "mystery system" that functioned as a kind of school for scholars visiting from foreign lands. Perhaps it is because it is so difficult to contest the central thesis of this book that my critics have concentrated on an issue that is essentially peripheral to the central discussion of the book: the question of race. *Not Out of Africa* is not a book about race or racism. It does not seek to promote racism in any form. It argues that the Egyptians were an African people and praises their achievements; it does not seek to deny the existence of the achievements of other African peoples in antiquity or in modern times. The book's title was borrowed from my 1992 *New Republic* article. The title was meant only to suggest that Greek philosophy does not come from Africa.[3] Nonetheless, my critics have insisted on making race (rather than history or philosophy) the center of their discussions of the book and its arguments. They believe that the reason there has been so much interest in the book has nothing to do with what is being taught in schools and universities; rather, they say, "the issue is race."[4] They assert that the real purpose of my book is to attack and disparage the work of scholars of African descent and to downplay the achievements of African civilizations, such as that of ancient Egypt.

The purpose of these assertions, if I am not mistaken, is to distract readers from the real issues discussed in the book and so far as possible to discredit me. But my readers should be aware that in virtually every case the assertions about race are made without specific reference to the contents of the book, as they must inevitably be, because in fact there is nothing in the book that could be cited to support them. Not that the absence of any racism has prevented some critics from finding evidence of it, even in the passages where I praise writers like Frederick Douglass and Edward Wilmot Blyden.[5] These critics resolutely refuse to believe that my purpose is to distinguish between history and myth. Apparently they cannot see that if I have been skeptical about, or even sought to refute, some of the more extravagant claims made by writers of African descent, such as George G. M. James or Y. A. A. ben-Jochannan, it is because I believe that their claims are unsupported by a fair consideration of all the evidence and not because I have any personal or ethnic animosity against them or their followers. Even if their claims about the debt of Greece to Egypt had been made by a person of European descent, I would have sought to show that such claims were unfounded. In fact, I have already done so, in that I have criticized the work of Martin Bernal in this book and still more extensively in the collection I edited with my colleague Guy Rogers, *Black Athena Revisited.*

It should (but cannot) go without saying that my aim has always been to subject ideas to scrutiny, not people or personalities. But in the present climate of debate, even the most abstract and impersonal disagreements quickly tend to be redefined as political or even personal quarrels, especially if scholars find that they can make a stronger or an apparently more persuasive case without much reference to evidence. Because many of my critics have written as they do because of personal commitment, a desire to change social policy, or to promote a particular cause, they assume that I must be doing the same. When I insist that in fact I have no particular cultural agenda to promote, they reply that I do but am simply not aware of it. Here the reviewers seem to be using the type of argument sometimes employed by Freudian psychotherapists, which allows the psychotherapist to determine what the patient means. Even if I state explicitly that *Not Out of Africa* was not written to promote Greek culture over all other cul-

tures, or to uphold white supremacy, or to reinstate an outmoded university curriculum based on the classics, which has
never, so far as I know, been in operation during my lifetime,
certain reviewers will insist that I am promoting such agendas at least unconsciously.[6]

In effect, *Not Out of Africa* has been "deconstructed" by critics into something that they can attack with all the force of
righteous moral indignation.[7] One leading Afrocentrist, during a "debate" sponsored by the New York City radio station
WBAI, accused me of wishing "to reenslave Africa!" The "debate" itself was conducted more in the style of an inquisition
than a discussion, with an actively hostile "moderator." Later,
one of my Wellesley colleagues asserted that in *Not Out of
Africa* I purposely constructed the argument to produce "a deliberate, eurocentric, and racist narrative."[8] Several critics
have also sought to show, mainly by assertion, that I have an
overt ideological or political agenda. In the preface (p. xii), I
observed that I have been called the leader of a Jewish "onslaught" against people of African descent. But now, quite re-
markably, I am supposedly continuing "what Martin Bernal
calls the Aryanist tradition of attacking African agency in
Greece."[9] Several critics have also deduced that I am part of a
"paranoid" right-wing white supremacist conspiracy. The
"facts" produced as "evidence" for this assertion are as follows:
(1) My book was praised by several well-known right-wing
commentators, including George Will and Roger Kimball, suggesting that "perhaps Will and Kimball believe that they have
found a savior of the pure White thesis."[10] Robert Bork mentions my question at the ben-Jochannan lecture.[11] (2) I am on
the advisory board of the National Association of Scholars

(which so far as I know has never met), and I am therefore "intimately connected with extreme conservatives" and "have powerful allies on the far right."[12] (3) I received small grants from the Olin and Bradley Foundations, which support a number of right-wing causes.

How fair are these criticisms? In the case of the first, I am being held accountable for what is said about my book by reviewers and commentators over whom I have no control and no influence. In the second and third, I am found guilty by association, even when there has been no association, and it is readily assumed that I agree with or am influenced by people who have found my work useful or interesting. Even if it were true (it isn't) that I shared *all* the views of the people with whom I am supposed to be so closely associated, or that these people told me what to think and what to write, my critics have failed to demonstrate (other than in their "deconstructed" versions of my work) how these alleged views and associations have affected my historical judgment. The success or failure of the arguments in *Not Out of Africa* depends not on who I am supposed to be or even who I am but on the evidence I present and the conclusions I draw from it. Even if it could be shown (and I invite my critics to do so) that I am an Aryanist Jew, or a Republican, or even an academic traditionalist, that would not necessarily affect the quality of the evidence I present but merely offer one possible explanation of why I (rather than anyone else) chose to concern myself with the issues raised in the book. The point is that *Not Out of Africa* is not about me but about ancient history, and as such it should be judged on the basis of its discussion and analysis of the evidence.

Some critics have also sought to show that I am intemperate, emotional, and lacking in control and therefore unreliable. Although several reviewers remarked that the tone of the book was calm and restrained (which is what I meant it to be), one reviewer stated (again without citing any specific instances) that the book was an "impassioned polemic ... through which rage boils."[13] Perhaps that was the impression given by the book's provocative cover, which was a legacy from my (also not very inflammatory) *New Republic* article.[14] The astonishing statement about the boiling rage[15] was immediately seized on by some critics to use as further "evidence" of my alleged political agenda. When George Will, in his favorable review, characterized the book "as using a howitzer to slay a hamster," some critics rushed to the "hamster's" defense, without remarking that in the very next sentence Will noted that "the hamster, the Afrocentrist fable, is unslayable by mere evidence."[16] One critic complained of my alarmist rhetoric and suggested that in some way I have equated modern identity politics "with the atrocity of genocide."[17] But where in fact did I actually do that? Is it where I said that symbolic myths have great power and that any myth that encourages resentment and antagonism toward others can be dangerous (p. 52)?

Reinforcing the idea that *Not Out of Africa* is an intemperate work is the suggestion that "the book was obviously written in a hurry" or "in seeming haste" and that it is a "compilation" of a "series of overlapping articles," which "shows signs of its origins in the cobbling together of articles written with passionate urgency for the popular and semipopular press."[18] Also, because the book is short, critics have said

I have chosen to present only such evidence as supports my case or that I simply have not done my homework.[19] My claims are based on "thin research—almost entirely in a handful of secondary sources," my conclusions drawn "on the basis of a very slender number of examples?"[20] None of these writers seems to have noticed that the book is not long because it did not need to be, especially because much of the detailed research on which it draws can be found in *Black Athena Revisited*. But even if these unfounded, and certainly rather ungenerous, assertions about haste and anger were true, again why would it matter, when the merit of the book can be judged on the basis of historical evidence?

Rather than address the questions raised by that research, my critics have suggested that the serious factual errors made by George G. M. James in *Stolen Legacy* and by Dr. Yosef A. A. ben-Jochannan in *Africa: The Mother of Western Civilization* can be explained or even excused entirely because these authors did not have access to research libraries and grants.[21] Certainly it is true that James, who taught at a series of Black colleges in the segregated South, was a victim of malicious and inexcusable racism,[22] but even that does not justify the numerous citations in his notes that do not support his argument.[23] Also, Dr. ben-Jochannan, who helped to rescue James's work from oblivion and who has based his own theories on James's ideas, has taught at Cornell, a university with major library and research resources.

Finally, some critics have insisted that there was no need to write *Not Out of Africa* because I have vastly exaggerated the threat posed by Afrocentric ancient history. One critic, without reflecting that some of his own writings were scrutinized in the book, suggested that I have raised "strawpeople arguments."[24] Another reviewer asked, apparently in all innocence, "at what institutions of higher learning, other than her own Wellesley campus and in Leonard Jeffries' City College classroom, is Afrocentric history taught?"[25] I have provided a preliminary answer to that question in the supplementary notes to p. 1 of this edition, which provide detailed evidence about the schools and universities where Afrocentric curricula have been adopted. But even if falsified history (of whatever sort) were taught in just a few places, it would be a cause for concern. It is entirely appropriate that a professor's use of university property, even of something as tangential as a website, come under scrutiny, if that professor uses it for the purpose of disseminating nonhistorical information, as is claimed in the current controversy about a professor's alleged placing of Holocaust denial propaganda on the Northwestern University website.[26]

If my critics' "deconstruction" of my work can be considered fair and reasonable, then surely I should be allowed to adopt the same approach in my critique of their reviews. I shall refrain (as some of them have not been able to do) from speculating about the possible effect on their work of their personal lives and backgrounds.[27] I will simply ask them some of the same questions they have asked me. How can they be so sure that *they* know what they are saying? What about *their* hidden agendas? Don't these include the promotion of ancient African culture (however defined) over all other cultures, the determined disparagement of ancient Greek civilization on racial or cultural grounds, and the desire to revise radically or even to replace existing school and university curricula

with courses of study and even with "facts" of their own devis-
ing? They want us to believe that African peoples think and
learn differently from other peoples; that Egyptian civilization was more monumental and therefore superior to Greek
civilization; that only people of African descent can properly
understand the history of Africa and its peoples. At the same
time, they are ready to excuse historical inaccuracy on the
part of certain Afrocentric writers on the grounds that under
the circumstances they could not have done any better. Can't
they see that most of these ideas would sound distinctly
racist if they were used by or about people of European descent?

Perhaps also they feel justified in ignoring or downplaying
the importance of the historical evidence because they sincerely believe that facts really do not matter so much as motives and that the person with the best motives (as defined by
themselves) will write the best or most "useful" kind of history (see also pp. 49–51, this volume). My critics do not seem
to be concerned that they are arguing for an even more sub-
jective form of history writing than the one that includes the
"historical patterns of racist exclusion of minority perspec-
tives" that they and all the rest of us should reject.[28] The quality of historical writing cannot be evaluated on the basis of
criteria such as an author's politics or ethnicity; if it could, we
would be back virtually in the days of Jim Crow. To make any
real progress in this discussion, it will be to everyone's ulti-
mate benefit to concentrate on the evidence, wherever it leads
us. Not everything is possible or even probable, and as far as
we know, some things have happened and other things have
not. Aristotle did not steal his philosophy from the Library at

Alexandria, and Greek philosophy was not heavily dependent on some as yet unknown Egyptian models. This book demonstrates that these statements are supported by historical evidence and that other statements are not, and because it is a book about what is known and what isn't, it should be judged on that basis.

TOPICS FOR FURTHER DISCUSSION

Progress can be made if we can agree from the start to use neutral terminology. Why not concentrate on questions of influence and refrain from using morally charged words like "stealing" or even "borrowing"? Imprecise statements such as "borrowed massively from Egypt," in addition to being essentially untrue, rely on metaphors that make it appear that the discussion is about tangible objects rather than about ideas.[29] The confusion obscures an important difference: If I borrow your car, you do not have it until I return it; if I borrow your ideas, you still have your ideas to keep and use, whatever I go off and choose to do with them. It is also important to remember that influence (unlike invasion) is most often a two-way process. We also need to define, so far as possible, just what we mean by the word *philosophy*. If we use it as the ancients did, it applies to all kinds of knowledge, and therefore anyone who has acquired learning of any kind can be a philosopher. But in this book I use the term philosophy in the more specialized, modern sense, to mean the study of causes and laws underlying reality or a system of inquiry designed specifically to study those laws and causes. The ancient Egyptians and

Babylonians were learned and had what we would now call advanced civilizations; they could have developed an abstract terminology for discovering causes and principles had they chosen to do so. But they did not study and analyze the nature of reality in abstract, nontheological language. This specialized notion of philosophy was invented, so far as anyone knows, by the ancient Greeks.

The next step is to address some basic issues. If there had been the kind of extensive Egyptian cultural influence on ancient Greece that the Afrocentrists claim, we would expect to find evidence of its existence in Egyptian civilization, such as parallel texts or direct echoes, as we have in the case of the Roman poets who from early times adapted and quoted Greek sources. But that is precisely what we do not find—in Egypt or anywhere else in the ancient Mediterranean—in the area of what is thought of as Greek philosophy. There is nothing in surviving Egyptian literature that resembles the dialectical methods and argumentative structures that Greek philosophers invented. This is not to say that the Egyptians are irrational and the Greeks rational, or that the Egyptians did not possess a profound theology and concept of justice, or that this theology and other wisdom are not expressed in surviving Egyptian literature. It is simply a statement that Egyptian (or Hebrew) wisdom literatures are essentially different in nature and form of expression from the philosophical writings of Plato and Aristotle, which are nondogmatic and ratiocinative in character.

As I suggest earlier in chapter 3, even if we assume that writers in Roman times knew what they were talking about when they claimed that Plato and other Greek thinkers studied with Egyptian priests, what the Greek thinkers learned there would not have been Greek philosophy. Rather, what the biographers seem to have imagined is that Greek philosophers went to Egypt and to the Near East to learn "Eastern wisdom." But the principal reason it is unlikely that Greek philosophy was heavily dependent on Egyptian thought is that there is no evidence of similar philosophical writings in Egypt. What are the chances that there was an Egyptian philosophy, similar to what has always been known as Greek, that has now vanished without a trace, especially given the ancient Greeks' interest in and fascination with all things Egyptian? Surely if there had been such an extensive body of literature, some of Plato's contemporaries would have known about it and Plato himself would have had no reason *not* to acknowledge it or indeed not to boast about it. Greeks tended to be so respectful of Egyptian learning that they were eager to use it whenever and wherever they could. But the kind of Egyptian learning that Plato referred to in his works takes the form of "wisdom" narratives, that is, the kind of moral tales that we still possess Egyptian examples of. In the *Phaedrus* and the *Philebus,* Socrates told a story about the god Theuth's invention of letters; in the *Timaeus* and in the incomplete dialogue *Critias,* Plato had Critias tell the story of Atlantis, which his ancestor Solon learned from an Egyptian priest during his visit to the Egyptian pharaoh Amasis. These stories are told, not in the usual question-and-answer dialogue form, but as long didactic narratives, almost certainly of Plato's own invention.[30] In view of the way Plato used Egyptian lore, it is misleading to insist that the presence of these tales in his dialogues indicates that he studied in Egypt, especially if we define philosophy as a system of argumentation. We need also to be aware that there are many reasons other than racism, anti-Semitism, politics, and the like that scholars choose not to discuss the question of cultural influence. Clearly, the main reason classical scholars have not reexamined all the possible Egyptian connections as fully as they might have is that they are occupied principally with trying to understand and teach about Greek and Roman civilizations. Students of ancient Greek philosophy concentrate on Plato's thought and dialectic and tend to devote proportionately less space to his narrative technique, including his use of stories about Egypt. One virtue of the present controversy is that it has encouraged classical scholars, Egyptologists, and Near Eastern scholars to expand their focus and to look again, and in depth, at possible sources of foreign influence. It is time to look again at the possible influence of Egyptian narrative style on Greek literature, particularly in the development (starting in the late fifth century B.C.) of the adventure novel.

In considering the extent and nature of Egyptian influence, a fuller assessment needs to be made of the extent of the connections of ancient Egypt with Nubia and other African civilizations (see p. 135, this volume). Discussion should continue about the Egyptian influence on Greek thought in medicine, mathematics, and science, although not without acknowledging the Greek contribution to those disciplines. We can assess the extent of influence in the case of medicine because we have documents from both Egyptian and Greek medical writers. From these we learn that Greek physicians knew about Egyptian medicines and adopted some (though by no means

all) of their theories and some of their drugs.[31] But in discussing the influence of Egyptian medicine, scholars must
also take into account the Greek use of *mistaken* Egyptian
ideas. Afrocentric writings emphasize only ideas that have
been shown to work or claim for the ancient Egyptians discoveries that were actually made by other peoples much later in
history, such as the invention of electricity and of gliders capable of transporting human beings.[32] The ancient Egyptians,
like all other peoples in history, had some bad ideas as well.
One example is the notion that a woman's womb wandered
within her abdominal cavity. The "medicines" used by Egyptian doctors to restore it to its proper place included human ex-
crement.[33]

It is important to remember that Egypt was not the only
ancient Mediterranean civilization with which the Greeks
came into contact. As students of Greek philosophy have long
known, and Martin Bernal now chooses to remind us, the
Greeks were influenced by many other peoples, including the
Hittites and the Phoenicians.[34] Although it is certainly true
that the Egyptians and other peoples had knowledge of medicine, mathematics, and astronomy long before the Greeks did,
the Greeks nonetheless made their own contribution and developed new theoretical formulations that scientists have relied on since that time.

Is it possible to discuss these sorts of issues without the
rancor and distrust that discussion of ancient African civilization seems to generate? I sincerely believe that it is. The first
requirement, however, is that the discussion be carried on by
scholars who have the necessary basic qualifications, specifically knowledge of the requisite ancient languages, litera-

tures, and civilizations. Too much distrust has already been generated by misunderstanding, ignorance, and oversimplification. Some critics have assumed that in this book I have equated radical Afrocentrism with Afro-American studies; that Herodotus is a more reliable source of information about Africa than he could possibly have been, because he "travelled throughout Africa" (he tells us that he only travelled as far as the first cataract of the Nile); that so-called Greek columns are really Egyptian columns.[35] Such statements can have a powerful effect on sympathetic audiences, but they do not contribute to anyone's understanding of what happened in the past. What evidence is there that modern classical scholars or Egyptologists are concerned either consciously or unconsciously with promoting European hegemony? Surely the purpose of studying the past is not primarily to discover our real or supposed origins; it is to find out, so far as we can, what happened in the past. We owe it to the peoples of ancient Egypt and ancient Greece to preserve the memory of their history in as scientific a manner as possible. That, and not self-promotion, is our duty and obligation.

NOTES

PREFACE

1. Martin Bernal, *Black Athena: The Afroasiatic Roots of Classical Civilization* (New Brunswick, N.J.: Rutgers University Press, vol. 1 [hereafter *BA* 1], 1987; vol. 2 [hereafter *BA* 2], 1991). For a review of the literature generated by *BA* 1, see Molly M. Levine, "The Use and Abuse of *Black Athena*," *American Historical Review* 97, no. 2 (1992): 440–60. The project as a whole is assessed in Mary R. Lefkowitz and Guy MacLean Rogers, eds., *Black Athena Revisited* (Chapel Hill: University of North Carolina Press, 1996) [hereafter, *BAR*].
2. Mary R. Lefkowitz, "Not Out of Africa," *The New Republic* (February 10, 1992): 29–36.

3. See also Richard Bernstein, *Dictatorship of Virtue: Multiculturalism and the Battle for America's Future* (New York: Alfred A. Knopf, 1994), 116–19.

4. Tony Martin, *The Jewish Onslaught: Despatches from the Wellesley Battlefront* (Dover, Mass.: The Majority Press, 1993), p. 30.

5. Molefi Kete Asante, "On the Wings of Nonsense," *Black Books Bulletin: WordsWork* 16, no. 1–2 (1993–94): 38.

6. Ibid., p. 39.

7. For a full-length treatment of some of the problems, see Mary R. Lefkowitz, *The Lives of the Greek Poets* (Baltimore: Johns Hopkins University Press, 1981).

CHAPTER 1: INTRODUCTION

1. See especially Paul R. Gross and Norman Levitt, *Higher Superstition: The Academic Left and Its Quarrels with Science* (Baltimore: Johns Hopkins University Press, 1994), pp. 203–14.

2. See Mary R. Lefkowitz, "Afrocentrists Wage War on Ancient Greeks," *Wall Street Journal*, April 7, 1993, p. A14.

3. Arthur M. Schlesinger, Jr., *The Disuniting of America* (New York: W. W. Norton, 1992), p. 99.

4. See especially John Miller, ed., *Alternatives to Afrocentrism* (Washington, D.C.: Center for the New American Community, 1994).

5. Carl J. Richard, *The Founders and the Classics: Greece, Rome, and the American Enlightenment* (Cambridge, Mass.: Harvard University Press, 1994), pp. 232–43.

6. On the important differences between ancient and mod-

ern ideas of democracy, see Paul A. Rahe, *Republics Ancient and Modern: Classical Republicanism and the American Revolution* (Chapel Hill: University of North Carolina Press, 1992), especially pp. 186–218. For a useful survey of modern critiques of Athenian democracy, see Jennifer Tolbert Roberts, *The Antidemocratic Tradition in Western Thought* (Princeton: Princeton University Press, 1994), pp. 291–314. On the failure of freedom in the non-Western world, see Orlando Patterson, *Freedom* (New York: Basic Books, 1991), pp. 20–44.

7. See Arnaldo Momigliano, *The Classical Foundations of Modern Historiography* (Berkeley: University of California Press, 1990), p. 30; Cynthia Farrar, *The Origins of Democratic Thinking* (Cambridge: Cambridge University Press, 1988), p. 131.

8. For one such instance, see Mary R. Lefkowitz, "Afrocentrism Poses a Threat to the Rationalist Tradition," *Chronicle of Higher Education* (May 6, 1992): A52.

CHAPTER 2: MYTHS OF AFRICAN ORIGINS

1. On their origins, see especially Aris N. Poulianos, *I Proelefsi ton Ellinon*, 4th ed. (Petralona, Khalkhidiki: Daphni, 1988).

2. Cf. especially the illustrations in Frank M. Snowden, Jr., *Blacks in Antiquity* (Cambridge, Mass.: Harvard University Press, 1970).

3. Herodotus 2.104.1. See especially Frank M. Snowden, Jr., "Bernal's 'Blacks,' Herodotus, and Other Classical Evidence," *Arethusa*, special issue (Fall 1989): 87–88.

4. Herodotus 2.55.1.

5. See especially Loring Brace et al., "Clines and Clusters versus Race," *Yearbook of Physical Anthropology* 37 (1994): 24–25; and Kathryn Bard, "Ancient Egyptians and the Issue of Race," *Bostonia* 7, no. 3 (Summer 1992): 69, also in *Black Athena Revisited*, ed. Mary R. Lefkowitz and Guy MacLean Rogers (Chapel Hill: University of North Carolina Press, pp. 111, 158–59.) [hereafter, *BAR*].

6. Compare Cheryl Johnson-Odim, "The Debate over Black Athena," *Journal of Women's History* 4, no. 3 (1990): 87, who assumes that because I discussed the question briefly, I was "obsessed with race."

7. Bernal, *BA* 1, p. 3; cited approvingly in Martha Malamud's review of *BA* 1 in *Criticism* 31, no. 3 (1989): 319.

8. Gerald Early, "Understanding Afrocentrism: Why Blacks Dream of a World without Whites," *Civilization* 2, no. 4 (July/August 1995): 35–36.

9. Cheikh Anta Diop, *Civilization or Barbarism: An Authentic Anthropology*, trans. Yaa-Lengi Meema Ngemi (Brooklyn, N.Y.: Lawrence Hill Books, 1991), p. 92.

10. Ibid., p. 151.

11. Diodorus Siculus 1.44.1.

12. Apollodorus, *The Library* 3.14.1.

13. Apollodorus, *The Library* 3.14.8.

14. In Aeschylus's drama *The Suppliants* and in most later sources, Hera is responsible for Io's transformation (299), but in his drama *Prometheus Bound*, Io blames Zeus (679–82).

15. For a reconstruction of the action in the lost plays of the trilogy, see R. P. Winnington-Ingram, *Studies in Aeschylus*

(Cambridge: Cambridge University Press, 1983), p. 62.

16. Diodorus Siculus 1.44.1.

17. On the origins of the Hyksos, see Lawrence E. Stager, "When Canaanites and Philistines Ruled Ashkelon," *Biblical Archaeology Review* 17, no. 2 (March/April 1991): 27–30.

18. Emily Vermeule, "The World Turned Upside Down," *New York Review of Books* 39, no. 6 (March 26, 1992): 43; also in *BAR,* p. 276.

19. Donald B. Redford, *Egypt, Canaan, and Israel in Ancient Times* (Princeton: Princeton University Press, 1992), p. 122.

20. Herodotus 2.41.2.

21. Bernal, *BA* 1, p. 84.

22. The weakness of this etymology was pointed out by several reviewers, e.g., "When is a Myth Not a Myth." in *BAR*, p. 34. For the actual meaning of the term, see Heinz J. Thissen, "Zum Umgang mit der ägyptischen Sprache in der griechisch-römischen Antike," *Zeitschrift für Papyrologie und Epigraphik* 97 (1993): 250.

23. Diop, *Civilization or Barbarism*, p. 379.

24. Jean-Jacques Barthélemy, *Voyage du jeune Anacharsis en Grèce*, vol. 1 (Paris: Libraire Dupont, 1826), p. 2. Cf. Bernal, *BA* 1, p. 186.

25. See, for example, Tony [Anthony C.] Martin, *The Jewish Onslaught: Despatches from the Wellesley Battlefront* (Dover, Mass.: The Majority Press, 1993), pp. 61, 63.

26. Herodotus uses the phrase *ap' Aigyptou* (2.43.2). If he had meant Egypt the country he would have said *ek Aigyptou.*

27. Bernal, *BA* 2, p. 108.
28. Jasanoff-Nussbaum, "Word Games," in *BAR*, p. 192.
29. At a lecture at Trinity College in Hartford in 1990, the audience was told that Socrates, Thomas Edison, and Abraham Lincoln were black; Thomas Duffy, "Fear and the Power of Don Muhammed," *Boston Magazine* (January 1995): 114.
30. Plato *Crito* 50c.
31. Mary R. Lefkowitz, *The Lives of the Greek Poets* (Baltimore: Johns Hopkins University Press, 1981), p. 88.
32. Ibid., p. 170; Aristophanes alludes to these jokes in his play *Acharnians*, 653–54.
33. Eugene M. Mitchell, "Greek to Me," letter to the editor, *New Republic* (March 2, 1992): 6.
34. Martin Bernal, "Socrates' Ancestry in Question," letter to the editor, *Academic Questions* (Summer 1994): 7.
35. On this topic, see also Lawrence Tritle, "Review Discussion," *Liverpool Classical Monthly* 17, no. 6 (June 1992): 94; also in *BAR*, p. 325.
36. Frank M. Snowden, Jr., *Blacks in Antiquity* (Cambridge, Mass.: Harvard University Press, 1970), p. 264. For various versions of the *Life of Aesop*, see Ben Edwin Perry, ed., *Aesopica* (Urbana: University of Illinois Press, 1952): Vita G.1 (I 35); Vita W.1 (I 81), Vita Lolliana (I 111); Vit. Min. 1a, 1b (I 213).
37. On Planudes, see Nigel G. Wilson, *From Byzantium to Italy* (London: Duckworth, 1992), pp. 143–44.
38. Suetonius *Life of Terence* 5.
39. *Moretum* 31–35, in the *Appendix Vergiliana*; see Augusto Rostagni, *Suetonio de Poetis e Biografi Minori* (Turin:

Chiantore, 1944), p. 40; Snowden, *Blacks in Antiquity*, p. 270.

40. Suetonius *Life of Terence* 1.

41. Cf. Virgil *Eclogue* 10.38–40, which describes a shepherd in Arcadia: "who cares if Amyntas is dark (*fuscus*), violets are black and bilberries are black (*niger*)." Here Virgil has in mind a passage from Theocritus describing a Syrian woman (see n. 52). But there were black slaves in Carthage, like Giddenis in Plautus *Poenulus* 1112: "pleasant-looking, with a black (*niger*) face and eyes." See Snowden, *Blacks in Antiquity*, p. 163.

42. Cf. especially Frank M. Snowden, Jr., *Before Color Prejudice* (Cambridge, Mass.: Harvard University Press, 1983), p. 108.

43. Y. A. A. ben-Jochannan, *African Origins of the Major "Western Religions"* (Baltimore: Black Classic Press, 1991 [1970]), p. 74.

44. Ben-Jochannan cites secondary source Charles Pelham Groves, *The Planting of Christianity in Africa*, vol. 1 (London: Lutterworth Press, 1964), p. 59; Groves in turn took the information from Beresford James Kidd, *A History of the Church to A.D. 461*, vol. 1 (Oxford: Clarendon Press, 1922), pp. 110–11.

45. Augustine, *Epist.* 17.2 (Migne *Patrologia Latina* 33, p. 83); apparently it was not uncommon in Numidia, and exists also in a Greek form, *Agathopus*; Paolo Mastandrea, *Massimo di Madauros* (Padua: Editoriale Programma, 1985), p. 67. On the Carthaginian language, see Adrian Gratwick, "Hanno's Punic Speech in the Poenulus of Plautus," *Hermes* 99, no. 1 (1971): 39.

46. See Epistle 16.2 by Maximus of Madaurus in the collection of Augustine's letters (*Patrologia Latina* 33, p. 82); Mastandrea, *Massimo*, p. 27. On the correspondence, see Robert A. Kaster, *Guardians of Language: The Grammarian and Society in Late Antiquity* (Berkeley: University of California Press, 1988), pp. 86, 311.

47. Mastandrea, *Massimo*, p. 27; for a different view, see W. H. C. Frend, *Martyrdom and Persecution in the Early Church* (Oxford: Basil Blackwell, 1965), p. 313. Of his comrades Miggin, Sanames, and Lucitas, only Miggin is mentioned on surviving inscriptions: nos. 2062, 2068a, 2088, 2095 in *Inscriptiones Latinae Christianae Veteres*, ed. E. Diehl (Berlin: Weidmann, 1961).

48. Peter Brown, *The Cult of the Saints* (Chicago: University of Chicago Press, 1981), pp. 31–34.

49. *Passio Sanctarum Perpetuae et Felicitatis* 2.1.

50. *Acta Proconsularia Sancti Cypriani* 2.1, in *The Acts of the Christian Martyrs*, ed. Herbert Musurillo, S.J. (Oxford, Clarendon Press: 1972), p. 170; cf. Introduction, pp. xxxi.

51. On Augustine's background see Peter Brown, *Augustine of Hippo* (Berkeley: University of California Press, 1969), pp. 19–34; on the spelling of his mother's name, see James O'Donnell, ed., *Augustine, Confessions* (Oxford: Clarendon Press: 1992), vol. 3, p. 148.

52. Brown, *Augustine of Hippo*, pp. 62–63; W. H. C. Frend, *The Donatist Church* (Oxford: Clarendon Press, 1952), p. 230.

53. For his writing style, see Brown, *Augustine of Hippo*, p. 23; on his views of Ethiopians, see Snowden, *Blacks in*

Antiquity, pp. 204–5.

54. On the other Cleopatras, see John Whitehorne, *Cleopatras* (London: Routledge, 1994).

55. According to Plutarch *Life of Antony* 27.4, in addition to Egyptian and Greek, she spoke the language of the Ethiopians, Troglodytes, Hebrews, Arabians, Syrians, Medes, and Parthians.

56. Lucy Hughes-Hallett, *Cleopatra: Histories, Dreams and Distortions* (New York: Harper Perennial, 1990), p. 17.

57. Whitehorne, *Cleopatras*, p. 175.

58. Joel A. Rogers, *World's Great Men of Color* (New York: Collier Books, 1972 [1946]), p. 130.

59. Ibid., p. 130.

60. Ibid., p. 129.

61. Was Rogers thinking of the ancient story (Ovid *Metamorphoses* 2.235–36) that the Ethiopians' skin turned black when Phaethon borrowed his father the Sun God's chariot, and brought it too near the earth?

62. See Frank M. Snowden, Jr., "Bernal's 'Blacks' and the Afrocentrists" in *BAR*, p. 120.

63. Rogers, *World's Great Men of Color*, p. 130.

64. John Henrik Clarke, "African Warrior Queens," *Journal of African Civilization* 6, no. 1 (1984): 123–34; also in Ivan Van Sertima, ed., *Black Women in Antiquity* (New Brunswick, N.J.: Transaction Publishers, 1984), pp. 123–34.

65. Ibid., pp. 126–27.

66. Ibid., p. 127.

67. Ibid., p. 128.

68. Ibid., p. 123.

69. Erich Martel, "What's Wrong with the Portland Baseline

Essays?" in *Alternatives to Afrocentrism* (Washington, D.C.: Center for the New American Community, 1994), p. 39.

70. The letter is cited in Martin, *Jewish Onslaught*, p. 59.

71. Ibid., p. 101.

72. Shelley P. Haley, "Black Feminist Thought and the Classics: Re-membering, Re-claiming, Re-empowering," in *Feminist Theory and the Classics*, ed. N. S. Rabinowitz and Amy Richlin (London: Routledge, 1993), p. 27.

73. Ibid., p. 28.

74. Athenaeus *The Doctors at Dinner* 13.576e–f.

75. Alan Cameron, "Two Mistresses of Ptolemy Philadelphus," *Greek, Roman, and Byzantine Studies* 30 (1990): 287–88.

76. Asclepiades, in A. S. F. Gow and D. L. Page, eds., *Hellenistic Epigrams* (Cambridge: Cambridge University Press, 1965), no. 828–31 = *Palatine Anthology* 5.210.

77. Gow-Page, *Hellenistic Epigrams*, vol. 2, p. 120, compare Bombyca, the "sun-burned" Syrian, Theocritus *Idyl* 10.26–28, and "darkening" (*melaneusa*) Philaenion (*Palatine Anthology* 5.121); but Philaenion was probably an African, since she has hair that is "more woolly than parsley"; cf. Snowden, *Blacks in Antiquity*, p. 21.

78. Sappho T1 Campbell = POxy.1800.fr.1; *phaiodes* describes colors that are somewhere between light and dark and is a synonym of *melas*; Gerhard Reiter, *Die griechischen Bezeichnungen der Farben weiss, grau, und braun*, Commentationes Aenipontanae (Innsbruck: Universitätsverlag Wagner, 1962), pp. 78–81.

79. Frank M. Snowden, Jr., "Asclepiades' Didyme," *Greek,*

Roman, and Byzantine Studies 32 (1991): 239–41.

80. Haley, "Black Feminist Thought," p. 29.

81. Daphne Patai and Noretta Koertge, *Professing Feminism* (New York: Basic Books, 1994), p. 50.

82. Haley, "Black Feminist Thought," p. 29.

83. Ibid., pp. 29–30.

84. Ibid., p. 39 n. 7.

85. The two references are Cameron, "Two Mistresses" (n. 50, above) and Sarah B. Pomeroy, *Women in Hellenistic Egypt* (New York: Schocken Books, 1984), p. 53.

86. Nancy Sorkin Rabinowitz, "Introduction," *Feminist Theory and the Classics*, ed. N. S. Rabinowitz and Amy Richlin (London: Routledge, 1993), p. 6.

87. Susan Haack, "Puzzling Out Science," *Academic Questions* 8, no. 2 (1995): 21–22.

88. Bernal, *BA* 1, p. 73.

89. Johnson-Odim, "The Debate over Black Athena," p. 86.

CHAPTER 3: ANCIENT MYTHS OF CULTURAL DEPENDENCY

1. Molefi Kete Asante, "On the Wings of Nonsense," *Black Books Bulletin: WordsWork* 16, nos. 1–2 (1993–94), p. 40.

2. For some examples of scholarship with racist overtones, see Bernal, *BA* 1, pp. 240–46.

3. On the absence of ideological sweeps, see Frank Turner, "Martin Bernal's *Black Athena*: A Dissent," *Arethusa*, Special Issue (Fall 1989): 108–9.

4. See Charles C. Gillespie, "The Scientific Importance of

Napoleon's Egyptian Campaign," *Scientific American* (September 1994): 78–85.

5. For illustrations, see Christiane Ziegler, Jean-Marcel Humbert, and Michael Pantazzi, *Egyptomania: Egypt in Western Art 1730–1930* (Ottawa: National Gallery of Canada, 1994), pp. 200–309.

6. Ibid., pp. 404–41.

7. Richard Jenkyns, "Bernal and the Nineteenth Century," in *BAR*, p. 419.

8. See J. P. Mallory, *In Search of the Indo-Europeans* (London: Thames and Hudson, 1989), pp. 9–23, 66–73.

9. See, for example, Detlev Fehling, *Herodotus and His "Sources,"* trans. J. G. Howie (Leeds: Francis Cairns, Ltd., 1989); O. Kimball Armayor, *Herodotus' Autopsy of the Fayoum: Lake Moeris and the Labyrinth of Egypt* (Amsterdam: J. Gieben, 1985).

10. Diodorus of Sicily 3.11.1–3.

11. John Gould, *Herodotus* (New York: St. Martin's Press, 1989), pp. 10–11.

12. Bernal, *BA* 1, p. 100.

13. Herodotus, 2.49.2. All references are to the Greek text, but they can easily be found in most English translations.

14. Herodotus 2.50.1.

15. For a similar use of the phrase, see Herodotus 1.10.3.

16. David Grene, trans., *Herodotus: The History* (Chicago: University of Chicago Press, 1987), p. 153. Compare Walter Blanco and Jennifer Tolbert Roberts, eds., *Herodotus: The Histories* (New York: W. W. Norton, 1992), p. 91: "Furthermore, practically all the names of

the gods. . . . " The misinterpretation may derive from George Rawlinson, trans., *Herodotus: The Persian Wars* [1858], ed. Francis Godolphin (New York: Modern Library, 1942), p. 142: "Almost all the names of the gods. . . ."

17. Christian Froidefond, *Le Mirage égyptien dans la littérature grecque d'Homère à Aristote* (Aix-en-Provence: Ophrys, 1971), pp. 151–52.

18. For example, Homer derives Odysseus's name from both "lament" (*odyromai*) and "be angry" (*odyssomai*); *Odyssey* 1.55, 1.62; Rudolf Pfeiffer, *History of Classical Scholarship from the Beginnings to the End of the Hellenistic Age* (Oxford: Clarendon Press, 1968), pp. 4–5.

19. Hesiod *Works and Days* 2; Aeschylus *Agamemnon* 1485; Pfeiffer, *History of Classical Scholarship*, p. 4. For other examples, see Eduard Fraenkel, *Aeschylus: Agamemnon*, vol. 3 (Oxford: Clarendon Press, 1950), p. 704.

20. Walter Burkert, *Greek Religion: Archaic and Classical*, trans. John Raffan (Cambridge, Mass.: Harvard University Press, 1985), p. 185.

21. Lefkowitz and Rogers, preface to *BAR*, p. ix.

22. Bernal, *BA* 1, p. 52; Herodotus 2.28.1, 59.3.

23. Jasanoff-Nussbaum, "Word Games," in *BAR*, pp. 193–94. But Herodotus and other Greeks occasionally discovered the correct *translation* of Egyptian names; see Heinz J. Thissen, "Zum Umgang mit der ägyptischen Sprache in der griechisch-römischen Antike," *Zeitschrift für Papyrologie und Epigraphik* 97 (1993): 239–52.

24. Alan B. Lloyd, *Herodotus Book II*, vol. 1 (Leiden: E. J. Brill, 1975–88), pp. 147–49.

25. Herodotus 2.57.3–58.

26. Herodotus 2.81.

27. Lloyd, *Herodotus Book II*, vol. 1, p. 57; vol. 2, p. 343.

28. John Gould, "Herodotus and Religion," in *Greek Historiography*, ed. Simon Hornblower (Oxford: Clarendon Press, 1994), pp. 91–106.

29. See Martin Kaiser, "Herodots Begegnung mit Ägypten," appendix in Siegfried Morenz, *Die Begegnung Europas mit Ägypten* (Zurich: Artemis-Verlag, 1969), pp. 263–64.

30. Herodotus 2.123.

31. John A. Wilson, *The Burden of Egypt* (Chicago: University of Chicago Press, 1951), p. 305.

32. For a particularly clear account, see Jaromir Malek, *The Cat in Ancient Egypt* (London: British Museum Press, 1993), p. 125.

33. Walter Burkert, *Lore and Science in Ancient Pythagoreanism*, trans. Edwin L. Minar, Jr. (Cambridge, Mass.: Harvard University Press, 1972), p. 126. Lloyd, *Herodotus Book II*, vol. 1, pp. 57–58, vol. 2, p. 59.

34. Herodotus 2.171.

35. Lloyd, *Herodotus Book II*, vol. 3, p. 209.

36. Ibid., vol. 3, pp. 206–7.

37. Herodotus 2.182.2. Lloyd, *Herodotus Book II*, vol. 3, pp. 239–40.

38. Herodotus 2.156.6.

39. Aeschylus frag. 333 *TGrF*.

40. Ulrich von Wilamowitz-Moellendorf, *Der Glaube der Hellenen* (Berlin: Weidmannsche Buchhandlung, 1932),

vol. 2, pp. 135–36.

41. Kaiser, in Morenz, *Die Begegnung Europas mit Ägypten*, pp. 254–55.

42. Strabo 17.1.12.

43. Lloyd, *Herodotus Book II*, p. 281.

44. Diodorus 1.44.1.

45. Diodorus 1.96.1, 3.

46. Herodotus 2.149.

47. Timothy Gantz, *Early Greek Myth: A Guide to the Literary and Artistic Sources* (Baltimore: Johns Hopkins University Press, 1993), p. 107.

48. Diodorus 1.96.4.–97.2.

49. Diodorus 1.97.7.

50. Diodorus 1.98.2.

51. Plutarch *Life of Lycurgus* 4.5.1.

52. Herodotus 1.30.1.

53. Plato *Timaeus* 20e–22c.

54. Plutarch *Life of Solon* 26.1; J. Gwyn Griffiths, *Plutarch's De Iside et Osiride* (Swansea: University of Wales Press, 1970), p. 285.

55. Iamblichus *Life of Pythagoras* 19. For translations, see Gillian Clark, ed. and trans., *Iamblichus: On the Pythagorean Life*, Translated Texts for Historians (Liverpool: Liverpool University Press, 1989); John Dillon and Hershbell Jackson, eds. and trans., *Iamblichus: On the Pythagorean Way of Life*, Texts and Translations 29: Graeco-Roman Religion Series 11 (Atlanta: Scholars Press, 1991).

56. Lloyd, *Herodotus Book II*, vol. 1, p. 50.

57. Froidefond, *Le Mirage Égyptien*, p. 126; Democritus 68 A 99, II 107–8 Diels-Kranz; cf. B5, II 137.

58. Democritus 68 B 7, II 144 Diels-Kranz.

59. Democritus 68 A 1, II 81; 68 A 40, II 94 Diels-Kranz.

60. Diodorus 1.98.2 = Oenipodes 41 A 7, I 394 Diels-Kranz.

61. Pythagoreische Schule 58 B 36, I 461 Diels-Kranz; Robert Palter, "*Black Athena*, Afro-Centrism, and the History of Science," *History of Science* 31 (1993): 240=*BAR*, p. 222.

62. Diodorus 1.41.1 = Oenopides 41 A 11, I 394 Diels-Kranz.

63. Eudoxus frag. 7, 8 in François Lasserre, *Eudoxos von Knidos*, Texte und Kommentare (Berlin: W. de Gruyter, 1966).

64. Eudoxus, frag. 287 Lasserre.

65. Eudoxus, frag. 301, 291 Lasserre.

66. Martin Bernal, "Animadversions on the Origins of Western Science," *Isis* 83 (1992): 603; Palter, "*Black Athena*, Afro-Centrism, and the History of Science," p. 251=*BAR*, pp. 232–233.

67. Strabo 17.1.29.

68. Diogenes Laertius 8.87

69. Diogenes Laertius 8.90 = T 18 Lasserre; the same information is supplied by Plutarch *De Iside et Osiride* 354e.

70. Diogenes Laertius 8.87, 90.

71. J. Gwyn Griffiths, "A Translation from the Egyptian by Eudoxus," *Classical Quarterly*, n.s. 15 (1965): 77–78.

72. Bernal, "Animadversions on the Origin of Western Science," p. 603.

73. Raymond O. Faulkner, trans., *The Ancient Egyptian Book of the Dead* [1985], ed. Carol Andrews (Austin: Uni-

versity of Texas Press, 1993).

74. Diodorus 1.96.3.

75. Alice Swift Riginos, *Platonica: The Anecdotes Concerning the Life and Writings of Plato* (Leiden: Brill, 1976), 64 n. 13.

76. Plato *Politicus* 264c; *Republic* 4.436a; *Phaedo* 80c.

77. Plato *Gorgias* 482b; *Phaedrus* 274e.

78. Plato *Timaeus* 21e–22b.

79. Plato *Laws* 2.656d–657b.

80. Lloyd, *Herodotus, Book II*, vol. 1, p. 56.

81. Rosalind Thomas, *Oral Tradition and Written Records in Classical Athens* (Cambridge: Cambridge University Press, 1989), pp. 170–71.

82. Herodotus 2.143.

83. Mary R. Lefkowitz, *The Lives of the Greek Poets* (Baltimore: Johns Hopkins University Press, 1981), p. 13.

84. The anecdote about Crantor is recorded by Proclus *Commentary on Timaeus* 1.75.

85. Bernal, *BA* 1, pp. 106–7.

86. A similar anecdote is attributed to the third-century writer Satyrus: when Sophocles was accused by his son Iophon of having become old, he responded by writing his great drama *Oedipus at Colonus* (*Life of Sophocles* 13); see Lefkowitz, *Lives of the Greek Poets*, p. 85.

87. Diogenes Laertius 3.6.

88. For Euripides' fragment about the Nile, see frag. 228 in Augustus Nauck, ed., *Tragicorum Graecorum Fragmenta* (Leipzig: B. G. Teubner, 1889), and Annette Harder, *Euripides' Kresphontes and Archelaos* (Leiden: E. J. Brill, 1985), pp. 186–87 (= frag. 1A).

89. Euripides *Iphigenia Among the Taurians* 1193. Lines of tragedy are often used for punch-lines in Greek comedy; cf. Mary R. Lefkowitz, "Aristophanes and Other Historians of the Fifth-Century Theater," *Hermes* 112, no. 2 (1984): 144–46.

90. Epistle 28 in the letters of the Socratic school in R. Hercher, ed., *Epistolographi Graeci* (Paris: Didot, 1871).

91. Tertullian, *On the Soul* 2.3; Garth Fowden, *The Egyptian Hermes* (Cambridge: Cambridge University Press, 1986), p. 200 n. 26. Brian P. Copenhaver, *Hermetica* (Cambridge: Cambridge University Press, 1992), pp. xxvii–xxix.

92. Plato *Timaeus* 47a.

93. Strabo 17.1.29.

94. Clement of Alexandria *Miscellanies* 1.15.69 = Eudoxus T 18 Lasserre.

95. Diogenes Laertius 3.6.

96. Froidefond, *Le Mirage Égyptien*, pp. 308, 335.

97. Diogenes Laertius 1.27, 37 (= Thales 11 A 1, I 68–69, 71 Diels-Kranz); Plutarch *On Isis and Osiris* 354e.

98. Homer *Iliad* 14. 201; Plutarch *On Isis and Osiris* 364d (= Thales 11 A 14, I 78 Diels-Kranz). Gwyn Griffiths, *Plutarch's De Iside et Osiride*, p. 428, thinks Thales may have gone to Egypt, but cf. Charles H. Kahn, *Anaximander and the Origins of Greek Cosmology* (New York: Columbia University Press, 1960), p. 91.

99. Wilson, *The Burden of Egypt*, p. 317.

100. Nikolaus Walter, *Der Thoraausleger Aristobulus*, Texte und Untersuchungen (Berlin: Akademie-Verlag, 1964), p. 44; Garth Fowden, *The Egyptian Hermes* (Cambridge: Cambridge University Press, 1984), p. 73; Mary R. Lef-

kowitz, "Ethnocentric History from Aristobulus to Bernal," *Academic Questions* 6, no. 2 (1993): 15–17.

101. Artapanus 726 frag. 3.3 in Felix Jacoby, ed., *Fragments of the Greek Historians* (Leiden: E. J. Brill, 1923); for a translation of the fragments, see James H. Charlesworth, ed., *The Old Testament Pseudepigrapha* (Garden City, N.Y.: Doubleday, 1985), vol. 2, pp. 898–903.

102. Musaeus 2 A 6–7, I 21 Diels-Kranz; also Aristophanes *Frogs* 1032–33; P. M. Fraser, *Ptolemaic Alexandria* (Oxford: Clarendon Press, 1972), vol. 2b, p. 984 n. 182.

103. Charlesworth, *Old Testament Pseudepigrapha*, vol. 2, pp. 823–24.

104. Fraser, *Ptolemaic Alexandria*, vol. 2a, p. 695; vol. 2b, pp. 967–68 nn. 113–14.

105. Sophocles frag. dubium 1025.1–2 in Nauck; Charlesworth, *Old Testament Pseudepigrapha*, vol. 2, p. 825.

106. Euripides frag. dubium 1131.1 in Nauck; Charlesworth, *Old Testament Pseudepigrapha*, vol. 2, p. 829.

107. Fraser, *Ptolemaic Alexandria*, vol. 2a, p. 695; vol. 2b, p. 966 n. 111.

108. Walter, *Der Thoraausleger Aristobulus*, frag. 3; Fraser, *Ptolemaic Alexandria*, vol. 2b, p. 966, n. 111; Charlesworth, *Old Testament Pseudepigrapha*, vol. 2, frag. 4. See also Emil Schürer, *A History of the Jewish People in the Age of Jesus Christ* [1884], ed. Geza Vermes, Fergus Millar, T. A. Burkill, et al. (Edinburgh, Clark, 1973), vol. 3, pp. 240–41; Arnaldo Momigliano, "Ebrei e Greci," in *Sesto Contributo* (Rome: Edizione di Storia e Letteratura, 1980), p. 537.

109. Fraser, *Ptolemaic Alexandria*, vol. 1, pp. 689–90; Arnaldo

Momigliano, *Alien Wisdom: The Limits of Hellenization* (Cambridge University Press, 1975), pp. 92–93, 115–16; Clara Krauss Reggiani, "I frammenti di Aristobulo, esegeta biblico," *Bolletino dei Classici* 3 (1982): 108–11.

110. Charlesworth, *Old Testament Pseudepigrapha*, frag. 12; Fraser, *Ptolemaic Alexandria*, vol. 2b, p. 966, n. 110 = Walter, *Der Thoraausleger Aristobulus*, frag. 3 and p. 44; Momigliano, *Alien Wisdom*, pp. 92–93, 115–16.

111. Riginos, *Platonica*, p. 65 n. 18. Henry Chadwick, *Early Christian Thought and the Classical Tradition* (Oxford: Clarendon Press, 1966), p. 13–14.

112. Philip Merlan, "The Pythagoreans," in *Cambridge History of Later Greek and Early Medieval Philosophy*, ed. A. H. Armstrong (Cambridge: Cambridge University Press, 1967), frag. 10L, pp. 99–100; R. T. Wallis, *Neoplatonism* (London: Duckworth, 1972), p. 35; Riginos, *Platonica*, p. 65 n. 17.

113. Howard Jacobson, *The Exagoge of Ezekiel* (Cambridge: Cambridge University Press, 1983), p. 8.

114. Chadwick, *Early Christian Thought*, p. 15; G. E. R. Lloyd, "The Debt of Greek Philosophy and Science to the Ancient Near East," in *Methods and Problems in Greek Science: Selected Papers* (Cambridge: Cambridge University Press, 1991), p. 281.

115. Clement of Alexandria *Miscellanies* 6.3.

116. Theodor Hopfner, *Plutarch über Isis und Osiris* (Darmstadt: Wissenschaftliches Gesellschaft, 1941), pp. 85–91.

117. Anthony Preus, "Greek Philosophy: Egyptian Origins," *Research Papers on the Humanities and Social Sciences*

3 (1992): 7–8.

118. Palter, "*Black Athena*, Afro-Centrism, and the History of Science," p. 230-BAR, p. 211.

119. Rudolf Anthes, "Affinity and Difference between Egyptian and Greek Sculpture and Thought in the Seventh and Sixth Centuries, B.C.," *Proceedings of the American Philosophical Society* 107 (1963): 74.

120. Preus, "Greek Philosophy: Egyptian Origins," pp. 11–14.

121. Diodorus 1.96.1, 3.

CHAPTER 4: THE MYTH OF THE EGYPTIAN MYSTERY SYSTEM

1. Walter Burkert, *Ancient Mystery Cults* (Cambridge, Mass.: Harvard University Press, 1987), pp. 40–41.

2. Siegfried Morenz, *Egyptian Religion*, trans. Ann E. Keep (Ithaca, N.Y.: Cornell University Press, 1973), pp. 88–90.

3. Charles H. Vail, *The Ancient Mysteries and Modern Masonry* (1909; reprint, Chesapeake, N.Y.: ECA Associates, 1991).

4. Plutarch *On Isis and Osiris* 351f–52c.

5. Ibid., 354b–c.

6. Epiphanius *Heresies* 51.22. Aion was worshipped in many forms; here he is the son of Pluto, the god of the Underworld; see Marcel le Glay, "Aion," *Lexicon Iconographicum Mythologiae Classicae* [hereafter *LIMC*] 1, no. 1 (1981): 409; Günther Zuntz, "Aion Ploutonios," *Hermes* 116, no. 3 (1988): 303. In the Hermetic treatises discussed below, he is god of boundless time, master of

the universe; see Brian P. Copenhaver, *Hermetica* (Cambridge: Cambridge University Press, 1992), pp. 167–68.

7. Nicholas J. Richardson, *The Homeric Hymn to Demeter* (Oxford: Clarendon Press, 1974), pp. 26–27. On the Alexandrian rite, see also Arthur Darby Nock, *Essays on Religion and the Ancient World*, ed. Zeph Stewart (Oxford: Clarendon Press, 1972), pp. 390–91. On Aion at Eleusis, see Burkert, *Ancient Mystery Cults*, pp. 37–38.

8. Apuleius *The Golden Ass* 11.21–30.

9. Ibid., 11.22.

10. Ibid., 11.23.

11. Ibid., 11.24.

12. J. Gwyn Griffiths, ed., *Apuleius of Madauros: The Isis-Book*, Études Préliminaires aux Religions Orientales dans l'Empire Romain (Leiden: E. J. Brill, 1975), pp. 297, 303–4, 309.

13. Ibid., pp. 302, 305.

14. Siegfried Morenz, *Die Zauberflöte: eine Studie zum Lebenszusammenanhang Ägypten–Antike–Abendland*, Münstersche Forschungen 5 (Münster: Bülau Verlag, 1952), pp. 86, 89.

15. Morton H. Bloomfield, *The Seven Deadly Sins* (East Lansing: Michigan State University Press, 1952), pp. 15–18; James Tatum, *Apuleius and the Golden Ass* (Ithaca, N.Y.: Cornell University Press, 1979), p. 91.

16. Homer *Odyssey* 11.

17. Virgil *Aeneid* 6.

18. Virgil *Aeneid* 6.258–61.

19. Morenz, *Die Zauberflöte*, p. 92.

20. Iamblichus *Life of Pythagoras* 18. For translations,

see Gillian Clark, ed. and trans., *Iamblichus: On the Pythagorean Life*, Translated Texts for Historians (Liverpool: Liverpool University Press, 1989); John Dillon and Hershbell Jackson, *Iamblichus: On the Pythagorean Way of Life*, Texts and Translations 29: Graeco-Roman Religion Series 11 (Atlanta: Scholars Press, 1991).

21. Apuleius 11.22.

22. Gwyn Griffiths, *Apuleius of Madauros*, p. 285.

23. Chaeremon 618 frag.6 in Felix Jacoby, ed., *Fragments of the Greek Historians* (Leiden: E. J. Brill, 1923). On Chaeremon, see P. M. Fraser, *Ptolemaic Alexandria* (Oxford: Clarendon Press, 1972), vol. 1, p. 810 and n. 46; Garth Fowden, *The Egyptian Hermes* (Cambridge: Cambridge University Press, 1984), pp. 54–56.

24. The vase represented Osiris; see Gwyn Griffiths, *Apuleius of Madauros*, pp. 227–30; Elfriede Regina Knauer, *Urnula Faberrime Cavata, Observations on a Vessel Used in the Cult of Isis*, Beiträge zur Altertumskunde, 63 (Stuttgart: B. G. Teubner, 1995), p. 15.

25. Clement of Alexandria *Miscellanies* 6.4; see also Fowden, *The Egyptian Hermes*, pp. 54–59.

26. James, *Stolen Legacy*, pp. 131–32, 135.

27. Cf. Fowden, *The Egyptian Hermes*, pp. 62–63.

28. Nock, *Essays on Religion*, p. 501.

29. For discussion and translation, Brian P. Copenhaver, *Hermetica* (Cambridge: Cambridge University Press, 1992).

30. Iamblichus *On the Mysteries of Egypt* 8.1.260–61; Copenhaver, *Hermetica*, p. xvi.

31. On ancient forgeries, see Ronald Syme, "Fraud and Im-

posture," in *Pseudepigrapha I*, Entretiens sur l'Antiquité Classique, vol. 18 (Vandoevres-Geneva: Fondation Hardt, 1972), pp. 13–16; Anthony Grafton, *Forgers and Critics* (Princeton: Princeton University Press, 1990), pp. 8–35. More specific examples in Mary R. Lefkowitz, *The Lives of the Greek Poets* (Baltimore: Johns Hopkins University Press, 1981), pp. 19–20; John Morgan, "Make-Believe and Make Believe: The Fictionality of the Greek Novels," in *Lies and Fiction in the Ancient World*, ed. Christopher Gill and T. P. Wiseman (Austin: University of Texas Press, 1993), pp. 208–9.

32. Iamblichus *On the Mysteries of Egypt* 8.5.267–68; Copenhaver, *Hermetica*, pp. 200–201.

33. Iamblichus *On the Mysteries of Egypt* 8.4.265.

34. *Hermetica* 16.2; translation in Copenhaver, *Hermetica*, p. 58. My translation follows the reading *energētikōn* (instead of *energētikous*) and attempts to represent the treatise writer's pun on *philosophia, logōn psophos*.

35. On the sympathy for Egypt in the Hermetic Corpus, see Fowden, *The Egyptian Hermes*, pp. 26–31.

36. Erik Iversen, *Egyptian and Hermetic Doctrine*, Opuscula Graecolatina (Copenhagen: Museum Tusculanum Press, 1984), pp. 23–25, 53–54.

37. Arnaldo Momigliano, *Alien Wisdom: The Limits of Hellenization* (Cambridge: Cambridge University Press, 1975), pp. 146–47.

38. Porphyry *Epistle to Anebo* 2.13.

39. Iamblichus, *On the Mysteries of Egypt* 1.2.7; 1.1.2.

40. Ibid., 7.1.

41. Tatum, *Apuleius*, pp. 183–84.

42. *Oxyrhynchus Papyrus* 1380. See Friedrich Solmsen, *Isis among the Greeks and Romans*, Martin Classical Lectures, vol. 25 (Cambridge, Mass.: Harvard University Press, 1979), pp. 53–60.

43. James, *Stolen Legacy*, pp. 31–35.

44. T. G. H. James, *Ancient Egypt: The Land and Its Legacy* (Austin: University of Texas Press, 1990), p. 132; Siegfried Morenz, *Egyptian Religion*, trans. Ann E. Keep (Ithaca, N.Y.: Cornell University Press, 1973), p. 36.

45. G. G. M. James, *Stolen Legacy*, refers to Vail, *Ancient Mysteries*, pp. 182–83, but these pages are about the significance of Masonic symbols.

46. Vail, *Ancient Mysteries*, p. 185.

47. James, *Stolen Legacy*, p. 35.

48. Michael Baigent and Richard Leigh, *The Temple and the Lodge* (New York: Arcade Publishing Co., 1989), pp. 123–45.

49. Lynn Dumenil, *Freemasonry and American Culture* (Princeton, N.J.: Princeton University Press, 1984), p. 33.

50. Frances Yates, *Giordano Bruno and the Hermetic Tradition* (Chicago: University of Chicago Press, 1964), p. 274.

51. Ibid., pp. 12–14.

52. Ibid., p. 6.

53. Ibid., pp. 14–17.

54. David Stevenson, *The Origins of Freemasonry* (Cambridge: Cambridge University Press, 1988), pp. 84–85.

55. D'Arcy Wentworth Thompson, *A Glossary of Greek Birds* (Oxford: Clarendon Press, 1895), p. 67; Karl-Theodor Zauzich, *Hieroglyphs without Mystery: An Introduction to Ancient Egyptian Writing*, trans. Ann Macy Roth (Austin: University of Texas Press, 1992), p. 94.

56. Diodorus 3.4.2; see Erik Iversen, *The Myth of Egypt and its Hieroglyphs in European Tradition* (1961, reprint, Princeton, N.J.: Princeton University Press, 1993), p. 44.

57. Plutarch *On Isis and Osiris* 354f.

58. Plutarch *On Isis and Osiris* 363f; Gwyn Griffiths, *Plutarch's De Iside et Osiride*, pp. 422–23.

59. Apuleius *The Golden Ass* 11.22.

60. Iversen, *The Myth of Egypt and Its Hieroglyphs*, p. 49; Chaeremon 618 frag. 2 in Jacoby, *Fragments of the Greek Historians*.

61. Horapollo *On Hieroglyphs* 1.6; translation in George Boas, *The Hieroglyphics of Horapollo*, Bollingen Series (New York: Pantheon Books, 1950), pp. 45–46. See also Iversen, *The Myth of Egypt and Its Hieroglyphs*, pp. 48–49.

62. Stevenson, *The Origins of Freemasonry*, p. 86.

63. For example, see Walter Leslie Wilmshurst, *The Meaning of Masonry* (New York: Bell Publishing Co., 1867), pp. 170–216; Vail, *The Ancient Mysteries and Modern Masonry*, passim; A. G. Mackey, *The History of Freemasonry* (1898, reprint, New York: Masonic History Company, 1906), pp. 176–98; John S. M. Ward, *Freemasonry and the Ancient Gods* (London: Simpkin, Marshall, Hamilton, Kent and Co., 1921), pp. 97–109.

64. Daniel J. Boorstin, "Afterlives of the Great Pyramid," *Wilson Quarterly* 16, no. 3 (Summer 1992): 137.

65. Horapollo 1.6; Paul Naudon, *Histoire générale de la Franc-Maçonnerie* (Paris: Presses Universitaires de France, 1981), p. 14 fig. 4.

66. Jean Terrasson, *Life of Sethos, Taken from Private Mem-*

oirs of the Ancient Egyptians, 2 vols., trans. Thomas Lediard (London: J. Walthoe, 1732); all references below are to this translation.

67. Edward J. Dent, *Mozart's Operas*, 2nd ed. (Oxford: Clarendon Press, 1960), pp. 224–25.

68. Terrasson's translation was full of mistakes, according to the article in *Nouvelle Biographie Générale* (Paris: Didot, 1868), p. 1010. On Diodorus's account of Egypt, see ch. 3.

69. Terrasson, *Sethos*, vol. 1, pp. i–v.

70. Ibid., vol. 1, p. xiii.

71. Ibid., vol. 1, pp. 64–85.

72. Ibid., vol. 1, pp. 86–97.

73. Ibid., vol. 1, pp. 84–85.

74. Ibid., vol. 1, pp. 152–96.

75. On nineteenth-century scientific fantasies about the meaning of the pyramids, see Boorstin, "Afterlives of the Great Pyramids," pp. 131–38.

76. Terrasson, *Sethos*, vol. 1, p. 155.

77. Morenz, *Die Zauberflöte*, p. 61; see above.

78. The best-known accounts are Virgil *Georgics* 4.453–527 and Ovid *Metamorphoses* 10.4–77, but the story was known in fifth-century Athens; see R. A. B. Mynors, *Virgil, Georgics* (Oxford: Clarendon Press, 1990), pp. 314–15.

79. Empedocles frag. 31 B 115, I 357–58 Diels-Kranz; translation in Jonathan Barnes, *Early Greek Philosophy* (Harmondsworth: Penguin, 1987), pp. 194–95; see also M. R. Wright, *Empedocles: The Extant Fragments* (New Haven: Yale University Press, 1981), pp. 271–72.

80. See Richardson, *The Homeric Hymn to Demeter*, pp.

344–48, and lines 208–12 of the hymn itself.

81. Terrasson, *Sethos*, vol. 1, pp. 174–76.

82. Ibid., vol. 1, pp. 250–81.

83. Ibid., vol. 1, p. 250.

84. Ibid., vol.1, pp. 331–42.

85. Ibid., vol. 2, pp. 90–97.

86. Ibid., vol. 2, pp. 427–60.

87. Paul Nettl, *Mozart and Masonry* (New York: Philosophical Library, 1957), p. 69.

88. Terrasson, *Sethos*, vol. 2, p. 460.

89. Sergio Donadoni, "The Eighteenth Century," in Sergio Donadoni, Silvio Curto, and Anna Maria Donadoni-Roveri, *Egypt from Myth to Egyptology*, trans. Elizabeth Poore and Francesco L. Rossi (Turin: Istituto Bancario San Paolo, 1990), p. 79; Nettl, *Mozart and Masonry*, pp. 70–71, notes that Naumann used Masonic elements in his portrayal of Inca Sun-priests (!) in his Swedish opera *Cora och Alonzo*.

90. Iversen, *The Myth of Egypt and Its Hieroglyphs*, p. 122.

91. Volkmar Braunbehrens, *Mozart in Vienna*, trans. Timothy Bell (New York: Grove Weidenfeld, 1986), p. 226.

92. See ibid., p. 3, on his middle name. On Masonry in Vienna, see pp. 232–39, and also H. C. Landon Robbins, *Mozart and the Masons: New Light on the Lodge of "Crowned Hope"* (London: Thames and Hudson, 1982), pp. 8–9; Otto Jahn, *W. A. Mozart*, rev. and enl., ed. Hermann Abert (Leipzig: Breitkopf & Härtel, 1923), pp. 69–79.

93. Iversen, *The Myth of Egypt and Its Hieroglyphs*, p. 122.

94. See the text reproduced in Judith A. Eckelmeyer, *The Cultural Context of Mozart's Magic Flute*, Studies in the History and Interpretation of Music (Lewiston, N.Y.: Ed-

win Mellen Press, 1991), vol. 2, p. 260.

95. Ibid., vol. 2, p. 466.

96. Ibid., vol. 2, p. 470.

97. Cf. Dent, *Mozart's Operas*, p. 254.

98. Katharine Thomson, *The Masonic Thread in Mozart* (London: Lawrence and Wishart, 1977), p. 29.

99. Ibid., pp. 30, 179–80; also see Nettl, *Mozart and Masonry*, p. 70; Jahn, *W. A. Mozart*, pp. 817–23.

100. Nettl, *Mozart and Masonry*, pp. 64, 72. On Schikaneder's other sources, see pp. 67–69, and Hans-Albrecht Koch, ed., *Wolfgang Amadeus Mozart, Die Zauberflöte* (Stuttgart: Philipp Reclam, Jr., 1991), p. 80.

101. Jacques Chailley, *The Magic Flute, Masonic Opera*, trans. Herbert Weinstock (New York: Alfred A. Knopf, 1971), p. 240.

102. Dent, *Mozart's Operas*, pp. 224–27.

103. Thomson, *The Masonic Thread in Mozart*, p. 164; Chailley, *The Magic Flute, Masonic Opera*, pp. 145, 276–79.

104. Scene 28, text translated from the original libretto reproduced in Eckelmeyer, *The Cultural Context of Mozart's Magic Flute*, vol. 2, p. 204; see also Dent, *Mozart's Operas*, p. 228.

105. Chailley, *The Magic Flute, Masonic Opera*, pp. 138, 238.

106. Braunbehrens, *Mozart in Vienna*, p. 231.

107. Chailley, *The Magic Flute, Masonic Opera*, pp. 119–21.

108. Thomson, *The Masonic Thread in Mozart*, pp. 160–62; Chailley, *Magic Flute, Masonic Opera*, pp. 158–65.

109. Thomson, *The Masonic Thread in Mozart*, pp. 127, 166.

110. Alexandre Lenoir, *La Franche-maçonnerie rendue à sa véritable origine, ou L'antiquité de la franche-maçonnerie*

prouvée par l'explication des mystères anciens et modernes (Paris: B. Fournier, 1814), pp. 4, 18.

111. Donadoni, "The Eighteenth Century," p. 78.

112. Terrasson, *Sethos*, vol. 1, pp. 175–76; Lenoir, *La Franchemaçonnerie*, p. 72.

113. The idea of Egyptian mysteries also survives (via Freemasonry) in certain Mormon doctrines; see John L. Brooke, *The Refiner's Fire: The Making of Mormon Cosmology* (Cambridge: Cambridge University Press, 1994), p. 301. But these theories conflate the elaborate Egyptian rituals for the dead with Greek mystery cults for the living (above, n. 14). For an example, see Hugh Nibley, *The Message of the Joseph Smith Papyri: An Egyptian Endowment* (Salt Lake City: Deseret Book Company, 1976), pp. xii–xiii, 65, 253.

CHAPTER 5: THE MYTH OF THE STOLEN LEGACY

1. Alexandre Lenoir, *La Franche-maçonnerie rendue à sa véritable origine, ou L'antiquité de la franche-maçonnerie prouvée par l'explication des mystères anciens et modernes* (Paris: B. Fournier, 1814), p. 244. On the artist Jean-Michel Moreau the younger (1741–1814), see Christiane Ziegler, Jean-Marcel Humbert, and Michael Pantazzi, *Egyptomania: Egypt in Western Art* (Ottawa: National Gallery of Canada, 1994), pp. 146–47. Jean Terrasson, *Life of Sethos, Taken from Private Memoirs of the Ancient Egyptians*, trans. Thomas Lediard (London: J. Walthoe, 1732), vol. 1, pp. 160–61.

2. Clement of Alexandria *Miscellanies* 6.3.

3. George G. M. James, *Stolen Legacy* (New York: Philosophical Library, 1954), pp. 1, 164, 158.

4. Halford H. Fairchild, "Knowing Black History Isn't Just for Blacks," *Los Angeles Times*, February 5, 1995, sec. M, p. 5.

5. Cf. Clarence Walker, "The Distortions of Afrocentric History," in *Alternatives to Afrocentrism*, ed. John Miller (Washington, D.C.: Center for the New American Community, 1994), pp. 32–36; Mary R. Lefkowitz, "The Myth of a 'Stolen Legacy,'" *Society* 31, no. 3 (1994): 27–33.

6. From "Assimilation," a commencement address at Case Western Reserve, as quoted by Howard Brotz, ed., *Negro Social and Political Thought, 1850–1920: Representative Texts* (New York: Basic Books, 1966), p. 234.

7. Ibid., pp. 235, 237.

8. As quoted by Edith Holden, *Blyden of Liberia* (New York: Vantage Press, 1966), p. 885.

9. Edward Wilmot Blyden, *Christianity, Islam and the Negro Race* (1887; reprint, Edinburgh: Edinburgh University Press, 1967), p. 154 n. 2.

10. Edward Wilmot Blyden, "The Negro in Ancient History," in *The People of Africa: A Series of Papers on Their Character, etc.*, ed. Henry Maunsell Schieffelin (New York: A. D. F. Randolph, 1871), pp. 3, 7–9.

11. As quoted by St. Clair Drake, *Black Folk Here and There* (Los Angeles: Center for Afro-American Studies, 1987), vol. 1, p. 133.

12. From Blyden's 1912 book *From West Africa to Palestine*, as quoted by Hollis R. Lynch, *Edward Wilmot Blyden:*

Pan-Negro Patriot 1832–1912 (London: Oxford University Press, 1967), p. 55.

13. Drake, *Black Folks Here and There*, vol. 1, pp. 131–32.

14. Wilson J. Moses, *The Golden Age of Black Nationalism* (Camden, Conn.: Shoe String Press, 1978; New York: Oxford University Press, 1988), pp. 161–67.

15. Loretta J. Williams, *Black Freemasonry and Middle-Class Realities*, University of Missouri Studies, vol. 20 (Columbia: University of Missouri Press, 1980), p. 88 n. 37.

16. Anon., "The First Mason, A Black Man," *Colored American Magazine* 6, no. 4 (1903): 285–86; Moses, *The Golden Age of Black Nationalism*, p. 300.

17. William H. Grimshaw, *Official History of Freemasonry Among the Colored Peoples of North America* (1903; reprint, New York: Greenwood Press, 1969), pp. 1–2.

18. As quoted by William A. Muraskin, *Middle-Class Blacks in a White Society: Prince Hall Freemasonry in America* (Berkeley: University of California Press, 1975), p. 197.

19. Robert A. Hill, ed., *Marcus Garvey and Universal Negro Improvement Association Papers* (Berkeley: University of California Press, 1983), vol. 1, p. lxvi.

20. Melville J. Herskovits, *The Myth of the Negro Past* (Boston: Beacon Press, 1941), p. 162. But some scholars doubt that there is any direct continuity between the two types of organization; see Williams, *Black Freemasonry and Middle-Class Realities*, p. 88 n. 37.

21. Hill, *Marcus Garvey and UNIA Papers*, vol. 1, p. lxii.

22. Tony Martin, *Race First: The Ideological and Organizational Struggles of Marcus Garvey and the Universal Negro Improvement Association* (Westport, Conn.:

Greenwood Press, 1976; Dover, Mass.: The Majority Press, 1986), pp. 82–83.

23. As quoted in ibid., p. 83.

24. As quoted by Howard Brotz, ed., *Negro Social and Political Thought*, pp. 561–62.

25. Garvey, "The Tragedy of White Injustice," in Robert A. Hill and Barbara Bair, eds., *Marcus Garvey: Life and Lessons* (Berkeley: University of California Press, 1987), stanzas 6 and 63, pp. 120, 137.

26. Ibid., p. 193.

27. See, for example, the report of the UNIA meeting of March 13, 1920, in Hill, ed., *Marcus Garvey and Universal Negro Improvement Association Papers*, vol. 2, p. 255.

28. Ibid., vol. 6, p. 164.

29. James, *Stolen Legacy*, pp. 153–54.

30. Henri Frankfort, *Kingship and the Gods* (Chicago: University of Chicago Press, 1948), pp. 33–34.

31. Herodotus 2.60.1; Alan B. Lloyd, *Herodotus Book II* (Leiden: E. J. Brill, 1975–88), vol. 2, p. 274.

32. James, *Stolen Legacy*, pp. 27, 30.

33. Ibid., p. 106; cf. Walter Leslie Wilmshurst, *The Meaning of Masonry* (New York: Bell Publishing Company, 1867), pp. 186–90.

34. James, *Stolen Legacy*, pp. 67, 89, 93.

35. Ibid., p. 81; cf., ch. 4.

36. Ibid., p. 101; see ch. 4.

37. Ibid., pp. 47, 119.

38. Ibid., p. 13.

39. Ibid., pp. 176–77.

40. P. M. Fraser, *Ptolemaic Alexandria* (Oxford: Clarendon Press, 1972), vol. 1, pp. 1, 6–7, 320–35.

41. James, *Stolen Legacy,* p. 2.

42. The Greek philosopher Pyrrho of Elis (ca. 360–271 B.C.) is said to have gone to India with Anaxarchus and to have been influenced by Brahmin ideas (Diogenes Laertius 9.61, 63). Everard Flintoff, "Pyrrho and India," *Phronesis* 85 (1980): 88–108, suggests possible parallels. But the hypothesis of foreign influence is not necessary, because there are Greek precedents for these same ideas; see Anthony A. Long, *Hellenistic Philosophy* (London: Duckworth, 1974), p. 80; Fernanda Decleva Caizzi, *Pirrone: Testimonianze,* Elenchos 5 (Milan: Bibliopolis, 1981), pp. 136–42.

43. James, *Stolen Legacy,* p. 154.

44. Ibid., p. 123.

45. See Raymond O. Faulkner, *The Ancient Egyptian Book of the Dead,* ed. Carol Andrews (Austin: University of Texas Press, 1985), pp. 11–12.

46. James, *Stolen Legacy,* p. 125.

47. Ibid., p. 126.

48. Ibid., pp. 136–37.

49. Clement *Miscellanies* 6.4. See ch. 4.

50. Siegfried Morenz, *Egyptian Religion,* trans. Ann E. Keep (Ithaca, N.Y.: Cornell University Press, 1973), p. 273.

51. James, *Stolen Legacy,* pp. 121–22.

52. Translation in Miriam Lichtheim, ed. and trans., *Ancient Egyptian Literature: A Book of Readings* (Berkeley: University of California Press, 1973), vol. 1, pp. 54–55; discussion in Frankfort, *Kingship and the Gods,* pp. 27–30.

53. Aristotle *Metaphysics* 11.1072b7; W. D. Ross, *Aristotle* (London: Methuen and Co., 1945), pp. 179–80.

54. Ibid., pp. 127–28.

55. Ingemar Düring, *Aristoteles* (Heidelberg: Carl Winter, 1966), p. 33.

56. Ross, *Aristotle*, p. 9.

57. For the ancient lists, see Valentin Rose, *Aristotelis Fragmenta* (Leipzig: B. G. Teubner, 1886), pp. 3–22.

58. James, *Stolen Legacy*, p. 70.

59. Ibid., p. 67.

60. Ibid., pp. 68, 74–75.

61. Ibid., pp. 71–72.

62. Ibid., p. 73.

63. Ibid., p. 81.

64. Ibid., p. 79; Diogenes Laertius 9.35.

65. James, *Stolen Legacy*, p. 89, cf. p. 2.

66. Ibid., p. 94.

67. Ibid., pp. 88–89.

68. Plato *Apology of Socrates* 19c.

69. Pausanias *Description of Greece* 10.24.1 attributes the saying "know thyself" (*gnōthi sauton*) to several of the legendary Seven Wise Men, but more likely it was simply proverbial.

70. Plato *Crito* 52b.

71. Diogenes Laertius 3.37–38, 57; 8.85.

72. By the end of the late fourth century B.C., Plato was accused by biographers of having "plagiarized" from many different ancient writers, some quite obscure; see Alice Swift Riginos, *Platonica: The Anecdotes Concerning the Life and Writings of Plato* (Leiden: Brill, 1976), pp. 166,

186.

73. Mary R. Lefkowitz, *The Lives of the Greek Poets* (Baltimore: Johns Hopkins University Press, 1981), pp. 75–76, 84–85, 88–91.

74. Exodus 14.7; James, *Stolen Legacy*, pp. 110–12.

75. James, *Stolen Legacy*, pp. 9–10, 39, 44.

76. Ibid., p. 26.

77. Ibid., p. 22.

78. Ibid., p. 17.

79. Ibid., p. 105.

80. Ibid., p. 151.

81. It is possible that James himself is not responsible for the misleading system of documentation, since the book was published after his death.

82. E. Zeller, *A History of Greek Philosophy from the Earliest Period to the Time of Socrates*, trans. S. F. Alleyne from the 1876 German edition (London: Longmans, Green, and Co., 1881); William Turner, *History of Philosophy* (Boston: Athenaeum Press, 1903); Eva Matthews Sanford, *The Mediterranean World in Ancient Times*, Ronald Series in History (New York: Ronald Press Co., 1938).

83. For examples of incomplete references to ancient sources, see James, *Stolen Legacy,* pp. 11, 109, 112; for incorrect citations, pp. 43, 69, 112–13, 123.

84. Ibid., pp. 144, 149.

85. The ancient Greek encyclopedia known as the Suda gives two different etymologies for Io: the moon (in the dialect of Argos) and (absurdly) the cry "io io" (no. 453, II p. 646 Adler).

86. James, *Stolen Legacy*, p. 149.

87. On the terminology, see Frank M. Snowden, Jr., *Blacks in Antiquity* (Cambridge, Mass.: Harvard University Press, 1970), pp. 4–5.

88. Ibid., p. 68.

89. Pierre Chantraine, *Dictionnaire étymologique de la langue grecque* (Paris: Éditions Klincksieck, 1984), vol. 2, p. 958.

90. Bernal, *BA* 1, p. 435.

91. Yosef A. A. ben-Jochannan, *Africa, Mother of Western Civilization* (Baltimore: Black Classic Press, 1971), p. 483.

92. Ibid., p. 406.

93. Ibid., p. 493.

94. Cheikh Anta Diop, *Civilization or Barbarism: An Authentic Anthropology*, trans. Yaa-Lengi Meema Ngemi (Brooklyn: Lawrence Hill Books, 1991), p. 338.

95. Ibid., pp. 337–40.

96. Ibid., pp. 341–43.

97. Ibid., p. 356.

98. Diop, *Civilization or Barbarism*, pp. 237–42, as discussed by Robert Palter, "*Black Athena*, Afro-Centrism, and the History of Science," *History of Science* 31 (1993): 260.

99. An extreme example is reported by Myron Magnet, *The Dream and the Nightmare: The Sixties' Legacy to the Underclass* (New York: William Morrow, 1993), p. 218: In a speech to high-school teachers, Wade Nobles, a director of a program for troubled youths, compared ancient Greek culture to a drink that has been regurgitated: "the Greeks gave back the vomit of the African way." According to Magnet, Nobles exhorted his audience not to become "vomit-drinkers."

100. George Orwell, *Nineteen Eighty-Four* (New York: Harcourt Brace, 1949), p. 41.

101. Ibid., p. 53.

CHAPTER 6: CONCLUSION

1. Molefi Kete Asante, *Kemet, Afrocentricity and Knowledge* (Trenton, N.J.: Africa World Press, 1990), p. 117.

2. See especially David A. Hollinger, *Postethnic America* (New York: Basic Books, 1995), especially pp. 105–29.

3. Mary R. Lefkowitz, "Combating False Theories in the Classroom," *Chronicle of Higher Education* (January 19, 1994): B1–B3; Raymond Winbush, letter to the editor, *Chronicle of Higher Education* (February 9, 1994): B4.

4. Plato *Republic* 515e–516a.

5. *Jeffries v. Harleston*, 828 F. Supp. 1066, 1098 (S.O.N.Y. 1993).

6. *Jeffries v. Harleston*, 52 F. 3rd 9 (2nd Cir. 1995). The Supreme Court refused to hear Jeffries's appeal of the decision.

7. *Waters v. Churchill*, 114 S. Ct. 1878 (1994).

8. Leonard Jeffries, from text of speech quoted in *New York Newsday*, August 19, 1991, p. 29.

9. Nathan Glazer, "Levin, Jeffries, and the Fate of Academic Autonomy," *William and Mary Law Review* 36, no. 2 (1995): 732.

10. See also Guy MacLean Rogers, "Racism and Anti-semitism in the Classroom," *Midstream* 40, no. 6 (August/September 1994): 8–10.

EPILOGUE

1. The internet debate was discussed in the *Chronicle of Higher Education* (April 12, 1996): A8 and in the *Washington Post,* April 29, 1996, p. A16, and May 28, 1996, p. A11. Some of the same material appeared in Martin Bernal, "The Afrocentric Interpretation of History: Bernal Replies to Lefkowitz," *Journal of Blacks in Higher Education (JBHE)* 12 (Spring 1996): 86–95; and in Mary Lefkowitz, "The Afrocentric Interpretation of History: Lefkowitz Replies to Bernal," ibid. (Summer 1996): 88–90.

2. Cf. John Elson, "Attacking Afrocentrism," *Time,* February 19, 1996, p. 66.

3. "Not Out of Africa." *The New Republic,* February 10, 1992, pp. 29–36, reprinted as "Ancient History: Modern Myths" in Mary R. Lefkowitz and Guy MacLean Rogers, eds., *Black Athena Revisited* (Chapel Hill: University of North Carolina Press, 1996). See pp. xi–xii, this volume.

4. Ibrahim Sundiata, "Afrocentrism: The Argument We're Really Having," *Dissonance,* September 30, 1996 [http://way.net/dissonance/sundiata.html], p. 4.

5. For example, Bernal, *JBHE*, p. 86.

6. Jacques Berlinerblau, "Black Athena Redux," *The Nation,* October 12, 1996, pp. 46, 48.

7. On the technique, see John M. Ellis, *Against Deconstruction* (Princeton, N.J.: Princeton University Press, 1989), pp. 141–45; Alan B. Spitzer, *Historical Truth and Lies About the Past* (Chapel Hill: University of North Carolina Press, 1996), pp. 2, 83, 90.

8. Selwyn R. Cudjoe, "Not a Racist Polemic," *Boston Globe,*

April 21, 1996, p. 85.

9. Molefi Kete Asante, "Ancient Truths: New Attacks on Afrocentrism Are as Weak as They Are False," *Emerge,* July/August 1996, p. 66.

10. Ibid., p. 68. George Will, "Intellectual Segregation," *Newsweek,* February 19, 1996, p. 78; Roger Kimball, "Greece for the Greeks: History Is Not Bunk," *Wall Street Journal,* February 14, 1996, p. A12.

11. Robert Bork, *Slouching Towards Gomorrah: Modern Liberalism and American Decline* (New York: ReganBooks/HarperCollins, 1996), pp. 244–45. See pp. 2–3, this volume.

12. Bernal, *JBHE,* pp. 87, 89; but in fact I have never met, corresponded with, or spoken to the "close associates" that he singles out by name, Jeane Kirkpatrick and Peter Diamandopoulos. Bernal has also published abbreviated versions of the *JBHE* review: "Whose Greece?" in the *London Review of Books,* December 12, 1996, pp. 17–18, and [Ithaca, N.Y.] *Bookpress* 6, no. 7 (November 1996): 11–12.

13. Sibyl S. Steinberg, *Publishers Weekly,* December 18, 1995, p. 37; Tom Carson, "Greece is the Word," *Village Voice,* April 16, 1996, p. 20; Glen Bowersock, *New York Times Book Review,* February 25, 1996, p. 6.

14. Carson, "Greece is the Word," p. 20; Jason Vickers, "*Not Out of Africa*: A Reaction," *Virtual Dashiki,* August/September 1996, p. 9. James L. Conyers, Jr., *Journal of Black Studies* 27 (September 1996): 130. But Malcolm X says that he argued that Homer was a Moor who "symbolized how white Europeans kidnapped black Africans, then blinded them so they could never get back to their own

people." He learned from his reading of the "old philosophers" that "Socrates, for instance, traveled in Egypt. Some sources say that he was initiated into some of the Egyptian mysteries" (see this volume, pp. 144–45); *The Autobiography of Malcolm X*, With the assistance of Alex Haley (New York: Ballantine Books, 1973), pp. 182, 188.

15. Nathan Glazer, letter to *New York Times Book Review*, March 17, 1996, p. 4.

16. Will, "Intellectual Segregation," p. 78.

17. Berlinerblau, "Black Athena Redux," pp. 46–47.

18. Bernal, *JBHE*, p. 88; August Meier, *Journal of American History* 83.3 (December 1996): 988.

19. Ibid., p. 988; Elson, "Attacking Afrocentrism," p. 66.

20. Meier, op. cit. p. 988; Sundiata, "Afrocentrism," p. 2.

21. Bernal, *JBHE*, pp. 87, 89.

22. Asa G. Hilliard III, "Biographical Notes," from the publisher's insert to George G. M. James, *Stolen Legacy* (New York: Philosophical Library, 1954).

23. This volume, pp. 148–49.

24. Asante, "Ancient Truths," p. 66; this volume, pp. 158–60; this volume, Supplementary Notes, note to p. 42.

25. Berlinerblau, "Black Athena Redux," p. 46.

26. *Chicago Tribune,* December 19, 1996, p. 1.

27. Compare Bernal, "Whose Greece?" (in *Bookpress*), p. 11.

28. Michael Eric Dyson, *Reflecting Black African American Cultural Criticism* (Minneapolis: University of Minnesota Press, 1993), pp. 161–62.

29. Martin Bernal, *Black Athena: The Afroasiatic Roots of Classical Civilization. Vol. I: The Fabrication of Ancient Greece* (New Brunswick, NJ: Rutgers University Press,

1987), p. 38.

30. Richard B. Rutherford, *The Art of Plato* (London: Duck-worth, 1995), pp. 288–90, with bibliography; see also this volume, Supplementary Notes, note to p. 81

31. Heinrich von Staden, *Herophilus: The Art of Medicine in Early Alexandria* (Cambridge: Cambridge University Press, 1989), pp. 1–31, especially pp. 5–6.

32. See this volume, Supplementary Notes, note to p. 1.

33. See Cyril P. Bryan, trans., *Ancient Egyptian Medicine: The Papyrus Ebers* (Chicago, Ares Publishers, 1974), pp. 86–87; Henry E. Sigerist, *A History of Medicine*, I, pp. 342–43; von Staden, *Herophilus*, pp. 18–19; von Staden, "Women and Dirt," *Helios* 19, no. 1–2 (1992): 20. Herodotus recalls how the Persian king Darius (558?–486 B.C.) found the Greek doctor Democedes superior to the best Egyptian doctors (3.129).

34. Bernal, "Whose Greece?" (in *London Review of Books*), p. 18; compare G. E. R. Lloyd, "The Debt of Greek Philosophy and Science to the Ancient Near East," pp. 281–98 in *Methods and Problems in Greek Science* (Cambridge: Cambridge University Press, 1991); Walter Burkert, *The Orientalizing Revolution: Near Eastern Influence on Greek Culture in the Early Archaic Age*, trans. M. E. Pinder and W. Burkert (Cambridge, Mass.: Harvard University Press, 1992), pp. 120–27.

35. Cudjoe, "Not a Racist Polemic," p. 85; Asante, "Ancient Truths," p. 70.

SUPPLEMENTARY NOTES

page

1. **Afrocentrism in the Schools.** Paul R. Gross and Norman Levitt, in *Higher Superstition: The Academic Left and Its Quarrels with Science* (Baltimore: Johns Hopkins University Press, 1994), 203–14, discuss some of the absurd claims made in Hunter Havelin Adams, *African and African American Contributions to Science and Technology*, Portland Baseline Essay in Science (Portland, Oregon: Multnomah School District, 1990). See also Bernard Ortiz de Montellano, "Spreading Scientific Illiteracy Among Minorities. Part I: Multicultural Pseudoscience," *Skeptical Inquirer* 16 (Fall 1991): 46–50; "Spreading Scientific Illiteracy Among Minorities. Part II: Magic Melanin," *Skeptical Inquirer* 16 (Winter 1991): 62–66; "Afrocentric Creationism," *Creation / Evolution* 29 (Winter 1991–92): 1–8; "Melanin, Afrocentricity, and Pseudoscience," *Yearbook of Physical Anthropology* 36

(1993): 33–58; "Afrocentric Pseudoscience: The Miseducation of African Americans," Paul R. Gross, Norman Levitt, and Martin W. Lewis, eds., *The Flight from Science and Reason. Annals of the New York Academy of Sciences,* Vol. 775 (New York: New York Academy of Sciences, 1996) pp. 561–72; "Avoiding Egyptocentric Pseudoscience: Colleges Must Help Set Standards for Schools," *Chronicle of Higher Education* (March 25, 1996): B1–B2. See also Erich Martel, "What's Wrong with the Portland Baseline Essays," in *Alternatives to Afrocentrism,* ed. John Miller (Washington D.C.: Center for Equal Opportunity, 1994), pp. 37–42 = pp. 30–34 in the second edition (1996).

1. **Who Teaches Afrocentric Ancient History?** Jacques Berlinerblau, in his review of *Not Out of Africa* in *The Nation,* October 28, 1996, p. 47, remarks that I did not specify where, besides City University and Wellesley College, Afrocentric materials have been used. I mentioned those universities because specific information was available about what was being taught in the classrooms. If it can be assumed that people who write about Afrocentric ancient history also teach what they have written, more universities could be added to the list, including Cornell University, Kent State, and California State University at Long Beach. I do discuss some of the views of Professor Molefi Asante of Temple University in this volume. Asante has served as a consultant for many schools and is the author of the "Social Studies" Essay in *The Camden African–Puerto Rican Centric Guide* (Camden, N.J., Camden Board of Education, n.d.), which is

based on the source materials criticized in this book. According to Andrew Sullivan, "Racism 101," *The New Republic,* November 26, 1990, pp. 18–21, the Portland Baseline Essays were adopted by schools in Atlanta, Pittsburgh, Indianapolis, and Washington, D.C. See also Chester E. Finn, Jr., "Cleopatra's Nose," *Commentary* 101, no. 6 (June 1996): 71–72. The *60 Minutes* segment "Out of Africa," aired 11/24/96, featured the Iowa-Maple School in Cleveland, Ohio. Twenty-one public schools in Detroit use an Afrocentric curriculum, according to David Butty, "Afrocentrism generates mixed results in Detroit and debate across nation," *The Detroit News* (May 19, 1996): http://www.detnews.com/menu/stories/48444.htm. Kansas City has two Afrocentric Schools, and plans for more; see Lynn Horsely, "Ladd elementary becomes second Afrocentric School," *Kansas City Star* (November 7, 1996): B 1, 4.

6. **Greek Democracy.** In his review of *Not Out of Africa* in the *Journal of Blacks in Higher Education (JBHE)* 12 (Spring 1996): 87, Martin Bernal complained that I did not observe that this country's founding fathers preferred republicanism to democracy. But I am talking about *ideals*, not actual Athenian democracy (which the founding fathers rejected). The founding fathers had read Plato and Aristotle, as well as Plutarch on Solon and Lycurgus. The purpose of this brief discussion was to remind readers why ancient Greek history has been the subject of proportionately more attention than the history of other ancient civilizations. But Bernal, with his characteristic tendency to read political meaning

into everything, insists that my motive here was to imply that Afrocentrists are the enemies of freedom! Of course I meant no such thing.

13. **Origins of the Egyptians**. Recent work on skeletons and DNA suggests that the people who settled in the Nile valley, like all of humankind, came from somewhere south of the Sahara; they were not (as some nineteenth-century scholars had supposed) invaders from the north. See Bruce G. Trigger, "The Rise of Civilization in Egypt," *Cambridge History of Africa,* vol. 1 (Cambridge: Cambridge University Press, 1982), pp. 489–90; S. O. Y. Keita, "Studies and Comments on Ancient Egyptian Biological Relationships," *History in Africa* 20 (1993), pp. 129–54.

22. **Minoans in Egypt**. Manfred Bietak, the archaeologist in charge of the excavations at Avaris, suggested that there may have been an alliance between the Hyksos dynasty and the Minoans: "In return for protecting the sea approaches to Egypt, the Minoans might have secured harbour facilities and access to those precious commodities (especially gold) for which Egypt was famous in the outside world," *Avaris: The Capital of the Hyksos: Recent Excavations at Tell el-Dab'a* (London: British Museum Press, 1996), p. 81.

25–26. **Heracles's Family Tree.** Although Martin Bernal often appears contemptuous of the opinions of classical scholars, on p. 88 of his *JBHE* review, he criticizes me for defying the "conventional wisdom" of "all" earlier scholars in translating *gegonotes to anekathen ap' Aigyptou* (Herodotus 2.43.2) as "descended on both sides from Aegyptus" (rather than, as would better suit his purposes, "descended on both sides from Egypt"). The problem is that the Greeks used the same word, *Aigyptos,* to designate both the hero and the country. Because *Aigyptos* means the country Egypt virtually everywhere else in Book II, most English translators have assumed it means Egypt rather than Aegyptus, but commentators on the Greek text have seen that it means the hero. The context of this passage makes it clear that the hero is meant, because Herodotus is talking not about the country Egypt but about the hero Heracles's family tree. With the verb meaning "to be descended from" (*ginesthai*), Herodotus usually employed *ek* ("out from") to designate place and *apo* ("away from") to designate person, particularly if the descent was remote. There is a close parallel at 6.35.1 *ta men anekathen ap' Aiakou te kai Aigines gegonos.* Other examples: *ek,* of place, 1.146.1, 1.173.1, 2.91.5, 2.154.2, 5.57.1, 7.92 (an exception, 4.95.3); *apo,* of person, 1.147.1, 3.55.2, 3.83.2, 3.84.1, 4.6.1, 4.10.3, 4.149.2, 5.7, 5.22.1, 6.35.1, 6.51, 6.52.8, 7.150.2, 8.22.2, 8.46.3, 8.139 (an exception, 7.93). See also Henry George Liddell, Robert Scott, and Henry Stuart Jones, *A Greek–English Lexicon,* 9th ed. (Oxford: Clarendon Press, 1940), s.v. *apo,* III.1; R. Kuehner and B. Gerth, *Ausführliche Grammatik der Griechischen Sprache* [1898], (Hannover: Hahnsche Buchhandlung, 1983), p. 457.

42. **Was Cleopatra Black**? Molefi Asante, in his review of *Not Out of Africa,* "Asante Answers the Eurocentrists," *Emerge* (July/August 1996): 68, dismissed my discussion of Cleopatra's origins as an "irrelevancy." But in his

Camden Social Studies Essay (p. 122), published several
years ago, he quoted John Henrik Clarke's statement
that she was of mixed African and Greek parentage.

47. **Ptolemy VIII's Memoirs.** See Ptolemy VIII Euergetes
II "Physcon" 234 frag. 4 in Felix Jacoby, ed., *Fragments of
the Greek Historians* (Leiden: E. J. Brill, 1923); and P. M.
Fraser, *Ptolemaic Alexandria* (Oxford: Clarendon Press,
1972), vol. 1, p. 515; vol. 2, p. 743, notes pp. 180–81.

49–52 **Cultural Relativism.** On this issue see especially
Keith Windschuttle, *The Killing of History: How a Discipline Is Being Murdered by Literary Critics and Social
Theorists* (Paddington, N.S.W.: Macleay Press, 1996), pp.
270–81; Stephen Miller, "The Future of Disinterest and
Foucault's Regime of Truth," *Partisan Review* 64, no. 1
(Winter 1997): 28–36. For some thoughtful reservations
about my treatment of the historical issues here and on
pp. 155–58, see Glenn Loury, "Color Blinded," *Arion* 4.4
(Winter 1997): 168–85.

57. **Impact of Decipherment on Western Thought.** In
my brief discussion of the significance of decipherment, I
only give the date when Champollion's Egyptian grammar began to be published (1836), as the time after
which it was no longer reasonable to maintain that hieroglyphics were a system of secret symbols. See E.
Iversen, *The Myth of Egypt and Its Hieroglyphs in European Tradition* [1961], (Princeton: Princeton University
Press, 1993), p. 146. Although Champollion had deciphered hieroglyphics in the early 1820s, the philosopher
Hegel (for one) was unable to learn enough about Champollion's work to alter his views about the "Western iden-

tity" of Egypt; see S. Harten, "Archaeology and the Un-
concious: Hegel, Egyptomania, and the Legitimation of
Orientalism," *Egypt and the Fabrication of European
Identity* (Los Angeles: UCLA Center for Near Eastern
Studies, 1995), pp. 3–4.

75. Solon's Laws. Diodorus got his information about the
first of these, a law about the registration of occupation
(1.77.5), from Herodotus (2.177.2). This law was a basic
feature of the Egyptian fiscal system, but there is no
clear Athenian counterpart to it. There is also the problem of chronology: Herodotus says that Solon visited
Egypt *after* he enacted his legislation (1.30.1). Perhaps
what Herodotus had in mind was the law on the idleness
of land (*argias*) attributed to Solon or to Peisistratus
(Plutarch, *Life of Solon*, 31.2). But there is no reason to
assume that Solon needed to go to Egypt to find out
about the land use; he had read the eighth-century B.C.
Greek poet Hesiod on the idea of the necessity of toil. See
A. B. Lloyd, *Herodotus Book II* (Leiden: E. J. Brill,
1975–88), vol. 1, pp. 55–56; vol. 3, pp. 220–21.

The other law Diodorus "supposes" (it is clear from his
language that he relying on conjecture) to have been borrowed by Solon was the *seisachthei*a (1.79.4), which is
roughly similar to the debt legislation of the pharaoh the
Greeks called Bocchoris (Bakenrenef, 727–15 B.C.). Here,
as in my previous example, the connection Diodorus
makes between the Greek and Egyptian laws appears to
be based solely on the kind of speculation that Diodorus
and his informants were always eager to make. The
vague similarities between the two sets of laws can

hardly be used as evidence for "massive" cultural borrowing; at most (and even this is doubtful) they might represent a specific instance of adaptation. Although Bernal suggests in his *JBHE* review, p. 88, that Diodorus's information might weaken my argument, he fails to keep in mind that the Greeks, especially in the Hellenistic period, were eager to associate themselves with the ancient civilization of Egypt in any way they could. How much they actually *knew* about earlier antiquity is another matter.

81. **Plato and Egypt**. Plato could have taken most of his information about Egypt from the works of other Greek writers, such as Homer, Herodotus, and the comic poets Aristophanes and Cratinus; see Luc Brisson, "L'Égypte de Platon," *Les Études philosophiques* N.S. 2–3 (1987): 168.

83. **Hermes Trismegistus**. On Hermes Trismegistus in his divine and human manifestations, see Garth Fowden, *The Egyptian Hermes* (Cambridge: Cambridge University Press, 1986), pp. 22–31. The Alexandrian Jewish writer Artapanus (third- to second-century B.C.) said that Moses was identified with Hermes during his lifetime (726 frag. 3.6 in Jacoby, ed., *Fragments of the Greek Historians* = Eusebius, *Praeparatio Evangelica* 9.27.6; translation in James H. Charlesworth, ed., *The Old Testament Pseudepigrapha* [Garden City, N.Y.: Doubleday, 1985], vol. 2, p. 899).

88. **Hellenistic Syncretism**. On the tendency to connect Greek philosophy with Egyptian and Hebrew wisdom

literature, see also G. E. R. Lloyd, "The Debt of Greek Philosophy and Science to the Ancient Near East," p. 281 in *Methods and Problems in Greek Science: Selected Papers* (Cambridge: Cambridge University Press, 1991).

95. **Isis at Eleusis?** In his *JBHE* review, p. 91, Bernal assumed that the scarabs and a symbol of Isis found in a ninth- or eighth-century tomb in Eleusis suggest that there was an established connection between Isis and Demeter; but all the presence of such objects indicates is that the occupant of the tomb (or his or her relatives) might have visited Egypt or traded with Egyptians. See George Mylonas, *Eleusis and the Eleusinian Mysteries* (Princeton, N.J.: Princeton University Press, 1961), p. 61. The question is further complicated in the case of the Eleusinian mysteries because so little is known about their theological content. Emily Vermeule listed the many specific instances that "seem to point to aspects of the complex Egyptian iconography of the other world becoming known to the Greeks and adapted in part by them, probably at intervals between the fifteenth and the fifth centuries B.C." in *Aspects of Death in Early Greek Art and Poetry* (Berkeley: University Of California Press, 1979), p. 77. But the archaeological and documentary evidence suggests that in Eleusis the ritual did not become concerned with life after death or take the form of an initiation before the beginning of the sixth century B.C. See Christiane Sourvinou-Inwood, "Reconstructing Change: Ideology and the Eleusinian Mysteries," in *Inventing Ancient Culture: Historicism, Periodization, and*

the Ancient World, edited by Mark Golden and Peter Toohey, pp.140–141 (London: Routledge, 1996).

96. **Lucius's Initiation**. In Apuleius 11.23, the words "I stepped on the threshold of Proserpina" allude to Egyptian funerary rituals. According to the instructions appended to chapter 125 of the "Book of the Dead," if a living man recites the contents, his soul will not be held back at any gate in the west and will be "ushered in with the kings of Upper and Lower Egypt"; translation in Miriam Lichtheim, *Ancient Egyptian Literature: A Book of Readings* (Berkeley: University of California Press, 1973), vol. 2, p. 132; see John Baines, "Restricted Knowledge, Hierarchy, and Decorum: Modern Perceptions and Ancient Institutions," *Journal of the American Research Center in Egypt* 27 (1990): 14. See also Jan Assman, "Death and Initiation in the Funerary Religion of Ancient Egypt," *Religion and Philosophy in Ancient Egypt* (Yale Egyptological Studies 3; New Haven, 1989), p. 154, on Egyptian elements in Apuleius's ritual. But there is a characteristic difference in timing: Lucius is initiated while alive; the Egyptian reciter of the scroll will be allowed to cross the threshold after his death. The close personal relationship that Lucius enjoys with the divinity is also characteristic of the syncretistic "Egyptian mysteries" described by Apuleius; see Françoise Dunand, "Les syncrétismes dans la religion de l'Égypte romaine," *Études préliminaires aux religions orientales dans l'Empire romain* 46 (1975): 170. As Kevin Clinton observed in *Myth and Cult: The Iconography of the Eleusinian Mysteries* (Stockholm: Swedish Institute in

Athens, 1992), p. 131, "Isis mysteries were formed in the Hellenistic period after Greek models." Clearly there were initiatory ceremonies for Egyptian priests from which ordinary people were excluded; the question is whether these had any influence on Greek rituals established many centuries later. The chronological problems involved in tracing lines of influence in medicine apply also to other aspects of culture; see Heinrich von Staden, *Herophilus: The Art of Medicine in Early Alexandria* (Cambridge: Cambridge University Press, 1989), pp. 3–4.

103. **Egyptian Elements in the *Hermetica*.** See also David Potter, *Prophets and Emperors: Human and Divine Authority from Augustus to Theodosius* (Cambridge, Mass.: Harvard University Press, 1994), p. 193: "These versions formed popular, and then scholarly, impressions of the history and culture of Egypt . . . beneath the Greek surface there are ideas and forms that have a very real Egyptian past."

121. **Mystical Egypt.** The notion of Mystical Egypt survives in the occult world; it is still possible to buy Paul Christian's *The History and Practice of Magic* [ca. 1870], (Kila, Mont.: Kessinger Publishing, n.d.) and a book closely based on it, *Egyptian Mysteries: An Account of an Initiation* (York Beach, Maine: Samuel Weiser, 1988). Nothing in either of these reprints warns the reader that the initiations described in the book are based on fiction (by Terrasson) rather than on history.

127. **Ethiopia and Egypt**. As the abolition movement gained strength and importance, writers of African de-

scent called attention to Psalms 68:31: "Princes shall come out of Egypt and Ethiopia shall soon stretch her hand unto God." They pointed out that the Egyptian learning was imported into Greece. See St. Clair Drake, *Black Folk Here and There* (Los Angeles: Center for African American Studies, 1987), vol. 1, pp. 130–143; Leo Spitzer, "The Sierra Leone Creoles, 1870–1900," pp. 119–122 in *Africa and the West,* ed. Philip D. Curtin (Madison: University of Wisconsin Press, 1972); August Meier, *Negro Thought in America, 1800–1915: Racial Ideologies in the Age of Booker T. Washington* (Ann Arbor: University of Michigan Press, 1963), pp. 51–52, 260–61; George M. Frederickson, *Black Liberation: A Comparative History of Black Ideologies in the United States and South Africa* (New York: Oxford University Press, 1995), pp. 57–93. August Meier, in his review of *Not Out of Africa* in *The Journal of American History* 83, no. 3 (December 1996): 988, criticized me for ignoring the work of some of the black intellectuals mentioned in these sources, who "presented virtually full-blown the arguments about Egypt that are today known as Afrocentric." The reason I chose to provide a representative sampling of such writing, rather than a detailed survey, was that I had already discussed in chapter 3 the origins of the notion of Egyptian cultural influence and shown that its value as historical evidence had been greatly overestimated. I chose instead to concentrate on the origins of the myth of the "stolen legacy," which cannot be found in the eloquent and learned work of writers like Edward Wilmot Blyden (which I discuss), or of George

Wells Parker, e.g., "The African Origin of the Grecian Civilization," *The Journal of Negro History* 2, no. 3 (1917): 334–44, or in works like William Leo Hansberry's *Africa and Africans as Seen by Classical Writers: African History Notebook, vol. 2*, ed. Joseph E. Harris (Washington, D.C.: Howard University Press, 1981), or in Chancellor Williams's *The Destruction of Black Civilization: Great Issues of a Race from 4500 B.C. to 2000 A.D.* (Chicago: Third World Press, 1987), e.g., p. 297. "Ethiopianism" in African-American thought undoubtedly made it easier accept the more extravagant claims about Greek philosophy having been stolen from Africa, but it was not the source of the notion of an Egyptian Mystery System, which comes, as I have shown, from Freemasonry.

131. Meier, in his *Journal of American History* review of *Not Out of Africa*, p. 988, stated that I seem "unable to explain just how the doctrines of eighteenth-century white European Masonry might have provided a source of the tenets of twentieth-century black American Afrocentrism." Yet he acknowledged a few sentences later that "Masonry had, of course, been an important institution among Afro-Americans since the late eighteenth century." The link is made explicit by Henry Olela in *From Ancient Africa to Ancient Greece: An Introduction to the History of Philosophy*, eds. Edward F. Collins and Alveda King Beal (Atlanta: Select Publishing for Black Heritage Corporation, 1981), p. 77, who cites Albert Mackey's *Encyclopedia of Freemasonry* as the historical source for his account of the Egyptian Mystery System (EMS). The

Kemet educational system described by Kwame Nantambu in *Egypt and Afrocentric Geopolitics: Essays on European Supremacy* (Kent, Ohio: Imhotep Publishing, 1996), pp. 26–28, also is drawn from the Terrasson-based initiations described by Paul Christian in *The History and Practice of Magic*. See also Ernest Allen, Jr., "Religious Heterodoxy and Nationalist Tradition: The Continuing Evolution of the Nation of Islam," *The Black Scholar* 26 no.3–4 (Fall-Winter 1996), p.7.

134. **Why a *Stolen* Legacy?** As David Lowenthal observed in *Possessed by the Past: The Heritage Crusade and the Spoils of History* (New York: Free Press, 1996), p. 75, "atrocities are invoked as heritage not only to forge internal unity but to enlist external sympathy."

135. **On the Connections Between Ancient Egypt and the Rest of Africa.** See Theodore Celenko, ed., *Egypt in Africa* (Bloomington, Ind.: Indiana University Press, 1996).

137. **Indian Philosophers.** Alexander undoubtedly saw Indian gymnosophists and was impressed by them; see Albrecht Dihle, "Indien," in *Reallexicon für Antike und Christentum* (Stuttgart: Anton Hiersman, 1996), vol. 18, pp. 7–8. But the stories about his encounters with them follow conventional Greek philosophical patterns; see Richard Stoneman, "Naked Philosophers: The Brahmans in the Alexander Historians and the Alexander Romance," *Journal of Hellenic Studies* 115 (1995): 110–14.

149. **Atoms and Atum.** In his *JBHE* review, p. 92, Bernal revived James's suggestion about atoms (literally, "uncut,

indivisible" particles, *atoma)* and Atum, adopting a fanciful suggestion by Anthony Preus in "Greek Philosophy: Egyptian Origins," *Research Papers on the Humanities and Social Sciences* 3 (Binghamton, N.Y.: Institute of Global Cultural Studies, 1992–93), p. 8. But even if the sounds in the words *atoma* and *Atum* were as similar as Preus and Bernal suppose, we cannot be sure that the Greeks actually knew about Atum. There is no reference to Atum in the fragments of Democritus, or in ancient testimony about him, or indeed in the work of any Greek writer whose works have come down to us. Democritus, in the passage Bernal cited in support of this suggestion, did not discuss atoms or "uncut" particles; he dealt with the question of whether nothingness exists because it occupies a space. The Greek said "aught is no more real than naught" (Einarson and DeLacy's translation of *mē mallon to den ē to mēden einai,* Democritus, frag. 156 Diels-Kranz = Plutarch, *Reply to Colotes,* 1108F). The complex Egyptian idea of the nonexistent seems in any case to be somewhat different from Democritus's simple concept of nothingness, because nonexistence refers to the world before creation and continues to be intermixed with the existent in the present world. It was only associated with the Greek mythological notion of Chaos (void) by Gnostics in the late Hellenistic period; see Eric Hornung, *Conceptions of God in Ancient Egypt: The One and the Many* [1971], trans. John Baines (Ithaca, N.Y.: Cornell University Press, 1982), pp. 172–85.

150. **Analogies between *The Book of the Dead* and Orphic grave tablets**. The use of similar metaphors in

second-millennium Egyptian illustrated texts and Hellenistic gold grave tablets suggest that the writers of the Greek tablets may have been inspired by Egyptian sources; but there are significant differences in the ways that the metaphors are used in the Greek tablets, and there are other possible sources of inspiration. See Günther Zuntz, *Persephone* (Oxford: Clarendon Press, 1971), pp.370–76.

151. G. G. M. James's Influence. James's argument is also recapitulated by Olela in *From Ancient Egypt to Ancient Greece*, pp. 101–102, and by Maulana Karenga in his *Introduction to Black Studies* (Inglewood, Calif.: Kawaida Publications, 1982), pp. 174–77. According to investigative reporter Brian Burrough (personal correspondence) five different companies are now publishing *Stolen Legacy*. The president of United Brothers and United Sisters Communications in Hampton, Va., H. Khalifa Khalifah, estimates that there are now more than 500,000 copies in circulation.

173. Academic Freedom. For the courts' views on academic freedom, see *Jeffries v. Harleston* 52 F3d at 14. For an illuminating discussion of the dangers of compromising academic freedom, see Neil W. Hamilton, "Contrasts and Comparisons Among McCarthyism, 1960s Student Activism, and Faculty Fundamentalism," *William Mitchell Law Review* 22, no. 2 (1996): 369–413.

BIBLIOGRAPHY

(* denotes suggested for further reading)

Adler, Karen S. "'Always Leading Our Men in Service and Sacrifice': Amy Jacques Garvey, Feminist Black Nationalist." *Gender & Society* 6, no. 3 (1992): 346–75.

Allen, Jr., Ernest. "Religious Heterodoxy and Nationalist Tradition: The Continuing Evolution of the Nation of Islam," *The Black Scholar* 26 no.3–4 (Fall-Winter 1996): 2–34.

Anthes, Rudolf. "Affinity and Difference Between Egyptian and Greek Sculpture and Thought in the Seventh and Sixth Centuries, B.C." *Proc. Am. Philos. Soc.* 107 (1963): 60–81.

Armayor, O. Kimball. *Herodotus' Autopsy of the Fayoum: Lake Moeris and the Labyrinth of Egypt.* Amsterdam: Gieben, 1985.

Asante, Molefi Kete. *Kemet, Afrocentricity and Knowledge.* Trenton, N.J.: Africa World Press, 1990.

———. "On the Wings of Nonsense." *Black Books Bulletin: Wordswork* 16, no. 1–2 (1993–94): 38–41.

————. "Social Sciences." *The Camden African–Puerto Rican Centric Guide.* Camden, N.J.: Camden Board of Education, n.d., pp. 110–26.

Assman, Jan. "Death and Initiation in the Funerary Religion of Ancient Egypt." *Yale Egyptological Studies* 3 (1989): 135–53.

Baigent, Michael, and Richard Leigh. *The Temple and the Lodge.* New York: Arcade Publishing, 1989.

Baines, John. "Restricted Knowledge, Hierarchy, and Decorum: Modern Perceptions and Ancient Institutions." *Journal of the American Research Center in Egypt* 27 (1990): 1–23.

Bard, Kathryn. "Ancient Egyptians and the Issue of Race." *Bostonia* 7, no. 3 (Summer 1992). Reprinted in Lefkowitz and Rogers, eds., *Black Athena Revisited,* pp. 105–11.

Barnes, Jonathan. *Early Greek Philosophy.* Harmondsworth, England: Penguin, 1987.

Barthélémy, Jean-Jacques. *Voyage du jeune Anacharsis en Grèce.* Vol. 1. Paris: Librarie Dupont, 1826.

ben-Jochannan, Yosef A. A. *Africa, Mother of Western Civilization* [1971]. Baltimore: Black Classic Press, 1988.

————. *African Origins of the Major "Western Religions":* Baltimore: Black Classic Press, 1991 [1970].

Berlinerblau, Jacques. "Black Athena Redux." *The Nation,* October 28, 1996, pp. 42–48.

Bernal, Martin. *Black Athena: The Afroasiatic Roots of Classical Civilization. Vol. I: The Fabrication of Ancient Greece.* New Brunswick, N.J.: Rutgers University Press, 1987.

————. *Black Athena: The Afroasiatic Roots of Classical Civilization. Vol. II: The Archaeological and Documentary Evidence.* New Brunswick, N.J.: Rutgers University Press, 1991.

————. "Animadversions on the Origins of Western Science." *Isis* 83 (1992): 596–607.

————. "Socrates' Ancestry in Question." Letter to the editor. *Academic Questions* (Summer 1994).

——. "The Afrocentric Interpretation of History: Bernal Replies to Lefkowitz." *Journal of Blacks in Higher Education* 12 (Spring 1996): 86–94.

——. "Rocking the Cradle." *The Bookpress* (Ithaca, N.Y.) 6, no. 7 (November 1996): 11–12.

——. "Whose Greece?" *London Review of Books,* December 12, 1996, pp. 17–18.

Bernstein, Richard. *Dictatorship of Virtue: Multiculturalism and the Battle for America's Future.* New York: Knopf, 1994.

Bietak, Manfred. *Avaris: The Capital of the Hyksos: Recent Excavations at Tell el-Dab'a.* London: British Museum Press, 1996.

Blanco, Walter, ed. and trans., and Jennifer Tolbert Roberts, ed. *Herodotus: The Histories.* New York: Norton, 1992.

*Blok, Josine. "Proof and Persuasion in *Black Athena*: The Case of K. O. Müller." *Journal of the History of Ideas* 57, no. 4 (1996): 705–24.

Bloomfield, Morton H. *The Seven Deadly Sins.* Lansing: Michigan State University Press, 1952.

Blyden, Edward Wilmot. "The Negro in Ancient History." In *The People of Africa: A Series of Papers on Their Character, Condition, and Future Prospects.* Edited by Henry Maunsell Schieffelin. New York: A. D. F. Randolph, 1871.

——. *Christianity, Islam and the Negro Race* [1887]. Edinburgh: Edinburgh University Press, 1967.

*Boas, George. *The Hieroglyphics of Horapollo.* Bollingen Series. New York: Pantheon Books, 1950.

Boorstin, Daniel J. "Afterlives of the Great Pyramid." *Wilson Quarterly* 16, no.3 (Summer 1992): 130–38.

Bork, Robert. *Slouching Towards Gomorrah: Modern Liberalism and American Decline.* New York: ReganBooks, 1996.

Boulenger, Fernand, ed. *Saint Basile: Aux Jeunes Gens sur la manière de tirer profit des lettres helléniques.* Paris: Les Belles Lettres, 1952.

Bowersock, Glen. *The New York Times Book Review,* February 25, 1996, p. 6.

Brace, C. Loring, with David P. Tracer, Lucia Allen Yaroch, John Robb, Kari Brandt, and A. Russell Nelson, "Clines and Clusters Versus 'Race'." *Yearbook of Physical Anthropology* 37 (1994). Reprinted in Lefkowitz and Rogers, eds., *Black Athena Revisited,* pp. 129–64.

Braunbehrens, Volkmar. *Mozart in Vienna.* Translated by Timothy Bell. New York: Grove Weidenfeld, 1986.

Breasted, James Henry. *Development of Religion and Thought in Ancient Egypt.* New York: Charles Scribner's Sons, 1912.

Brisson, Luc. "L'Égypte de Platon." *Les Études philosophiques* N.S. 2–3 (1987): 153–68.

Brooke, John L. *The Refiner's Fire: The Making of Mormon Cosmology.* Cambridge: Cambridge University Press, 1994.

Brotz, Howard, ed. *Negro Social and Political Thought 1850–1920: Representative Texts.* New York: Basic Books, 1966.

Brown, Peter. *Augustine of Hippo: A Biography.* Berkeley: University of California Press, 1969.

———. *The Cult of the Saints: Its Rise and Function in Latin Christianity.* Chicago: University of Chicago Press, 1981.

Brunés, Ton. *The Secrets of Ancient Geometry—and Its Use.* Translated by Charles H. Napier. Copenhagen: Rhodos, 1967.

Bryan, Cyril P. *Ancient Egyptian Medicine: The Papyrus Ebers.* Chicago: Ares Publishers, 1974.

Burkert, Walter. *Lore and Science in Ancient Pythagoreanism.* Translated by Edwin L. Minar, Jr. Cambridge, Mass.: Harvard University Press, 1972.

———. *Greek Religion: Archaic and Classical.* Translated by John Raffan. Cambridge, Mass.: Harvard University Press, 1985.

———. *Ancient Mystery Cults.* Cambridge, Mass.: Harvard University Press, 1987.

———. *The Orientalizing Revolution: Near Eastern Influence on Greek Culture in the Early Archaic Age.* Translated by M. E. Pinder and W. Burkert. Cambridge, Mass.: Harvard University Press, 1992.

*Burstein, Stanley M. *Graeco-Africana: Studies in the History of Greek Relations with Egypt and Nubia.* New Rochelle, N.Y.: Aristide Caratzas, 1995.

Butty, David. "Afrocentrism generates mixed results in Detroit and debate across nation," *The Detroit News,* May 19, 1996 [http://www.detnews.com/menu/stories/48444.htm].

Cameron, Alan. "Two Mistresses of Ptolemy Philadelphus." *Greek, Roman and Byzantine Studies* 30 (1990): 287–92.

Campbell, David A. *Greek Lyric.* Loeb Classical Library. Cambridge, Mass.: Harvard University Press, 1982.

Carson, Tom. "Greece is the Word." *The Village Voice,* April 16, 1996, pp. 20–21.

*Celenko, Theodore, ed. *Egypt in Africa.* Bloomington: Indiana University Press, 1996.

Chadwick, Henry. *Early Christian Thought and the Classical Tradition.* Oxford: Clarendon Press, 1966.

Chailley, Jacques. *The Magic Flute, Masonic Opera.* Translated by Herbert Weinstock. New York: Knopf, 1971.

Chantraine, Pierre. *Dictionnaire étymologique de la langue grecque.* Paris: Éditions Klincksieck, 1984.

Charlesworth, James H. *The Old Testament Pseudepigrapha.* Garden City, N.Y.: Doubleday, 1985.

Christian, Paul (a.k.a. Jean Baptiste). *The History and Practice of Magic* [1870]. Kila, Mont.: Kessinger Publishing, n.d.

Clark, Gillian, ed. and trans. *Iamblichus: On the Pythagorean Life.* Translated Texts for Historians. Liverpool: Liverpool University Press, 1989.

Clarke, John Henrik. "African Warrior Queens." *Journal of African Civilization* 6, no. 1, 1984: 123–34. = *Black Women in Antiquity*. Edited by Ivan van Sertima. New Brunswick, N.J.: Transaction Books, 1988.

Clinton, Kevin. *Myth and Cult: The Iconography of the Eleusinian Mysteries*. Stockholm: Swedish Institute in Athens, 1992.

Conyers, James L., Jr., review in *Journal of Black Studies* 27 (September 1996): 130–31.

*Copenhaver, Brian P. *Hermetica*. Cambridge: Cambridge University Press, 1992.

Cornford, Francis. *Plato's Cosmology: The Timaeus of Plato*. Translated with a running commentary. London: Routledge & Kegan Paul, 1937.

Coughlin, Ellen. "Not Out of Africa." *Chronicle of Higher Education* (April 12, 1996): A8.

Cronon, E. David. *Black Moses: Marcus Garvey and the Universal Negro Improvement Association*. Madison: University of Wisconsin Press, 1955.

Cudjoe, Selwyn. "Not a Racist Polemic . . . ." *Boston Globe*, April 21, 1996, p. 85.

Curtin, Philip D., ed. *Africa and the West*. Madison: University of Wisconsin Press, 1972.

Decleva Caizzi, Fernanda. *Pirrone, Testimonianze*. Elenchos 5. Milan: Bibliopolis, 1981.

De Clifford, Norman Frederick. *Egypt: the Cradle of Ancient Masonry*. Philadelphia: Lincoln Publishing, 1902.

*Dent, Edward J. *Mozart's Operas*, 2d ed. Oxford: Clarendon Press, 1960.

de Ste. Croix, G. E. M. "Were the Early Christians Persecuted?" *Past and Present* 26 (November 1963): 6–38.

Diels, Hermann, and Walther Kranz, eds. *Die Fragmente der Vorsokratiker*. Berlin: Weidmannsche Verlagsbuchhandlung, 1956.

Dihle, Albrecht. "Indien." In *Reallexicon für Antike und Christen-tum.* Vol. 18. Stuttgart: Anton Hiersman, 1996, pp. 1–56.

Dillon, John, and Jackson P. Hershbell. *Iamblichus: On the Pythagorean Way of Life.* Texts and Translations 29: Graeco-Roman Religion Series 11. Atlanta: Scholars Press, 1991.

Diop, Cheikh Anta. *Precolonial Black Africa* [1960]. Translated by Harold Salemsen. Brooklyn, N.Y.: Lawrence Hill Books, 1987.

―――. *Civilization or Barbarism: An Authentic Anthropology* [1981]. Translated by Yaa-Lengi Meema Ngemi. Brooklyn, N.Y.: Lawrence Hill Books, 1991.

*Donadoni, Sergio, Silvio Curto, and Anna Maria Donadoni-Roveri. *Egypt from Myth to Egyptology.* Translated by Elizabeth Poore and Francesco L. Rossi. Turin: Istituto Bancario San Paolo, 1990.

*Drake, St. Clair. *Black Folk Here and There.* Los Angeles: Center for Afro-American Studies, 1987.

Duffy, Thomas. "Fear and the Power of Don Muhammed." *Boston Magazine,* January 1995, pp. 68–69, 114–15.

Dumenil, Lynn. *Freemasonry and American Culture.* Princeton, N.J.: Princeton University Press, 1984.

Dunand, Françoise. "Les syncrétismes dans la religion de l'É-gypte romaine." *Études préliminaires aux religions orien-tales dans l'Empire romain* 46 (1975): 152–85.

Düring, Ingemar. *Aristoteles.* Heidelberg: Carl Winter, 1966.

Dyson, Michael Eric. *Reflecting Black African American Cultural Criticism.* Minneapolis: University of Minnesota Press, 1993.

*Early, Gerald. "Understanding Afrocentrism: Why Blacks Dream of a World Without Whites." *Civilization,* July/August 1995, pp. 31–39.

Eckelmeyer, Judith A. *The Cultural Context of Mozart's Magic Flute.* Studies in the History and Interpretation of Music. Lewiston, N.Y.: Edwin Mellen Press, 1991.

Eliot, George. *Middlemarch*. New York: Collier Books, 1962.

*Ellis, John M. *Against Deconstruction*. Princeton, N.J.: Princeton University Press, 1989.

Elson, John. "Attacking Afrocentrism." *Time,* February 19, 1996, p. 66.

Fairchild, Halford H. "Knowing Black History Isn't Just for Blacks." *Los Angeles Times,* February 5, 1995, sec. M, p. 5.

Farrar, Cynthia. *The Origins of Democratic Thinking*. Cambridge: Cambridge University Press, 1988.

Faulkner, Raymond O., trans. *The Ancient Egyptian Book of the Dead*. Edited by Carol Andrews [1985]. Austin: University of Texas Press, 1990.

Fehling, Detlev. *Herodotus and His "Sources."* Translated by J. G. Howie. Leeds: Francis Cairns, 1989.

Fénelon, François. *Les Aventures de Télémaque* [1699]. Nouvelle édition. Edited by A. Chassang. Paris: Hachette, 1918.

Finn, Chester E., Jr. "Cleopatra's Nose." *Commentary* 101, no. 6 (June 1996): 71–72.

FGrHist. *Die Fragmente der griechischen Historiker*. Edited by Felix Jacoby. Leiden: Brill, 1923–57.

"The First Mason, A Black Man." *Colored American Magazine* 6, no. 4 (1903).

Flintoff, Everard. "Pyrrho and India." *Phronesis* 85 (1980): 88–108.

*Fowden, Garth. *The Egyptian Hermes*. Cambridge: Cambridge University Press, 1986.

Fraenkel, Eduard. *Aeschylus: Agamemnon*. Oxford: Clarendon Press, 1950.

Frankfort, Henri. *Ancient Egyptian Religion: An Interpretation*. New York: Columbia University Press, 1948.

———. *Kingship and the Gods*. Chicago: University of Chicago Press, 1948.

Fraser, P. M. *Ptolemaic Alexandria*. Oxford: Clarendon Press, 1972.

*Frederickson, George M. *Black Liberation: A Comparative History of Black Ideologies in the United States and South Africa*. New York: Oxford University Press, 1995.

Frend, W. H. *The Donatist Church*. Oxford: Clarendon Press, 1952.

———. *Martyrdom and Persecution in the Early Church*. Oxford: Basil Blackwell, 1965.

*Froidefond, Christian. *Le mirage égyptien dans la littérature grecque d'Homère à Aristote*. Aix-en-Provence, France: Ophrys, 1971.

Gantz, Timothy. *Early Greek Myth: A Guide to the Literary and Artistic Sources*. Baltimore: Johns Hopkins University Press, 1993.

Gates, Henry Louis, Jr. "Black Demagogues and Pseudo-Scholars." *The New York Times,* July 20 1992, p. A15.

Gillespie, Charles C. "The Scientific Importance of Napoleon's Egyptian Campaign." *Scientific American,* September 1994, pp. 78–85.

Gimbutas, Marija. *The Language of the Goddess*. San Francisco: Harper & Row, 1989.

Glazer, Nathan. "Levin, Jeffries, and the Fate of Academic Autonomy." *William and Mary Law Review* 36, no. 2 (January 1995): 703–32.

———. Letter to *The New York Times Book Review,* March 17, 1996, p. 4.

Gould, John. *Herodotus*. New York: St. Martin's Press, 1989.

———. "Herodotus and Religion." In *Greek Historiography*, edited by Simon Hornblower, 91–106. Oxford: Clarendon Press, 1994.

Gow, A. S. F., and D. L. Page. *The Greek Anthology: Hellenistic Epigrams*. Cambridge: Cambridge University Press, 1965.

Grafton, Anthony. *Forgers and Critics*. Princeton, N.J.: Princeton University Press, 1990.

———. *Defenders of the Text*. Cambridge, Mass.: Harvard University Press, 1991.

Gratwick, Adrian S. "Hanno's Punic Speech in the Poenulus of Plautus." *Hermes* 99 (1971): 25–45.

Grene, David, trans. *Herodotus: The History.* Chicago: University of Chicago Press, 1987.

Grimshaw, William H. *Official History of Freemasonry Among the Colored Peoples of North America* [1903]. New York: Greenwood Press, 1969.

*Gross, Paul R., and Norman Levitt. *Higher Superstition: The Academic Left and Its Quarrels with Science.* Baltimore: Johns Hopkins University Press, 1994.

Gross, Paul R., Norman Levitt, and Martin W. Lewis, eds. *The Flight from Science and Reason.* Annals of the New York Academy of Sciences. Vol. 775. New York: New York Academy of Sciences, 1996.

Groves, Charles Pelham. *The Planting of Christianity in Africa.* London: Lutterworth Press, 1964.

Gwyn Griffiths, J. "A Translation from the Egyptian by Eudoxus." *Classical Quarterly* N.S. 15 (1965): 75–78.

———. *Plutarch's De Iside et Osiride.* Swansea: University of Wales Press, 1970.

———, ed. *Apuleius of Madauros: The Isis-Book.* Études préliminaires aux religions orientales dans l'empire romain. Leiden: Brill, 1975.

Haack, Susan. "Puzzling Out Science." *Academic Questions* 8, no. 2 (1995): 20–31.

Haley, Shelley P. "Black Feminist Thought and the Classics: Remembering, Re-claiming, Re-empowering." In *Feminist Theory and the Classics,* edited by N. S. Rabinowitz and Amy Richlin, 23–43. London: Routledge, 1993.

Hamilton, Neil W. "Contrasts and Comparisons Among McCarthyism, 1960s Student Activism, and Faculty Fundamentalism." *William Mitchell Law Review* 22, no. 2 (1996): 369–413.

Hansberry, William Leo. *Africa and Africans as Seen by Classical Writers: The William Leo Hansberry African History Notebook, Vol. 2.* Edited by Joseph E. Harris. Washington, D.C.: Howard University Press, 1981.

Harder, Annette. *Euripides' Kresphontes and Archelaos.* Leiden: Brill, 1985.

*Harris, J.R., ed. *The Legacy of Egypt* Ed.2. Oxford: Clarendon Press, 1971.

Harten, Stuart. "Archaeology and the Unconscious: Hegel, Egyptomania, and the Legitimation of Orientalism," in *Egypt and the Fabrication of European Identity.* Edited by Irene A. Bierman, 3-33. Los Angeles: Center for Near Eastern Studies, UCLA 1995.

Harvey, A. E. *The New English Bible: Companion to the New Testament.* Cambridge/Oxford: Cambridge University Press/ Oxford University Press, 1970.

Hengel, Martin. *Judaism and Hellenism.* Translated by John Bowden. Philadelphia: Fortress Press, 1974.

Hercher, R., ed. *Epistolographi Graeci.* Paris: Didot, 1871.

Herskovits, Melville J. *The Myth of the Negro Past* [1941]. Boston: Beacon Press, 1958.

Hill, Robert A., ed. *Marcus Garvey and Universal Negro Improvement Association Papers.* Berkeley: University of California Press, 1983.

Hill, Robert A., and Barbara Blair. *Marcus Garvey: Life and Lessons.* Berkeley: University of California Press, 1987.

Hofstadter, Richard. *The Paranoid Style in American Politics.* New York: Knopf, 1965.

Holden, Edith. *Blyden of Liberia.* New York: Vantage Press, 1966.

Hollinger, David A. *Postethnic America.* New York: Basic Books, 1995.

Honolka, Kurt. *Papageno: Emmanuel Shikaneder.* Translated by Jane Mary Wilde. Portland, Oreg.: Amadeus Press, 1990.

Hopfner, Theodor. *Plutarch über Isis und Osiris* [1941]. Darmstadt: Wissenschafliches Buchgesellschaft, 1967.

Hornung, Eric. *Conceptions of God in Ancient Egypt: The One and the Many* [1971]. Translated by John Baines. Ithaca, N.Y.: Cornell University Press, 1982.

Horsely, Lynn. "Ladd elementary becomes second Afrocentric School," *Kansas City Star,* November 7, 1996, pp. B 1, 4.

Hughes-Hallett, Lucy. *Cleopatra: Histories, Dreams and Distortions.* New York: Harper Perennial, 1990.

"Iamblichus." *Egyptian Mysteries* [1870]. York Beach, Maine: Samuel Weiser, 1988. Excerpted from Christian, The History and Practice of Magic, book II.

*Iversen, Erik. *The Myth of Egypt and Its Hieroglyphs in European Tradition* [1961]. Princeton, N.J.: Princeton University Press, 1993.

———. *Egyptian and Hermetic Doctrine.* Opuscula Graecolatina. Copenhagen: Museum Tusculanum Press, 1984.

Jackson, D. "The Cleopatra Caper." *East Bay Express,* October 4, 1991, p. 4.

Jackson, John G. *Introduction to African Civilization* [1970]. New York: Citadel Press, 1990

Jacob, Margaret C. *The Radical Enlightenment.* London: Allen & Unwin, 1981.

Jacobson, Howard. *The Exagoge of Ezekiel.* Cambridge: Cambridge University Press, 1983.

Jahn, Otto. *W. A. Mozart.* Revised and enlarged. Edited by Hermann Abert. Leipzig: Breitkopf & Härtel, 1923.

James, George G. M. *Stolen Legacy.* New York: Philosophical Library, 1954.

James, T. G. H. *Ancient Egypt: The Land and Its Legacy.* Austin: University of Texas Press, 1990.

*Jasanoff, Jay, and Alan Nussbaum. "Word Games." In Lefkowitz and Rogers, eds., *Black Athena Revisited*, pp. 177–205.

Jenkyns, Richard. "Bernal and the Nineteenth Century." In

Lefkowitz and Rogers, eds., *Black Athena Revisited*, pp. 411–20.

Johnson-Odim, Cheryl. "The Debate Over Black Athena." *Journal of Women's History* 4, no. 3 (Winter 1993): 84–89.

Kahn, Charles H. *Anaximander and the Origins of Greek Cosmology*. New York: Columbia University Press, 1960.

Kaiser, Martin. "Herodots Begegnung mit Ägypten." In Morenz, *Die Begegnung Europas mit Ägypten*, pp. 243–65.

Karenga, Maulana. *Introduction to Black Studies*. Inglewood, Calif.: Kawaida Publications, 1982.

Karenga, Maulana. *Selections from the Husia: Sacred Wisdom of Ancient Egypt*. Los Angeles: Kwanda Publications, 1984.

*Kaster, Joseph. *The Wisdom of Ancient Egypt: Writings from the Time of the Pharaohs* [1968]. London: Michael O'Mara Books, 1995.

Kaster, Robert A. *Guardians of Language: The Grammarian and Society in Late Antiquity*. Berkeley: University of California Press, 1988.

Keita, S. O. Y. "Studies and Comments on Ancient Egyptian Biological Relationships." *History in Africa* 20 (1993): 129–54.

Kidd, Beresford James. *A History of the Church to A.D. 461*. Oxford: Clarendon Press, 1922.

Kimball, Roger. "Greece for the Greeks: History Is Not Bunk." *Wall Street Journal*, February 14, 1996, p. A12.

Kirk, G. S., J. E. Raven, and M. Schofield, eds. *The Presocratic Philosophers*, 2d ed. Cambridge: Cambridge University Press, 1983.

Knauer, Elfriede Regina. *Urnula Faberrime Cavata: Observations on a Vessel Used in the Cult of Isis*. Beiträge zur Altertumskunde, 63. Stuttgart: Teubner, 1995.

Koch, Hans-Albrecht, ed. *Wolfgang Amadeus Mozart, Die Zauberflöte*. Stuttgart: Philipp Reclam, Jr., 1991.

Lambropoulos, Vassilis. *The Rise of Eurocentrism: Anatomy of Interpretation*. Princeton, N.J.: Princeton University Press,

1993.

Landon Robbins, H. C. *Mozart and the Masons: New Light on the Lodge of "Crowned Hope."* London: Thames & Hudson, 1982.

———. *1791: Mozart's Last Year,* 2d ed. London: Thames & Hudson, 1989.

Lasserre, François. *Eudoxos von Knidos.* Texte und Kommentare. Berlin: de Gruyter, 1966.

*Lefkowitz, Mary R., and Guy MacLean Rogers, eds. *Black Athena Revisited.* Chapel Hill: University of North Carolina Press, 1996.

Lefkowitz, Mary R. *The Lives of the Greek Poets.* Baltimore: Johns Hopkins University Press, 1981.

———. "Aristophanes and Other Historians of the Fifth-Century Theater." *Hermes* 112 (1984): 143–53.

———. "Was Euripides an Atheist?" *Studi Italiani di Filologia Classica* 5, no. 2 (1987): 149–66. Series III.

———. "Commentary on Vlastos." Proceedings of the Boston Area Colloquium in Ancient Philosophy. Lanham, Md.: University Press of America, 1991.

———. "Not Out of Africa." *The New Republic,* February 1992, pp. 29–36. Reprinted as "Ancient History: Modern Myths," in Lefkowitz and Rogers, eds., *Black Athena Revisited*, pp. 3–23.

———. "Afrocentrism Poses a Threat to the Rationalist Tradition." *Chronicle of Higher Education* (May 6, 1992): A52.

———. "Ethnocentric History from Aristobulus to Bernal." *Academic Questions* 6, no. 2 (1993): 12–20.

———. "Afrocentrists Wage War on Ancient Greeks." *Wall Street Journal,* July 4, 1993, p. A14.

———. "Combating False Theories in the Classroom." *Chronicle of Higher Education* (January 19, 1994): B1-B3.

———. "The Myth of a 'Stolen Legacy'." *Society* 31, no. 3 (1994): 27–33.

———. "Whatever Happened to Historical Evidence?" In Gross, Levitt, and Lewis, eds., *The Flight from Science and Reason*, pp. 301–12.

———. "The Afrocentric Interpretation of Western History: Lefkowitz Replies to Bernal." *Journal of Blacks in Higher Education* 12 (Summer 1996): 88–91.

le Glay, Marcel. "Aion." In *Lexicon Iconographicum Mythologiae Classicae* (LIMC) I. Zürich: Artemis Verlag, 1981, pp., 398–411.

Lenoir, Marie Alexandre. *La franche-maçonnerie rendue à sa véritable origine, ou L'antiquité de la Franche-maçonnerie prouvée par l'explication des mystères anciens et modernes.* Paris: Fourniet, 1814.

Lerner, Gerda. *The Creation of Patriarchy.* New York: Oxford University Press, 1986.

*Levine, Molly. "The Use and Abuse of *Black Athena*." *American Historical Review* 97, no. 2 (1992): 440–60.

*Lichtheim, Miriam. *Ancient Egyptian Literature: A Book of Readings.* Berkeley: University of California Press, 1973.

Lloyd, Alan B. *Herodotus, Book II.* Leiden: Brill, 1975–88.

Lloyd, G. E. R. "The Debt of Greek Philosophy and Science to the Ancient Near East." In *Methods and Problems in Greek Science: Selected Papers*, 281–98. Cambridge: Cambridge University Press, 1991.

Long, Anthony A. *Hellenistic Philosophy.* London: Duckworth, 1974.

Loprieno, Antonio. *Ancient Egyptian: A Linguistic Introduction.* Cambridge: Cambridge University Press, 1995.

Loury, Glenn. "Color Blinded," *Arion* 4.4 (Winter 1997): 168–85.

Lowenthal, David. *Possessed by the Past: The Heritage Crusade and the Spoils of History.* New York: Free Press, 1996.

Lynch, Hollis R. *Edward Wilmot Blyden: Pan-Negro Patriot 1832–1912.* London: Oxford University Press, 1967.

———. "Preface to the Atheneum Edition." In *Philosophy and*

Opinions of Marcus Garvey, edited by Amy Jacques-Garvey. New York: Atheneum, 1971.

MacGregor, Alexander. "Gellius 17.8.7: The Roots of Africa." *Classical Journal* 87 (1991): 9–12.

Mackey, A. G. *The History of Freemasonry* [1898]. New York: Masonic History Company, 1906.

Magnet, Myron. *The Dream and the Nightmare: The Sixties' Legacy to the Underclass.* New York: William Morrow, 1993.

Malamud, Martha. "Review of *Black Athena 1.*" *Criticism* 31, no. 3 (1989): 317–22.

Málek, Jaromir. *The Cat in Ancient Egypt.* London: British Museum Press, 1993.

Manfredini, Mario, and Luigi Piccirilli. *Plutarco, La Vita di Solone.* Rome: Arnaldo Mondadori, 1977.

Manuel, Frank. *The Eighteenth Century Confronts the Gods.* Cambridge, Mass.: Harvard University Press, 1959.

Martel, Erich. "What's Wrong With the Portland Baseline Essays?" In *Alternatives to Afrocentrism,* edited by John Miller, 37–42. Washington, D.C.: Manhattan Institute, 1993=pp. 30–34 in the second edition (1996).

Martin, Tony. *Race First: The Ideological and Organizational Struggles of Marcus Garvey and the Universal Negro Improvement Association* [1976]. Dover, Mass.: The Majority Press, 1986.

———. *The Jewish Onslaught: Despatches from the Wellesley Battlefront.* Dover, Mass.: The Majority Press, 1993.

Mastandrea, Paolo. *Massimo di Madauros.* Padua: Editoriale Programma, 1985.

Mazrui, Ali A. *Political Values and the Educated Class in Africa.* Berkeley: University of California Press, 1978.

Means, Sterling. "Black Egypt and Her Negro Pharaohs." In *Ethiopia and the Missing Link in African History,* 53–65. Baltimore: Black Classic Press, 1945.

Meier, August. *Negro Thought in America, 1880–1915: Racial Ideologies in the Age of Booker T. Washington.* Ann Arbor: University of Michigan Press, 1963.

———. *Journal of American History* 83, no. 3 (December 1996): 988.

Merlan, Philip. "The Pythagoreans." In *Cambridge History of Later Greek and Early Medieval Philosophy*, edited by A. H. Armstrong, 84–106. Cambridge: Cambridge University Press, 1967.

*Miller, John, ed. *Alternatives to Afrocentrism*, 2d ed. Washington, D.C.: Center for the New American Community, 1996.

Miller, Stephen. "The Future of Disinterest and Foucault's Regime of Truth." *Partisan Review* 64, no. 1 (Winter 1997): 28–36.

Migne, J. P., ed. *Patrologia Latina.* Paris: Garnier Frères, 1844–64.

———, ed. *Patrologia Graeca.* Paris: Migne, 1857–66.

Mitchell, Eugene M. "Greek to Me." Letter to the editor. *The New Republic,* March 2, 1992, p. 6.

Momigliano, Arnaldo. *Alien Wisdom: The Limits of Hellenization.* Cambridge: Cambridge University Press, 1975.

———. "Ebrei e Greci." In *Sesto Contributo*, 527–47. Rome: Edizione di Storia e Letteratura, 1980.

———. *The Classical Foundations of Modern Historiography.* Berkeley: University of California Press, 1990.

*Morenz, Siegfried. *Die Zauberflöte: Eine Studie zum Lebenszusammenanhang Ägypten-Antike-Abendland.* Münstersche Forschungen 5. Münster: Bülau Verlag, 1952.

*———. *Die Begegnung Europas mit Ägypten.* Zurich: Artemis-Verlag, 1969.

———. *Egyptian Religion.* Translated by Ann E. Keep. Ithaca, N.Y.: Cornell University Press, 1973.

Morgan, John. "Make-Believe and Make Believe: The Fictionality of the Greek Novels." In *Lies and Fiction in the Ancient*

World, edited by Christopher Gill and T. P. Wiseman, 175–229. Austin: University of Texas Press, 1993.

Moses, Wilson J. *The Golden Age of Black Nationalism* [1978]. New York: Oxford University Press, 1988.

Muraskin, William A. *Middle-Class Blacks in a White Society: Prince Hall Freemasonry in America*. Berkeley: University of California Press, 1975.

Musurillo, Herbert, ed. and trans. *The Acts of the Christian Martyrs*. Oxford: Clarendon Press, 1972.

Mylonas, George. *Eleusis and the Eleusinian Mysteries*. Princeton, N.J.: Princeton University Press, 1961.

Mynors, R. A. B. *Virgil, Georgics*. Oxford: Clarendon Press, 1990.

Nauck, August. *Tragicorum Graecorum Fragmenta*, 2d ed. Leipzig: Teubner Verlag, 1889.

Nantambu, Kwame. *Egypt and Afrocentric Geopolitics: Essays on European Supremacy*. Kent, Ohio: Imhotep Publishing, 1996.

Naudon, Paul. *Histoire générale de la Franc-Maçonnerie*. Paris: Presses Universitaires de France, 1981.

Nettl, Paul. *Mozart and Masonry*. New York: Philosophical Library, 1957.

Nibley, Hugh. *The Message of the Joseph Smith Papyri: An Egyptian Endowment*. Salt Lake City: Deseret Book Company, 1976.

Nock, Arthur Darby. *Essays on Religion and the Ancient World*. Edited by Zeph Stewart. Oxford: Clarendon Press, 1972.

O'Donnell, James J., ed. *Augustine, Confessions*. Oxford: Clarendon Press, 1992.

Olela, Henry. *From Ancient Africa to Ancient Greece: An Introduction to the History of Philosophy*. Edited by Edward F. Collins and Alveda King Beal. Atlanta: Select Publishing for Black Heritage Corporation, 1981.

*Ortiz de Montellano, Bernard. "Spreading Scientific Illiteracy Among Minorities. Part I: Multicultural Pseudoscience,"

Skeptical Inquirer 16 (Fall 1991): 46–50.

*———. "Spreading Scientific Illiteracy Among Minorities. Part II: Magic Melanin." *Skeptical Inquirer* 16 (Winter 1991): 62–66.

*———. "Afrocentric Creationism." *Creation/Evolution* 29 (Winter 1991–92): 1–8

*———. "Melanin, Afrocentricity, and Pseudoscience." *Yearbook of Physical Anthropology* 36 (1993): 33–58.

*———. "Afrocentric Pseudoscience: The Miseducation of African Americans." In Gross, Levitt, and Lewis, eds., *The Flight from Science and Reason,* pp. 561–72.

———. "Avoiding Egyptocentric Pseudoscience: Colleges Must Help Set Standards for Schools." *Chronicle of Higher Education* (March 25, 1996): B1–B2.

Orwell, George. *Nineteen Eighty-Four.* New York: Harcourt Brace, 1949.

*Palter, Robert. "*Black Athena,* Afro-Centrism, and the History of Science." *History of Science* 31 (1993): 227–87. Reprinted in Lefkowitz and Rogers, eds., *Black Athena Revisited,* pp. 209–66.

Parker, George Wells. "The African Origin of the Grecian Civilization." *Journal of Negro History* 2, no. 3 (1917): 334–44.

———. *Children of the Sun* [1918]. Atlanta: Black Classic Press, 1978.

Patai, Daphne, and Noretta Koertge. *Professing Feminism.* New York: Basic Books, 1994.

Patterson, Orlando. *Harvard Educational Review* 41, no. 3 (1971): 297–315.

———. *Freedom.* New York: Basic Books, 1991.

Perry, Ben Edwin. *Aesopica.* Urbana: University of Illinois Press, 1952.

Pfeiffer, Rudolf. *History of Classical Scholarship from the Beginnings to the End of the Hellenistic Age.* Oxford: Clarendon Press, 1968.

Pomeroy, Sarah B. *Women in Hellenistic Egypt.* New York: Schocken Books, 1984.

Potter, David. *Prophets and Emperors: Human and Divine Authority from Augustus to Theodosius.* Cambridge, Mass.: Harvard University Press, 1994.

Poulianos, Aris N. *I Proelefsi ton Ellinon,* 4th ed. Petralona, Khalkhidiki: Daphni, 1988.

Pratt, John Clark, and Victor A. Neufeldt, eds. *George Eliot's Middlemarch Notebooks.* Berkeley: University of California Press, 1979.

Preus, Anthony. "Aristotle on Africa." *Research Papers on the Humanities and Social Sciences* 7. Binghamton, N.Y.: Institute of Global Cultural Studies, 1992.

———. "Greek Philosophy: Egyptian Origins." *Research Papers on the Humanities and Social Sciences* 3. Binghamton, N.Y.: Institute of Global Cultural Studies, 1992–93.

Rabinowitz, Nancy Sorkin. "Introduction." In *Feminist Theory and the Classics,* edited by N. S. Rabinowitz and Amy Richlin, 1–20. London: Routledge, 1993.

Rahe, Paul A. *Republics Ancient and Modern: Classical Republicanism and the American Revolution.* Chapel Hill: University of North Carolina Press, 1992.

Rawlinson, George, trans. *Herodotus: The Persian Wars.* Edited by Francis Godolphin. New York: Modern Library, 1942.

Redford, Donald B. *Egypt, Canaan, and Israel in Ancient Times.* Princeton, N.J.: Princeton University Press, 1992.

Reggiani, Clara Krauss. "I frammenti di Aristobulo, esegeta biblico." *Bolletino dei Classici* 3 (1982): 87–134.

Reiter, Gerhard. *Die griechischen Bezeichnungen der Farben weiss, grau, und braun.* Commentationes Aenipotanae. Innsbruck: Universitätsverlag Wagner, 1962.

Richard, Carl J. *The Founders and the Classics: Greece, Rome, and the American Enlightenment.* Cambridge, Mass.: Harvard University Press, 1994.

Richardson, Nicholas J. *The Homeric Hymn to Demeter*. Oxford: Clarendon Press, 1974.

*Riginos, Alice Swift. *Platonica: The Anecdotes Concerning the Life and Writings of Plato*. Leiden: Brill, 1976.

*Rigoni, Mario Andrea, and Elena Zanco, eds. and trans. *Orapollo: I geroglifici*. Classicii della Bur. Milan: Bilioteca Universale Rizzoli, 1996.

Roberts, Jennifer Tolbert. *The Antidemocratic Tradition in Western Thought*. Princeton, N.J.: Princeton University Press, 1994.

Rogers, J. A. *World's Great Men of Color*. New York: Collier Books, 1946.

Rose, Valentin. *Aristotelis Fragmenta*. Leipzig: Teubner, 1886.

Ross, W. D. *Aristotle*. London: Methuen, 1945.

Rostagni, Augusto. *Suetonio de Poetis e Biografi Minori*. Turin: Chiantore, 1944.

*Roth, Ann Macy. "Building Bridges to Afrocentrism: A Letter to My Egyptological Colleagues." In Gross, Levitt, and Lewis, eds., *The Flight from Science and Reason*, pp. 313–26.

Rutherford, Richard B. *The Art of Plato*. London: Duckworth, 1995.

Sacks, Kenneth S. *Diodorus Siculus and the First Century*. Princeton, N.J.: Princeton University Press, 1990.

Sanford, Eva Matthews. *The Mediterranean World in Ancient Times*. Ronald Series in History. New York: Ronald Press, 1938.

Schlesinger, Arthur M., Jr. *The Disuniting of America*. New York: Norton, 1992.

Schürer, Emil. *A History of the Jewish People in the Age of Jesus Christ*. Revised and edited by Geza Vermes and Fergus Millar. Translated by T. A. Burkill et al. Edinburgh: Clark, 1973.

Schwartz, Amy. "Fantasylands." *Washington Post,* April 28, 1996, p. A 11.

Ševčenko, Ihor. "A Shadow Outline of Virtue." In *Ideology, Letters, and Culture in the Byzantine World*, 53–73. London: Variorum Reprints, 1982.

Sigerist, Henry E. *A History of Medicine*. Vol. 1. New York: Oxford University Press, 1951–61.

*Snowden, Frank M., Jr. *Blacks in Antiquity*. Cambridge, Mass.: Harvard University Press, 1970.

*———. *Before Color Prejudice*. Cambridge, Mass.: Harvard University Press, 1983.

———. "Bernal's 'Blacks,' Herodotus, and Other Classical Evidence." *Arethusa* (Fall 1989): 83–95. Special issue edited by Molly M. Levine and John Peradotto.

———. "Asclepiades' Didyme." *Greek, Roman and Byzantine Studies* 32 (1991): 239–53.

———. "Whither Afrocentrism." *Georgetown* (Winter 1992): 7–8.

Solmsen, Friedrich. *Isis Among the Greeks and Romans*. Martin Classical Lectures. Cambridge, Mass.: Harvard University Press, 1979.

Sourvinou-Inwood, Christiane. "Reconstructing Change: Ideology and the Eleusinian Mysteries," in *Inventing Ancient culture: Historicism, periodization, and the ancient world*, edited by Mark Golden and Peter Toohey, 132–64. London: Routledge, 1996.

Sparrow, John. "Mark Pattison and the Idea of a University." *Notes and Queries* 15 (1968): 432–35.

Stager, Lawrence E. "When Canaanites and Philistines Ruled Ashkelon." *Biblical Archaeology Review* 17 (March/April 1991): 24–40.

Steinberg, Sibyl. Review. *Publishers Weekly*, December 18, 1995, p. 37.

Stevenson, David. *The Origins of Freemasonry*. Cambridge: Cambridge University Press, 1988.

Stoneman, Richard. "Naked Philosophers: The Brahmans in the Alexander Historians and the Alexander Romance." *Jour-*

nal of Hellenic Studies 115 (1995): 99–114.

Spitzer, Alan B. *Historical Truth and Lies About the Past: Reflections on Dewey, Dreyfus, de Man, and Reagan.* Chapel Hill: University of North Carolina Press, 1996.

Sullivan, Andrew. "Racism 101." *The New Republic,* November 26, 1990, pp. 18–21.

Sundiata, Ibrahim. "Afrocentrism: The Argument We're Really Having." *Dissonance,* September 30, 1996 [http://way.net/dissonance/ sundiata.html].

Syme, Ronald. "Fraud and Imposture." In *Pseudepigrapha I,* 3–17. Entretiens sur l'Antiquité Classique. Vol. 18. Vandoevres-Geneva, 1972.

Tatum, James. *Apuleius and The Golden Ass.* Ithaca, N.Y.: Cornell University Press, 1979.

Terrasson, Jean. *Life of Sethos.* Translated by Thomas Lediard. London, J. Walthoe, 1732.

TGF, See Nauck, *Tragicorum Graecorum Fragmenta.*

*Thissen, Heinz. "Zum Umgang mit der ägyptischen Sprache in der griechisch-römischen Antike," *Zeitschrift für Papyrologie und Epigraphik* 97 (1993).

Thomas, Rosalind. *Oral Tradition and Written Record in Classical Athens.* Cambridge Studies in Oral and Literate Culture. Cambridge: Cambridge University Press, 1989.

Thompson, D'Arcy Wentworth. *A Glossary of Greek Birds.* Oxford: Clarendon Press, 1895.

*Thomson, Katharine. *The Masonic Thread in Mozart.* London: Lawrence & Wishart, 1977.

Trevor-Roper, H. R. "The Uses of Fakery." Review of *Forgers and Critics* by Anthony Grafton. *New York Review of Books,* December 6, 1990, pp. 26–28.

Trigger, Bruce. "The Rise of Civilization in Egypt." In *Cambridge History of Africa.* Vol. 1. Cambridge: Cambridge University Press, 1982. pp. 489–90.

———. "Brown Athena: A Postprocessual Goddess?" *Current An-*

thropology 33, no. 1 (1992): 121–23.

Turner, Frank M. "Martin Bernal's Black Athena: A Dissent." *Arethusa* (Fall 1989): 97–109. Special issue.

Turner, William. *History of Philosophy.* Boston: Athenaeum Press, 1903.

Vail, Charles H. *The Ancient Mysteries and Modern Masonry* [1909]. Chesapeake, N.Y.: ECA Associates, 1991.

Vermeule, Emily. *Aspects of Death in Early Greek Art and Poetry.* Sather Classical Lectures, 46. Berkeley: University of California Press, 1979.

———. "The World Turned Upside Down." *New York Review of Books* 39, no. 6 (March 26, 1992). Reprinted in Lefkowitz and Rogers, eds., *Black Athena Revisited*, pp. 269–79.

Vickers, Jason. "*Not Out of Africa*: A Reaction." *Virtual Dashiki,* August/September 1996, pp. 3, 9.

Von der Mühll, Peter. "Antiker Historismus in Plutarchs Biographie des Solon." In *Ausgewählte Kleine Schriften.* Basel: Friedrich Reinhardt Verlag, 1975.

*von Staden, Heinrich. *Herophilus: The Art of Medicine in Early Alexandria.* Cambridge: Cambridge University Press, 1989.

———. "Women and Dirt." *Helios* 19, no. 1–2 (1992): 7–30.

*Walker, Clarence E. *Deromanticizing Black History.* Knoxville: University of Tennessee Press, 1991.

Wallis, R. T. *Neoplatonism.* London: Duckworth, 1972.

Walter, Nikolaus. *Der Thoraausleger Aristobulus.* Texte und Untersuchungen. Berlin: Akademie-Verlag, 1964.

———. "Fragmente jüdisch-hellenistischer Exegeten: Aristobulus, Demetrios, Aristeas." *Jüdische Schriften aus hellenistisch-römischer Zeit.* Gerd Mohn: Gütersloher Verlagshaus, 1975.

Warburton, W. *The Divine Legation.* Edited by R. Hurd. London: Cadell & Davies, 1811.

Ward, John S. M. *Freemasonry and the Ancient Gods.* London:

Simpkin, Marshall, Hamilton, Kent & Co., 1921.

West, Stephanie R. "Joseph and Asenath: A Neglected Greek Romance." *Classical Quarterly* 24 (1974): 70–81.

Whitehorne, John. *Cleopatras*. London: Routledge, 1994.

Wilamowitz-Moellendorf, Ulrich von. *Der Glaube der Hellenen*. Berlin: Weidmannsche Buchhandlung, 1932.

Will, George. "Intellectual Segregation." *Newsweek,* February 19, 1996, p. 78.

Williams, Chancellor. *The Destruction of Black Civilization: Great Issues of a Race from 4500 B.C. to 2000 A.D.* Chicago: Third World Press, 1987.

Williams, Loretta J. *Black Freemasonry and Middle-Class Realities*. University of Missouri Studies 20. Columbia: University of Missouri Press, 1980.

Wilmshurst, Walter Leslie. *The Meaning of Masonry*. New York: Bell Publishing, 1867.

Wilson, John A. *The Burden of Egypt*. Chicago: University of Chicago Press, 1951.

Wilson, Nigel G. *From Byzantium to Italy*. London: Duckworth, 1992.

———, ed. *St. Basil on Greek Literature*. London: Duckworth, 1975.

Winbush, Raymond. Letter to the Editor. *Chronicle of Higher Education* (February 9, 1994): B4.

*Windschuttle, Keith. *The Killing of History: How a Discipline Is Being Murdered by Literary Critics and Social Theorists*. Paddington, N.S.W.: Macleay Press, 1996.

Winnington-Ingram, R. P. *Studies in Aeschylus*. Cambridge: Cambridge University Press, 1983.

Wright, M. R. *Empedocles: The Extant Fragments*. New Haven: Yale University Press, 1981.

X, Malcolm. *The Autobiography of Malcolm X*, With the assistance of Alex Haley. New York: Ballantine Books, 1973.

Yates, Frances. *Giordano Bruno and the Hermetic Tradition*.

Chicago: University of Chicago Press, 1964.

*Yurco, Frank. "Were the Ancient Egyptians Black or White?" *Biblical Archaeology Review* 15, no. 5 (1989): 24–29, 58.

Zauzich, Karl-Theodor. *Hieroglyphs Without Mystery: An Introduction to Ancient Egyptian Writing*. Translated by Ann Macy Roth. Austin: University of Texas Press, 1992.

Zeller, E. *A History of Greek Philosophy from the Earliest Period to the Time of Socrates*. London: Longmans, Green, 1881.

*Ziegler, Christiane, Jean-Marcel Humbert, and Michael Pantazzi. *Egyptomania: Egypt in Western Art*. Ottawa: National Gallery of Canada, 1994.

Zuntz, Günther. "Aristeas Studies I." In *Opuscula Selecta*, 110–25. Manchester: Rowman & Littlefield, 1972.

———. "Aion Ploutonios." *Hermes* 116 (1988): 291–303.

———. *Persephone*. Oxford: Clarendon Press, 1971.

GLOSSARY OF ANCIENT NAMES, PLACES, AND TERMINOLOGY

(Mythical names are in bold type)

Aegyptus, Greek hero for whom Egypt is named; brother of **Danaus** (q.v.).

Aeneas, Trojan hero who settled in Italy, hero of the Roman poet Virgil's epic the **Aeneid.**

Aesop, legendary author of an ancient collection of fables; virtually nothing is known about his life.

Aeschylus of Athens (525/4?–456/5 B.C.), tragic poet.

Africa, ancient Roman name of unknown etymology for the province of Carthage, later generalized to the whole continent.

Alexander the Great of Macedon (356–323 B.C.), king and great general who, starting in 334, conquered the Eastern Mediterranean, Persia, and Egypt.

Alexandria "near Egypt," Greek city founded in 331 B.C. by Alexander the Great on the Canobic branch of the Nile

Delta; the Library at Alexandria, primarily a collection of Greek books, began to be assembled about 297 B.C. by Demetrius of Phaleron.

Amun (**Amun-Re, Ammon**), chief god of the Egyptian pantheon.

Anaxagoras of Clazomenae (ca. 500–428 B.C.), philosopher resident in Athens, known for his theories of mind and ontology.

Anaxarchus of Abdera (mid fourth century B.C.), a Democritean philosopher who accompanied Alexander the Great on his Asian campaigns.

Antony (Marcus Antonius, 83–31 B.C.), Roman statesman and general who married Cleopatra (q.v.).

Apollo, Greek god of prophecy, poetry, and music, with major shrines at Delphi and Delos, identified by the Greeks with the Egyptian god Horus.

Apuleius of Madaurus in North Africa (b. ca. 135 A.D.), orator and author of *The Golden Ass*, a novel that describes its hero's conversion to the cult of the Egyptian goddess Isis.

Archimedes of Syracuse (ca. 287–212 B.C.), Greek mathematician and inventor.

Argos, city-state in the Peloponnesus, home of Io and refuge for Danaus and his daughters.

Aristobulus (second century B.C.), an Alexandrian Jew who sought to show that Greek writers such as Homer and Plato had borrowed from the Old Testament.

Aristophanes (ca. 450–386 B.C.), the best-known Athenian comic poet.

Aristotle of Stagira (384–322 B.C.), philosopher who studied in Athens with Plato and who served as tutor to Alexander the Great (q.v.) before returning to Athens and founding his own school of philosophy, political theory, and natural science.

Atlantis, mythical island in the Atlantic ocean, whose constitution and situation are described by Plato in his dialogues *Timaeus* and *Crito*.

Athena, Greek goddess of war, cities, and handicrafts, whose principal shrine is in Athens, identified by the Greeks with the Egyptian goddess **Neit**.

Augustine of Hippo in North Africa (354–430 A.D.), Latin philosopher and theologian who incorporated Neoplatonism into Christianity.

Book of the Dead, modern title of a collection of Egyptian funerary texts known in antiquity as the *Book of Coming Forth by Day*.

Cadmus, mythical Phoenician hero who founded the Greek city Thebes.

Carthage, a rich and powerful Phoenician colony on the north coast of Tunisia, destroyed by the Romans in 146 B.C. but later rebuilt as a Roman colony.

Cecrops, mythical king of Athens.

Charon, mythical ferryman of the souls of the dead to the Greek underworld.

Clement of Alexandria (150–215 A.D.), Christian theologian who advocated the primacy of Hebrew scripture over pagan religious writings.

Cleopatra VII (69–30 B.C.), the last of the Ptolemaic dynasty who ruled Egypt from the death of Alexander the Great (q.v.); daughter of Ptolemy XII, granddaughter of Ptolemy IX, and wife of Antony (q.v.); she relied on the support of Roman generals.

Cyprian (ca. 200–258 A.D.), Christian martyr, bishop of Carthage.

Cyrene, Greek colony on the coast of Libya, a large and important city-state.

Danaus, mythical Greek hero from whose name is derived one of the names by which the Greeks are designated **(Danaoi)**. Son of **Belus**, brother of **Aegyptus** (for whom Egypt is named) and brother-in-law of **Phoenix** (for whom Phoenicia is named), he fled from Egypt to Argos in Greece with his fifty daughters.

Daedalus, descendant of **Cecrops**, artist and craftsman who fled from Athens to the court of King **Minos** of Crete.

Demeter, Greek goddess of grain, mother by **Zeus** of **Perse-phone,** identified by the Greeks with the Egyptian goddess **Isis.**

Democritus of Abdera (b. ca. 460), Greek philosopher and mathe-matician who was an important proponent of ancient atomic theory.

Didyme (308–246 B.C.), a "native" mistress of Ptolemy II Philadel-phus.

Diodorus of Sicily, Greek author of a "universal" history who vis-ited Egypt in 60–56 B.C.

Diogenes Laertius (third century A.D.?), author of a compendium of biographical sketches of famous Greek philosophers and thinkers.

Dionysus, Greek god of wine and the theater, identified by the Greeks with the Egyptian god Osiris.

Duat, the Egyptian underworld.

Eleusis, near Athens, site where the famous Mysteries of Deme-ter and Persephone were annually celebrated.

Empedocles of Acgragas in Sicily (ca. 492–432 B.C.), Greek poet and philosopher to some extent inspired by Pythagoreanism.

Epaphus, son of Io and Zeus, born in Egypt.

Erechtheus, mythological Athenian hero.

Ethiopia, according to the Greeks, the land of the "burnt-face people," a region south of Egypt including Nubia.

Eudoxus of Cnidus (ca. 390–340 B.C.), an accomplished Greek as-tronomer and mathematician.

Euripides of Athens (480–405 B.C.), tragic playwright.

Eusebius of Caesarea (ca. 260–339 A.D.), biblical scholar and his-torian of the Christian church.

Gnosticism, a term used to describe the religion of a number of ancient cults that in different ways combined elements from several religions, including Judaism, Christianity, and Neoplatonism.

Gymnosophists ("naked wise men"), Brahmin sages encountered by Alexander the Great when he invaded India in 326 B.C.

Hannibal (247–183/2 B.C.), Carthaginian general who invaded the Italian peninsula.

Heracles, mythical Greek hero who became a god.

Hermes, the Greek messenger god, identified by the Greeks with the Egyptian god **Thoth.**

Hermes Trismegistus ("Thrice-great"), (1) a composite of the Greek god Hermes and the Egyptian god Thoth, or (2) his grandson, a mortal man, who served as an intermediary between the god Hermes/Thoth and man; the purported author of treatises now known as the Hermetic corpus.

Herodotus of Halicarnassus (fifth century B.C.), author of a historical account of the hostility between the Greeks and the Persians; he visited Egypt and travelled as far as the first cataract of the Nile.

Hieroglyphics, the earliest form of Egyptian script, whose pictorial signs designated sounds and concepts; in practice, hieroglyphic characters are arranged artistically rather than in the order in which the sounds occur.

Homer (eighth century B.C.?), legendary poet to whom the epics *the Iliad* and the *Odyssey* were attributed.

Horapollo (fifth century A.D.), author of a treatise on the symbolic meaning of hieroglyphs, which preserves some accurate information along with considerable fantasy.

Hyksos, name given by the Jewish historian Josephus (first century A.D.) to a Semitic (probably Canaanite) people who ruled Egypt from 1674 to 1566 B.C.

Iamblichus (ca. 250–326 A.D.), Neoplatonist philosopher, author of a biography of the legendary Greek philosopher Pythagoras and a treatise on the Egyptian mysteries.

Indo-European, term used to designate a family of languages that includes Greek, Latin, and Sanskrit.

Io, daughter of the river-god **Inachus**, who was turned into a

cow by her lover, the god **Zeus**, and who travelled to Egypt,
where she became the mother of **Epaphus** (q.v.).

Isis, nurturing goddess (who could assume the form of a cow),
sister and wife of **Osiris** and mother of **Horus**, identified
by the Greeks with their goddess **Demeter**.

Josephus (first century A.D.), Jewish historian who wrote in Greek.

Kemet ("the black land"), name used by ancient Egyptians for
the land the Greeks called *Egypt.*

Lycurgus, traditional lawgiver to the Greek city-state Sparta.

Melampus, mythical Greek seer.

Memphite Theology, Egyptian theological text of the eighth century B.C., mythological account of the creation of the world
by the god **Ptah**.

Minoan, term derived from the name of the mythical Cretan king
Minos, used to designate the civilization of Crete during
the second millennium B.C.

Moses, legendary Hebrew lawgiver, born in Egypt, founder of ancient Israel.

Musaeus ("man of the Muses"), mythological Greek singer and
poet.

mysteries, Greek cults involving initiation.

Namphamo of Numidia, a Carthaginian saint.

Neoplatonism, modern name given to revival of Platonic philosophy by Greek writers from the third century to the sixth
century A.D.

Oenopides of Chios (fifth century B.C.), Greek astronomer and scientist.

Orpheus, legendary Greek singer and poet (closely associated
with **Musaeus**).

Osiris, Egyptian god of the Underworld, brother and husband of
the goddess **Isis** and father of **Horus**; he was identified by
Greeks with their god **Dionysus**.

Perpetua of Carthage (d. 203 A.D.), Christian martyr.

Persephone (**Kore, Proserpina**), Greek goddess of the Underworld, daughter of the goddess **Demeter** and the god **Zeus**.

Philo of Alexandria (first century A.D.), Jewish philosopher who wrote in Greek.

Plato of Athens (ca. 429–347 B.C.), Greek philosopher who invented the dialogue form and perfected the abstract terminology developed by earlier Greek philosophers, such as his teacher Socrates.

Plutarch of Chaeronea in Boeotia (ca. 50–120 A.D.), Greek philosopher and biographer, author of treatise on Isis and Osiris.

Ptah, creator god of Memphis in Egypt, identified by Greeks with their god **Hephaestus**.

Ptolemy VIII Euergetes II (ca. 182/1–116 B.C.), Macedonian Greek pharaoh of Egypt, author of memoir about his ancestor Ptolemy II Philadelphus (308–246 B.C.).

Ptolemy IX Soter II (142–80 B.C.), son of Ptolemy VIII, grandfather by an unknown mistress of Cleopatra VII (q.v.).

Ptolemy XII Neos Dionysos (Auletes), son of Ptolemy IX by an unknown mistress; father of Cleopatra VII (q.v.).

Ptolemy Chennos (first-century A.D.), biographer of Aristotle.

pyramid (Greek word for "wheat cake"), a funerary monument for Egyptian royalty; a stone structure with four triangular sides meeting in a point.

Pythagoras of Samos, mathematician, musician, and philosopher; legendary founder of a religious and philosophical movement based in Metapontum in southern Italy.

Semele, daughter of **Cadmus** (q.v.), mother by **Zeus** of the god **Dionysus**.

Sethos (Greek version of an Egyptian name like Sebithos), (1) according to Herodotus (2.141), a priest of **Ptah** who ruled Lower Egypt during the early seventh century B.C. (2) name used by the Abbé Terrasson for the fictional hero of his historical novel.

Socrates of Athens (469–399 B.C.), philosopher, teacher of Plato, who wrote nothing but debated ethical questions with great profundity; he was tried and executed by the Athenians on charges of impiety.

Solon of Athens (early sixth century B.C.), sage, lawgiver, and poet; after instituting political reforms that helped the poor, he is said to have travelled around the Mediterranean.

Strabo of Cappadocia (b. ca. 64 B.C.), geographer who provided a valuable picture of life in the Mediterranean in the first century B.C.

Tacitus (56–ca. 118 A.D.), Roman historian who described the first century of the Empire.

Terence (Publius Terentius Afer, d. 159 B.C.), playwright who adapted Greek comedies for the Roman stage.

Tertullian of Carthage (ca. 160–240 A.D.), Christian theologian and ethicist.

Thales of Miletus (seventh century B.C.), one of the legendary Seven Wise Men, the first important Greek scientist.

Theuth (Thoth), Egyptian moon-god, patron of scribes and scholars, identified by the Greeks with their god **Hermes.**

Virgil (Publius Vergilius Maro, 70–19 B.C.), Roman poet, author of the *Aeneid*.

Zeus, principal deity of the Greek pantheon, identified by the Greeks with the Egyptian god **Amun** (q.v.).

For more detailed information, see George Hart, *A Dictionary of Egyptian Gods and Goddesses* (New York: Routledge, 1986); *The Dictionary of Ancient Egypt*, eds. Ian Shaw and Paul Nicholson in association with the British Museum (New York: Harry N. Abrams, 1995); *The Oxford Classical Dictionary*, 3d ed., eds. Simon Hornblower and Anthony Spawforth (New York: Oxford University Press, 1996); Pierre Grimal, *The Dictionary of Classical Mythology*, trans. A. R. Maxwell-Hyslop (New York: Basil Blackwell, 1987); *The Oxford Dictionary of the Christian Church*, 2d ed., eds. F. L. Cross and E. A. Livingstone (New York: Oxford University Press, 1983).

INDEX

Acts of the Apostles, 40–41
Aegyptus (hero), 17–18, 25–26, 149, 242–43
Aeneas, 97, 98
Aeschylus, 70, 71
Aesop, 30, 31, 45
Africa: East, 135, 191, 250; North, 14–16, 30–34. *See also* Egypt, Ethiopia, Nubia
Afro-American Studies, 193
Afrocentrism, radical, *xi, xii, xiii, xvi,* 2, 5, 7, 9, 10, 14, 32, 54, 92, 124, 156–59, 164, 192; Ethiopianism in 250–1; in education, 186, 239–42
Aion, 95, 216n6
Alexander, 2, 3, 34, 135, 137, 144
Alexandria, 2, 3, 4, 7, 72, 80, 85, 88, 94, 95, 99, 107, 123, 131, 135, 137, 139, 140, 144, 150–51
Amasis, 70, 75, 81
Amun (Ammon), 75, 101, 102, 105
Anacharsis, 24–25
analogy, 67, 74, 78
ancestry, African, 16, 20, 27, 29, 33, 37, 43
anti-Semitism, 52, 172, 182, 191
Antony (Marcus Antonius), 38, 39, 41
Aphrodite, 65, 75
Apollo, 65, 70
Apuleius, *Golden Ass. See* Lucius
Archimedes, 153
architecture, 193
Argos, 13, 17–20, 23
arguments: from ethnicity, 48–52; possibility, 4–5, 27–29, 45, 50–51; resemblance, 63, 66, 73, 76,

81, 138–39, 142, 153;
silence, 45, 137, 144. *See
also* logic
Aristobulus, 84, 86, 87, 90, 125
Aristophanes, 28
Aristotle, 2–4, 6, 8, 135, 137–44,
146–47, 150–51, 153, 157,
165, 167–68, 173–74, 187
Aryanism, 182
Asante, Molefi Kete, *xii, xiii,
xvii,* 55, 158, 159, 160, 174,
241, 243–44
Asia, 13, 18, 31
astrology, 77–78, 107, 145
astronomy, 76, 77, 89, 98, 113,
115
Athena, 65, 70
Athens, 14, 17–18, 20, 23, 27–29
Atlantis, 75, 82
atom, 149, 252–53
Atum, 141, 149, 252–53
Augustine, Saint, 32–34
Avaris, 22, 242. *See also* Hyksos

Babylon, 77
barbaroi. *See* Foreign
Barthélemy, Jean-Jacques. *See*
Anacharsis
ben-Jochannan, Yosef A. A., 2–3,
32–33, 151, 181, 185
Berbers, 31–32, 34. *See also*
Africa, North
Berlinerblau, Jacques, 240
Bernal, Martin, *xi, xvii,* 23–26,
28–29, 51–52, 62, 65, 79, 80,
82, 150, 177, 181, 192,
241–42, 245–46, 253
bias, historical, 48, 161–64
Bible, 87

biographers, ancient, 75–84, 146
blacks: in antiquity, 13–48,
125–34; in modern times,
127–34. *See also*
Afrocentrism
Blyden, Edward Wilmot,
127–28, 180
Book of the Dead, 8, 80, 138–40,
143, 146, 150, 253–54. *See
also* Underworld
books, sacred, 96, 98–104. *See
also* Hermes Trismegistus;
Hermetica
Bork, Robert, 182
Born, Ignaz von, 117–18
borrowing, cultural, 89, 158,
188. *See also* Influence
Bruno, Giordano, 107
Burkert, Walter, 65

Cadmus, 13, 17, 20–21, 63, 74
Carthage, 14, 31–34, 132, 134
Casaubon, Isaac, 57, 100
Cecrops, 17, 18, 23
Chaeremon, 98
chariots, 146–47
Charon, 74
chronology, problematic, 7, 9, 58,
81, 82, 144, 158
citations, inaccurate, 38–40, 148.
See also research
methodology
Clarke, John Henrik, 40, 41, 244
classicists, *xv,* 16, 46–48
Clement of Alexandria, 88, 99,
100, 107, 115, 123–24,
139–40, 163
Cleopatra, 9, 14, 34–52, 157,
243–44; her grandmother,

35–37, 43, 45–47, 51
Colchis, 18, 20
colony, 14, 17, 41
color, of skin, 13–14, 20, 28–31,
    35–40, 42–47, 50, 126–34,
    159, 174, 200*n*41,
    204*nn*77–78
comedy, Athenian, 27–28
competence, academic, 165–66,
    168, 170, 173
Conboy, Kenneth, 171
conjecture, historical. *See*
    evidence
conspiracy theories, 6–8, 51,
    124, 133–34, 137, 182,
    193
cosmogony, 151, 152
creation, 140–43, 146
cults, mystery, 93–97, 104. *See
    also* Eleusinian Mysteries;
    Mystical Egypt
cultural history, 4, 8–9, 49–51,
    159–60, 181–82, 191, 193.
    See also history
curriculum, university, 99, 139,
    151, 165–75
Cuvier, Baron de, 56
Cyprian, Saint, 32, 34
Cyrene, 14, 132, 134

Daedalus, 73, 74
Danaids (daughters of Danaus),
    18–20, 23, 60–70
Danaus, 17–20, 23–26, 69–70, 74
dead: beliefs about, 73, 247–49;
    hero's visit to, 95–98,
    114–15. *See also* Book of the
    Dead, *On the Soul*;
    transmigration of souls

debate, 1, 11, 160
deconstruction, 186–87
Demeter, 67–70, 73–74
demiurge, 146, 152
democracy, 4, 6, 186–87
Democritus, 73, 77–78, 143–44,
    253
dependency, cultural, 76, 81, 83,
    88, 90, 123, 134, 142, 146,
    152
diaspora, 129, 130
Didyme, 45, 47, 50
Diodorus of Sicily, 17–18, 21–22,
    54, 57–60, 72–78, 90, 134,
    245–46
Diogenes, 79, 80, 84–85
Dionysus, 21, 63–64, 67–68,
    73–74
Diop, Cheikh Anta, 16–24,
    151–53, 157–60, 166
diversity, 161–64
Dodona, 66
Douglass, Frederick, 127, 180
Du Bois, W. E. B., 128
Duat, 67, 80, 138. *See also* Book
    of the Dead

ecliptic of sun, 78
education, in ancient Egypt. *See*
    Diop, Cheikh Anta;
    Terrasson, Jean
education, in United States, 1–6,
    48–52, 158–75
Egypt, as African culture, 16–17,
    41–48, 51–52, 126–34, 151,
    155–58, 250–51; Greek
    admiration for, 71–73,
    83–85, 246; origins of, 242
elements, the four, 96, 97,

113–14, 119, 122
Eleusinian Mysteries, 95, 97,
    114–15, 120, 247
Empedocles, 68, 114
empowerment, 4, 125, 163
Epiphanius, 95
Erechtheus, 17–18
Ethiopia, 13, 29, 31, 34, 47, 59,
    61, 78, 127, 250
ethnic history, 4, 8, 48–52,
    125–26, 158–60, 166–67,
    174–75
etymology, 23–24, 26, 149,
    207n18, 231n85
Eudoxus, 73, 78–80, 84
Euripides, 82–83, 87
Eusebius, 24, 88
evidence, 1–11, 39–40, 42–43,
    47–53, 58, 61, 63, 74, 76, 78,
    84–85, 134–54, 157–60, 183,
    193
eye, as symbol, 136, 146

faculty, responsibilities of,
    164–75
Fairchild, Halford, 125
Felicity, martyr, 32–33
Ficino, Marsilio, 107
fiction, historical, 75, 82, 93,
    101–3. See also James,
    George G. M.; Terrasson,
    Jean
flat-earth theory, 165–68, 174
foreign (to Greece), 14, 20,
    27–29, 33, 35, 45, 47, 50
forgeries, 101, 142, 218n31
freedom, academic, 161–75, 254;
    of speech, 165, 171–74. See
    also responsibility

Freemasonry. See Masonry
Freudianism, 181

Garvey, Marcus Mosiah, 10, 129,
    130–34
geology, 145
geometry, 76–79, 85, 89, 98,
    112–13, 144
Gobineau, Comte de, 56
Great Seal of the United States,
    110
Greece: legacy of, 6; origins of,
    12–13, myths about,
    14–26
gymnosophists, see India

hair, 13, 127
Haley, Shelley, 43–48
Ham, 127
Hannibal, 30–31, 36, 157
hawk, as symbol, 108–10
Hebrew, 18, 65, 86–89. See also
    Jews
Hecataeus, 79, 81
Helen of Troy, 83
Heracles, 25–26, 242–43
Heraclitus, 143, 152–53
Hermes: books of, 99; Greek god,
    81
Hermes Trismegistus, 57, 83,
    107, 113, 246
Hermetica, 100–104, 107–11,
    179, 249
hero pattern, 114–18
Herodotus, 9, 13, 23, 25–26, 54,
    57–77, 79, 81, 85, 89,
    126–27, 135, 143, 193,
    242–43
hieroglyphics, 25, 57, 96, 99, 101,

104, 108–11, 113, 149,
244–45
historians, Afrocentric. *See*
Asante, Molefi Keti; Diop,
Cheikh Anta; Garvey,
Marcus Mosiah; James,
George G. M.; Rogers, Joel A.
historians, Greek. *See* Diodorus
of Sicily; Hecataeus;
Herodotus
historians, Jewish, 84–90
historicism, new, 50
history, politics in, 16, 46, 161,
191, 241; teaching of,
177–78, 183, 186–88. *See
also* cultural history; ethnic
history; evidence
Hollinger, David, 160, 174
Homer, 73–75, 82, 85, 97, 147
Horapollo, 109–10
Horus, 70, 108–9, 112, 114–17
Hyksos, 22–24

Iamblichus, 76, 80, 98, 100–101,
103, 145
identity politics, 46, 177–78,
181–82
Inachus, 18, 20, 24, 25
India, 137, 228*n*42, 252
Indo-European, 12, 26, 58, 65
indoctrination, 11
influence, 53–55, 63, 66, 73–75,
84, 88–89, 122, 124, 150,
157, 160–61, 164, 179,
188–89, 190–92
initiation, 69, 93–98, 110,
113–19, 122, 157, 247–48.
See also Eleusis, Lucius
internet debate, 177

invasion of Greece 20–23, 26
Io, 18, 20, 22–25
Isis, 23, 35, 67, 70, 73–74, 94–96,
104–5, 112–16, 118–20,
247–49

James, George G. M., 10, 93–94,
99, 100, 104–6, 124–25,
134–54, 157, 164, 181, 185
Jeffries, Leonard, 171–72, 174
Jews, *xii, xvii,* 45, 51, 85–90,
125, 162, 163, 164. *See also*
anti-Semitism; Hebrew
Johnson-Odim, Cheryl, 52,
180*n*6

Kemet (Egypt), 151, 158, 174
Khoiak festival, 69
Kimball, Roger, 182
"know thyself," 145, 229*n*69
Koertge, Noretta, 46

laws, 75, 81, 85, 162, 163, 164
legacy. *See* stolen legacy
Lenoir, Alexandre, 120, 122–23
Library, at Alexandria, 135, 137,
139–40, 144, 150, 151, 157,
187–88
Libyans. *See* Cyrene
linguistics, 24, 26
lodge, 105–6, 117, 136
logic, 65, 76
Lucius, in Apuleius, 95–98, 114,
179, 248–49
Lycurgus, 73, 75–76

Macedonian, 21, 34, 35, 50. *See
also* Alexander; Ptolemies
Magic Flute, 56, 118, 119. *See*

also Mozart, Wolfgang
 Amadé
magic, 144
Maiden (Kore). *See* Eleusinian
 Mysteries; Persephone
martyrs, African, 32–33
Masonry, *xiv*, 10, 25, 92, 94,
 105–6, 110–11, 117–23,
 128–30, 134, 136, 179,
 251–52
Master Mason, 136, 144
mathematics, 79, 84, 93, 112. *See
 also* Archimedes; Eudoxus;
 Pythagoras
medicine, Egyptian 191–92
Mediterranean, 14, 16, 18, 22,
 31, 34, 35, 45
Meier, August, 250–51
Melampus, 63, 73–74
melanin, 173
Memphis, 112–13, 115–16, 120,
 122, 136, 140
Memphite theology, 140–45, 150
Minoan, 22, 242
Mithraism, 97
Monnica, 32, 34
Mormons, 224*n*113
Moses, 7, 9, 86–88, 125, 136, 143,
 162, 246
Mozart, Wolfgang Amadé, 56,
 117–19
Musaeus, 73, 86, 88
Mut, 75
mysteries: Egyptian "Mystery
 System," *xv*, 10, 92–95,
 104–6, 122–24, 134–36,
 138–39, 143–46, 148,
 150–51, 157, 160, 179, 249,
 252; Greek *(see* Eleusinian

Mysteries; initiation).
Mystical Egypt, 106, 107, 111,
 121, 136, 152, 249
myth, *xv–xvi*, 16, 18, 22, 24–25,
 42–43, 52, 123, 125–26, 134,
 153, 155, 156, 158, 161

names, etymology of, 63–64,
 67–68, 73, 76, 86
Namphamo, 32, 33
Napoleon, 56
narratives, Egyptian, 190–91
National Association of
 Scholars, 183
Naucratis, 68
Near East, 16, 52
Neit, 65
Neoplatonism, 103
Nile Delta, 18, 22
Nile, 18, 22, 62, 68, 72, 77–78,
 81, 83, 85, 99, 104, 127, 151
Not Out of Africa, article, 180,
 184; book, cover, 184;
 criticism, 179–88; praise,
 182–83, title, 180
Nubia, 44, 45, 191
Numidia, 33

Octavian, 35, 46
Oenopides, 73, 78
On the Soul (Aristotle), 8, 68, 74,
 76, 80, 89, 138, 139, 143
opposites, theory of, 140, 143,
 145, 152–53
oracle, 65, 66
origins, of Greek culture, 14–26,
 61–71
Orpheus, 72–73; Orphism,
 253–54

Orwell, George, 153–54
Osiris, 21, 63–64, 67, 69, 70, 73–74, 94, 97, 105, 112, 114–18, 120, 217*n*24

Palter, Robert, 89
Patai, Daphne, 46
Pelops, 13
Perpetua, Saint, 32, 33
Persephone, 95, 96, 98. *See also* Eleusinian Mysteries
Persia, 62, 71, 77, 79, 85
phallus, 63
philosophy, *xi, xii, xiv–xv,* 2, 4, 6, 7, 9–10, 54, 77, 86–87, 89, 91–93, 99, 100–104, 106, 110, 123–25, 127, 132, 135–37, 139, 140–42, 146–48, 151, 157, 188–89. *See also* Aristotle; Plato; Socrates
Phoenicia, 14, 17, 20–21, 29, 31, 33–34
piety, 89
plagiarism, alleged, 123–24, 139, 142, 146, 150
Plato, 7, 9, 26, 29, 73, 75–76, 79, 80–84, 87–88, 101, 104, 107, 114, 125, 139, 143–47, 151–52, 190–91
Plutarch, 39, 41, 47, 75–76, 85, 94, 108
Portland Baseline Essays, 42. 239–41
portraits: of Socrates, 29; of Cleopatra, 39–40
Preus, Anthony, 253
priests, Egyptian, 10, 75, 80, 81, 93–96, 98–99, 104, 107,

112–23, 115–16, 118–19, 139–40, 150, 152
processions, 95, 99, 107, 115
propaganda, 39, 155, 167
Proserpina. *See* Persephone
Ptah, 140–41
Ptolemies, 34–37, 39, 41, 44–45, 47, 50, 72, 77, 244
Punic. *See* Carthage
puns, 64
pyramid, 110, 113–14, 119, 122, 127
Pythagoras, 67–69, 77–78, 98, 104, 113, 143

race, 9, 14, 16, 29, 49, 127, 130, 132, 133, 148
racism, *xiii,* 2, 4, 5, 55, 156, 172, 174, 180, 182, 191
relativism, 48–49, 158, 244
religion, Greek, 62–71, 73–74, 76, 84, 89, 138. *See also* Eleusinian Mysteries
Republic (Plato), 146. *See also* Plato
research methodology: ancient 60, 71–72, 77, 125; Afrocentric, 153. *See also* arguments
responsibility, academic, 3–11, 161–75
right-wing politics, 182–83
ritual, "Egyptian," 69, 248–49. *See also* Eleusinian Mysteries; initiation; Lucius; Masonry
Rogers, Joel A., 30, 36–42
Romans, 6, 25, 30–35, 47–48

Sappho, 45
Schlesinger, Arthur, 4
self-esteem, 4. *See also*
   empowerment
Semitic, 14, 21–23, 26, 31, 33.
   See also Carthage; Jews;
   Phoenicia
Sethos, 111–20, 122, 126, 145.
   See also Terrasson, Jean
Shakespeare, 38–39, 40, 47
silenus, 29–30
Simeon, 149
skin. *See* color
slaves, 28, 33, 36–37
snub-nose, 29–30
Socrates, 9, 14, 26–30, 136,
   143–45, 147, 157, 159, 164,
   167, 200*n*29, 235*n*14
Solon, 73, 75–76, 79, 81, 245–46
Sophocles, 86
souls. *See* dead; *On the Soul*;
   transmigration of souls
stolen legacy, 2, 4, 9–10, 54, 70,
   71, 88, 92–94, 123–26,
   131–32, 134–39, 141, 143,
   146–48, 150–51, 153–58,
   160–61, 163–64, 168, 174,
   235*n*14, 250–52
Strabo, 72, 79, 84
Suppliants (Aeschylus), 23. *See
   also* Danaids
symbols, 52, 105–6, 108, 110–11,
   118, 136

Tacitus, 48
tenure, 165, 169, 171, 172
Terence, 30, 31, 36
Terrasson, Jean, 10, 24, 111–20,
   122, 123, 126–29, 136, 143,

145, 157, 249, 252
Tertullian, 32–33
Thales, 85, 113, 143
Thamos, 56, 118
Thebes, 13, 17, 20, 21, 113, 115
theology. *See* Memphite theology
Thesmophoria, 69–70
Thoth, 81, 83, 100. *See also*
   Hermes
Timaeus (Plato), 146, 151, 152,
   190
translations, problematic, 24,
   63–64, 100, 199*n*26, 206*n*16,
   218*n*34
transmigration of souls, 67–69.
   See also Pythagoras
treatises, Egyptian, 99, 100, 103,
   104, 107, 139. *See also*
   Hermes, books of;
   Hermetica
trials. *See* initiations
Trismegistus. *See* Hermes
truth, determination of,
   xiv, 10–11, 50–52, 155,
   157–60, 166–67. *See also*
   arguments; evidence;
   history

Underworld, 95–98. *See also*
   dead; Duat
Universal Negro Improvement
   Association (UNIA), 129–30.
   See also Garvey, Marcus
   Mosiah
universities, 1, 3, 11, 16, 43, 48,
   52, 135–36, 150–51, 155,
   157, 161, 163, 170, 173, 174,
   240–41
utopias, 85, 129–30

Vail, Charles, 94, 95, 105
vestments, 94, 96. *See*
Lucius
Virgil, 97, 120
Volney, Count, 127

Wellesley College, *xii, xvii,* 2, 4,
42, 43
Will, George, 182, 184
wisdom literature, Egyptian,
189–90, 247, 253; Near
Eastern, 189, 247; *see also*
India

X, Malcom, 235n14
Xenophon, 29

Zeus, 64–66, 75

Printed in the United States
96892LV00002B/368/A